Re-Examining Progressive Halakhah

Studies in Progressive Halakhah
General Editor: **Walter Jacob**, published in association with
the Solomon B. Freehof Institute of Progressive Halakhah

Dynamic Jewish Law
Progressive Halakhah—Essence and Application

Rabbinic-Lay Relations in Jewish Law

Conversion to Judaism in Jewish Law
Essays and Responsa

Death and Euthanasia in Jewish Law
Essays and Responsa

The Fetus and Fertility in Jewish Law
Essays and Responsa

Israel and the Diaspora in Jewish Law
Essays and Responsa

Aging and the Aged in Jewish Law
Essays and Responsa

Marriage and Its Obstacles in Jewish Law
Essays and Responsa

Crime and Punishment in Jewish Law
Essays and Responsa

Gender Issues in Jewish Law
Essays and Responsa

RE-EXAMINING
PROGRESSIVE HALAKHAH

❖ ❖ ❖

Edited by

Walter Jacob
and
Moshe Zemer

Berghahn Books
New York • Oxford

First published in 2002 by

Berghahn Books

© 2002 Walter Jacob and Moshe Zemer

Library of Congress Cataloging-in-Publication Data

Re-examining progressive Halakhah / edited by Walter Jacob and Moshe Zemer.
 p. cm. -- (Studies in progressive halakhah)
 Includes index.
 ISBN 1-57181-404-3 (pbk. : alk. paper)
 1. Jewish law--Interpretation and construction. 2. Jewish law--Reform Judaism. I. Jacob, Walter, 1930- II. Zemer, Moshe, 1932- III. Studies in progressive halakhah (Unnumbered)

BM521 .R4 2002
296.1'8--dc21
                                                            2002018421

British Library Cataloguing in Publication Data

A catalogue record for this book is available from the British Library.

Printed in the United States on acid-free paper

CONTENTS

Dedicated to the loving memory of
KENNEY JACOB

ACKNOWLEDGMENTS

We continue to be grateful to the Rodef Shalom Congregation for supporting the Freehof Institute of Progressive Halakhah and for assisting in technical matters connected with the publication of this volume. Our thanks as well to Barbara Bailey for her efforts with the typescript.

INTRODUCTION

The last two centuries have brought radical changes to our understanding of the world. The physical and social sciences have provided us with new insights. Philosophical systems, very different from those of earlier ages have been developed. This has had a major effect on our view of Judaism and its traditions.

Judaism was partially shielded from the earlier changes brought about by the Renaissance. The medieval world of scholasticism in which religion contained the absolute and all encompassing truth had given way to the critical spirit. As few Jews were in contact with the intellectual world of that period, Judaism, for the most part, could continue as before. The mode of reasoning as displayed in the commentaries on the Talmud or in the responsa literature remained very much the same. There were changes in both of these areas, but they had nothing to do with the intellectual climate of the surrounding world.

The eighteenth-century rumblings that eventually led to the Emancipation changed all of this. For most Jews of Central Europe, the change came in a single generation. The rabbis, the traditional leaders, were not prepared for the new intellectual world and sought to stop its influence, but such efforts were destined to fail. New views had to be developed. The process occurred first in the Reform movement, but eventually spread to all other groups within Judaism. They affected the rituals of the synagogue, the relationship of Jews to non-Jews, the *halakhah*, and much else.

Changes and adjustments in the practical application of the halakhah were relatively easy, but the foundations also needed attention and that came more slowly. The guiding principles on which decisions were based and which thereby guided all of Jewish life, had to be reviewed. The hermeneutics that served through the ages needed a critical view. Were they still valid? Could they be adjusted to a different world?

It was also important to understand the outside influences that played a role in the development of contemporary *halakhah* and to understand how the *halakhah*, in the new, freer world, could exercise some influence on other systems of law.

Equally important from the very beginning of the new age was self-criticism. The scholarly dialogue through the last two centuries has been highly critical. This has been helpful as veneration of the past, its leaders, and their decisions has often stood in the way of open discussion.

This volume is intended to take us onto the road of investigating the essentials of modern *halakhah*. It is done with an appreciation of earlier traditions, but with an open mind and a willingness to explore many different avenues. Other volumes that will treat the foundations of Liberal *halakhah* are planned.

Chapter 1

❖ ❖ ❖

TAKING PRECEDENT SERIOUSLY
On Halakhah as a Rhetorical Practice

Mark Washofsky

The concept of precedent is both characteristic of and unique to the activity of law. By "precedent," I mean the practice of deciding disputed questions on the basis of earlier decisions. By "characteristic," I mean that deference to precedent is endemic to every system of thought and practice that we call law. Every legal system, each in its own fashion, recognizes precedent as a factor which to some extent constrains the freedom of decision enjoyed by the present judge. And by "unique," I mean that in no other intellectual discipline does the doctrine of precedent enjoy the respect and acceptance that law accords to it. No other field of inquiry is as receptive to the argument from precedent, the claim that something ought to be done or an issue ought to be resolved in a particular way now precisely because it was done or resolved that way in the past. Other disciplines, to be sure, have *histories*, records of past achievement which command the respect of the practitioners of the field. Yet the past as such has no recognized power to confer legitimacy in these disciplines; "truth," as conceived by philosophers and scientists, is not arrived at through a process of conversation with the past but by methods of inquiry accepted as proper in that particular subject area. "Whatever conclusion you reach, the fact that Plato (or anyone else) held a certain view will not be for you a reason to adopt that view yourself. You must make up your own mind as to which view is correct, and however informative the positions of your predecessors, it does not count in favor of any position ... that some or all of them held it."[1] Truth, in other words, is a standard entirely independent from time; truth may be present in the words and writings of the sages of the past, but it is separate from those words and theoretically can be attained without recourse to them. For jurists, by contrast, the past *does* confer legitimacy.[2] An argument from precedent is not only acceptable before a court of law, it is often the crucial factor that determines the judge's ruling.

Why law should differ so essentially in this regard from other intellectual practices[3] is a question that has provoked much interest among legal theorists. Some note that the practice of following confers a number of important benefits upon a legal system.[4] Among these are fairness (similar cases and circumstances ought to be treated in a similar fashion); predictability or stability (the knowledge that courts will continue to apply existing rules introduces an element of certainty into the law, allowing individuals to plan their affairs accordingly); and efficiency (following precedent allows judges to conserve their decision-making energies, saving their limited time and resources for the creative resolution of problems that are truly new and different and which demand much careful attention). Reasoning by analogy (the search for "prototypical cases," another way of saying "precedent") limits the judge, reducing the likelihood that a decision will be controlled by prejudice or bias. Precedent, by serving as an agreed-upon fixed point in legal reasoning, also facilitates agreement among members of a legal community who may diverge on many other matters. It is also possible to justify the doctrine of precedent as a value in and of itself, on the grounds that culture, of which law is a principal constitutive element, is historical in nature, founded upon a kind of partnership between the contemporary generation and all those that have preceded it. We respect and seek guidance from the past, in other words, because it is our dialogue with the past that makes us what we are as cultural beings.[5]

Yet despite its ubiquity and obvious importance in law, the doctrine of precedent is a deeply problematic one in every legal system. I would divide this problematic into two major categories, the theoretical and the practical. The theoretical problem lies in an apparent contradiction between the practice of deciding according to past cases on the one hand and the very conception of "law" on the other. The *law*, as we generally understand it, exists prior to and separately from the rulings of the judges. This is because we do not tend to understand the judge's role as that of legislator; the duty of the judge is to find and to apply the law, not to make it. A legislator creates law through an exercise of political authority. The creation of law is an expression of legislative will which need not be justified according to the terms of existing law; by definition, the act of the legislator cannot be legally "incorrect."[6] The court, on the other hand, does not establish law on the basis of its own will. It resolves questions of law by justifying its answers as correct interpretations of the existing legal materials. A judge therefore owes primary fidelity to the law and *not* to the rulings of other judges who, after all, are also engaged in finding and applying the law. If the law is something other than the judge's ruling, then it is possible for a judge to err, to *mis*interpret the law and to render an *in*correct decision. If I find that a previous judge ruled incorrectly, why should I be constrained to follow that ruling merely because it preceded me in time? Are not both of us, I and the earlier judge alike, equally bound to decide our cases "according to the law"? If that earlier decision is, in my considered opinion, *not* according to the law, why should it exercise binding authority over my own good judgment? Against all of this, the doctrine of precedent asserts that to some significant extent the ruling of a prior judge *is* law, *is* binding upon me, precisely as though it was an act of legislation. This idea would seem to run counter to our conception of law.

The practical problem flows from our contemporary view of law as a progressive phenomenon; that is, law changes and has always changed to meet the needs of its community. And this is as it should be. Judges must be free to innovate, for even if we concede that a particular decision may have been "right" at one time, we do not thereby concede that the same decision is right for *all* time. We would agree with Justice Holmes that "it is revolting to have no better reason for a rule of law than that so it was laid down in the time of Henry IV. It is still more revolting if the grounds upon which it was laid down have vanished long since, and the rule simply persists from blind imitation of the past."[7] Yet precedent, which requires the judge to decide a question in precisely the way it was decided before, precisely *because* it was decided that way before, would seem to run counter to any sensible notion of legal progress.

I would argue that every successful legal system is characterized by a creative tension between a healthy respect for the doctrine of precedent and a cast of mind and a set of techniques to address and solve the problems that precedent causes.[8] By this I mean that a legal system must possess the means by which to reconcile its reverence for the past with the need to preserve judicial freedom. And "reconciliation" here is a must, for law cannot do without either side of the tension. Without precedent, the tendency for past decisions to influence or even constrain the decisions of present-day judges, the system is hardly a system of "law" as we understand law. And without some measure of judicial freedom from the constraint of precedent, judges would never be able to distinguish between the "law" and the at-times mistaken application of the law by their predecessors, nor would they be able to derive new solutions to new legal problems.

How does Jewish law (*halakhah*) reflect and respond to this challenge? Does Jewish law recognize the power of judicial precedent to constrain the decision-making freedom of present-day authorities, the *poskim*? If these constraints exist, how do the *poskim* cope with or, when necessary, evade them in the search for what they regard as the correct answer to a halakhic question? How do they respond to a perceived conflict between precedent, the accepted and settled understanding of halakhic texts and rules, and a situation that seems to call for a new approach to the law? These questions form the basis of the essay which follows. I ask them in part because I think that the issue of precedent in Jewish law holds some profoundly important implications for us as practitioners of liberal *halakhah*. Indeed, the answers to these questions will do much to determine whether we have a right to call our enterprise *halakhah* in any genuine and plausible sense of that term. While "liberal *halakhah*," like most other intellectual disciplines, is difficult to define with precision and while we may disagree profoundly over any number of its aspects, I think I am on safe ground in suggesting that its practitioners are united upon two core propositions: first, that an authentic Jewish practice must express itself largely, though not exclusively, in halakhic terms; and second, that this *halakhah* does not and need not conflict with the progressive values that must form the basis of our Jewish experience. Accordingly, our scholars have written extensively on numerous questions of Jewish law, seeking to demonstrate that the *halakhah* is sufficiently flexible and dynamic to support liberal and progressive solutions to questions of ritual and ethical observance.[9] These solutions, by their nature, often involve the sort of creative interpretation that will elicit new meanings from the literary sources, frequently departing from the decisions of past authorities.[10] It is here that the doctrine of precedent poses a potentially serious and even crippling difficulty to us. Putting it bluntly: to the extent that *pesak*, halakhic decision-making, is constrained by the weight of past decisions, then the Orthodox are right and we are wrong: Jewish law is *not* sufficiently flexible and dynamic to support the kind of *pesak* that we favor, so that our attempts to read it as such amount to a distortion of the essence and substance of the *halakhah*. On the other hand, should precedent operate in a strictly limited fashion within Jewish law, then we would have strong grounds on which to contend that the *halakhah* supports a maximum degree of freedom of interpretation and that *our* interpretations, even though new and "unprecedented," are as halakhicly legitimate as those of Orthodox *poskim*.

The results of my inquiry are decidedly mixed. While academic scholars of Jewish law, drawing upon theoretical and programmatic statements scattered through the Talmud and the post-Talmudic literature, declare that the *halakhah* recognizes no doctrine of binding precedent, sufficient evidence exists to suggest beyond much doubt that precedent, the collected weight of post-Talmudic Jewish jurisprudence, exerts a powerful constraining force upon the decision rendered by the contemporary authority. Yet I also hope to show that this situation closely parallels that which prevails in two other representative legal traditions—European "civil law" and Anglo-American "common law." In both of these systems we find the creative tension, of which I spoke earlier, between the healthy respect for precedent and other tendencies that serve to free the judge from slavish dependence upon the rulings of the past. A balance is struck, therefore, between tradition and continuity on the one hand and legal progress and flexibility on the other. I want to argue that Jewish law, too, achieves this balance through the use of techniques that are particularly well-suited to its history and development. I will conclude with some observations on the application of these findings to our liberal halakhic endeavor.

Precedent in the Civil Law Tradition

"Civil law" is the term generally used to describe the legal traditions of continental Western Europe (excluding Scandinavia), Latin America, and other jurisdictions such as Louisiana and Quebec whose law is presently or was at one time identical with or heavily influenced by Justinian's *Corpus iuris civilis.*[11] Of the many substantive and procedural differences between the civil law and other legal systems, the one that concerns us here has to do with what we might call the ideology of lawmaking. In civil law systems, legislation holds pride of place as the dominant source of the law.[12] This flows partly from its Roman antecedents.[13] Justinian viewed his Code as the single, exclusive source of authoritative law in his empire, which sought "to replace and did replace all former statements of law, both in literature and in legislation."[14] The ideology of this "post-classical" period of Roman jurisprudence therefore saw the Emperor as the source of all law. Where legalists had previously preferred that their law remain flexible and adaptable to new circumstances, "under an absolute monarchy all law tends to be thought of as royal command. ... Thereby further juristic controversy would be precluded, the uncertainty attending all juristic law [*i.e.,* law as it had been developed by prior legal scholars— MW] would be got rid of, and stability of law would be produced. What had previously floated on the mobile waters of juristic doctrine would now be solidly based on statute."[15] Civil law ideology is based as well upon the intellectual trends that dominated the West during the late-eighteenth and nineteenth centuries and that led to the widespread activity of legal codification in Europe during this period. One of these, nationalism, expressed itself in the politico-legal doctrine of state positivism: only the sovereign state can make law, and only statutes enacted by the legislative power can *be* law.[16] Customary law, which predates the organization of the political state and certainly exists prior to the enactment of the legal codes, is the great exception to this rule. All civil law jurisdictions recognize custom as the other "source" of law; hence, the theorists tend to divide the civil law into the broad categories of "written law" (*ius scriptum*) or legislation and "unwritten law" (*ius non scriptum*) or custom.[17] Yet they tend to dismiss custom as being of slight importance compared to legislation.[18] The second great intellectual trend was the rationalism that dominated Continental philosophical thought during the Enlightenment and that was congenial toward codification. Ever since Justinian, the civil law has assumed a systematic and formally rational style, one accessible to philosophers who are not necessarily lawyers, as opposed to "the common law, with its mass of cases and its lack of theory, especially until the nineteenth century, (which) is largely impenetrable to anyone not specifically trained in the common law."[19] Codification contributes to this systematic outlook; when the law has become fully rational and set forth in clear terms, the answer to a legal problem should consist in the simple application of the relevant statute rather than the interpretation of a line of cases.[20]

The supremacy of legislation as a source of law parallels the comparatively inferior position of the judiciary in civil law jurisdictions. Just as the Roman law judge was frequently a layperson not especially trained in the law,[21] the civil law judge does not exert a significant influence over legal development. Limited by the doctrine of the separation of powers, the judge is not to make law or interpret unclear legislation; he is rather to refer such difficulties to the legislature, the ultimate source of the law. [22] He simply applies the law to the facts of the case and reaches a decision in that case alone, in a supposedly deductive manner. He must base his case solely upon "the law," and this does not include previous judicial decisions.[23] In interpreting the law, the judge must give paramount weight to the intent of the legislator rather than to the practice of the courts, which may be rejected or modified at any time, depending upon the case.[24] The doctrine of binding precedent (*stare decisis*) is rejected in civil law theory.[25]

Civil law practice, on the other hand, accords the rulings of judges a much greater degree of influence than the theory would seem to allow. Judges perforce must interpret the law when applying its provisions to cases. And if there is no formal doctrine of binding precedent, civil law judges are in fact guided by prior decisions. Lawyers and judges alike refer to prior cases in briefs and decisions; "the fact is that courts do not act very differently toward reported decisions in civil law jurisdictions than do courts in the United States."[26] The situation in France, where the force of precedent is somewhat weaker than it is in other civil law countries,[27] serves as an example. In theory, precedent does not bind a French judge; he may even be forbidden to treat a prior decision as the obligatory reason for his ruling in the instant case.[28] Indeed, the decision of a regular court will be reversed for "absence of legal basis" if the only justification it offers for it is an earlier decision of the high court (*Cour de Cassation*).[29] Yet the citation of precedents is common in French law, where the prior decisions of the courts are the most important factor in predicting how the present court will interpret the relevant legislation.[30] It is understood that while the *Cour de Cassation* can change its mind whenever it so chooses, it will not do so readily. The reasons for this are similar to the reasons for the emphasis upon precedent in common law countries: the requirements of reasonable certainty and predictability in the law; the desire of judges to conserve intellectual energy or to avoid embarrassing reversals by higher courts; the demand that like cases be treated alike; and the consideration that justice not only be done but should appear to have been done.[31] Thus, the "caricature" that civil law systems are free from the constraint of precedent "is certainly no longer remotely accurate, if ever it was." Rather, "precedents are generally recognized at least as providing strong (but defeasible or outweighable) force."[32]

The clash between the ideology and the practice of the civil law underscores the inevitability of precedent even in legal systems that formally renounce it as a source of law. It also suggests the ways in which the civil law, intentionally or not, negotiates the "creative tension" between respect for precedent and the need to escape it. The civil law begins with an assertion that law is fundamentally a legislative endeavor. Legislation, especially codification that strives to impose order and system upon the legal materials, is the innovative force within civil law, for it is the essence of legislation that its power lies in the here and now, with the authority of the current legislator, rather than in the rulings of past judges or the statements of ancient authorities. It is thus a force for reform, for an observed defect in the law can be remedied much more simply and quickly through comprehensive legislative act than through the slow and piecemeal development of judicial interpretation.[33] Yet reliance upon precedent remains a vital part of the judicial function. This demonstrates that the respect for tradition and the desire to solve legal issues by proceeding on the basis of prior decisions is a basic element in the conception of "law" even in jurisdictions which officially refuse to bind their judges by the rulings of the past. Precedent, we might say, is not binding, but it is persuasive, a means of mapping the way for the judge so that he will not likely stray very far from the paths blazed by his predecessors. If legislation insures that the law in civil law countries remains flexible, forward-looking, and open to change, the practice of judicial precedent insures that it remains *law*, a conversation in which the sages of the past are asked to confront the problems of the present.

Precedent in the Anglo-Saxon Legal Tradition

While the civil law is rooted in legislation and codification illuminated by the writings of university-trained jurists,[34] the "common law," the basic legal doctrine of English-speaking countries, emerged from "a unique, 'unwritten' constitution and the recorded, but orally rendered decisions of an extraordinarily gifted and respected judiciary."[35] In saying this we should take care not to overlook the significant role played by legislation in common law systems. Still, it is correct to state that England's common law, originating in the efforts of the Plantagenet magistrates to extend the authority of the king's courts, is to a great extent the product of judges rather than legislators or academicians. It is a system of case law, and the distinguishing characteristic of such a system is precedent.[36] This is only natural: if the basis of a legal system lies in the rulings of judges rather than in the abstract principles and provisions of an enacted code, those rulings constitute the major source material upon which a judge can draw for his decisions. "A judge in a subsequent case *must* have regard to (prior decisions); they are not, as in some other legal systems, merely material which he *may* take into consideration."[37] To the extent that a precedent is recognized as binding, especially—but not necessarily[38]—upon a court that ranks lower in the legal hierarchy than the tribunal which issued the original ruling, the court applies the doctrine of *stare decisis* ("let the decision stand"): the prior decision becomes a formal reason for the ruling in a subsequent case and therefore a formal constraint upon the subsequent judge's freedom of decision. By "formal," I mean a reason that is sufficient in itself: if a precedent is "binding" the subsequent judge *must* decide in accordance with the legal rule or "holding" of the earlier decision,[39] whether or not he or she likes or agrees with it.[40] It is in this sense that a system of case law differs so starkly from the civil law tradition, for there is little doubt that, say, a French judge would overrule the decision of a prior court should he consider it wrongly decided.[41] Common law systems differ as to just how binding the "binding" precedent is,[42] and there is no unanimity among legal theorists as to how precisely to identify that part of the prior decision which in fact obliges the subsequent judge to decide in the same way.[43] Yet most common law countries have adopted some version of the doctrine of *stare decisis* and recognize a significant body of binding precedents.[44]

Not all precedents are regarded as binding. Common law theorists speak of "persuasive" precedent, a ruling "which the judges are under no obligation to follow, but which they will take into consideration, and to which they will attach such weight as it seems to them to deserve."[45] Among these are the decisions of foreign courts, particularly those of other common law countries, and those parts of judicial decisions regarded as *dicta*, or extraneous to the decision's legal holding. And it has been suggested that, at one time, *all* precedents in the English tradition were held to be persuasive rather than binding in nature. I refer here to the so-called "declaratory theory" of the common law, according to which a judicial decision is regarded as evidence of the pre-existing law rather than as an act of law-creation. Thus, Sir Matthew Hale (d. 1676) writes that judicial decisions

> do not make a law, properly so called; for that only the king and parliament can do; yet they have a great weight and authority in expounding, declaring, and publishing what the law of this kingdom is; especially when such decisions hold a consonancy and congruity with resolutions and decisions of former times. And though such decisions are less than a law, yet they are a greater evidence thereof than the opinion of any private persons.[46]

Similarly Blackstone (d. 1780): "the common law, properly so called" consists of "general customs" established by "immemorial usage." The decisions of the judges, the "living oracles," are "the principal and most authoritative evidence, that can be given, of the existence of such a custom as shall form a part of the common law." Judges, therefore, while obligated by practice to follow prior decisions, may overturn these "where the former determination is most evidently contrary to reason." But even in such a case, the judge does not legislate; "for if it be found that the former decision is manifestly absurd or unjust, it is declared, not that such a sentence was *bad law*, but that it was *not law*; that is, that it is not the established custom of the realm, as has been erroneously determined."[47] In this view, a precedent is "binding" only to the extent that it is *right*, a correct application or interpretation of the law that exists prior to and apart from the judge's decision and that acts as a standard by which lawyers can measure that decision's correctness. Yet the declaratory theory has gone out of fashion; it seems much more reasonable now to concede that common law is *judge-made* rather than "judge-declared." The judicial decisions are precedents because they lay down the legal rule to be followed. This view proceeds from the jurisprudential theory generally known as legal positivism, rooted in the nineteenth- and twentieth-century reactions against the more "mystical" conceptions of law championed by earlier theorists.[48] Positivism asserts that law is a human artifact; it is "legal" because it is *posited*, enacted, created by an authoritative law-making agency.[49] From now on, a precedent is not judged "correct" to the extent that it accords with the law; a precedent *is* law, having been established by proper judicial authority, whether or not the subsequent judge thinks the earlier case was rightly decided.[50] A precedent cannot be "wrong." A precedent *binds* as an act of legal power; it need not "persuade." Thus, referring back to that "theoretical problem" of which I spoke earlier, the doctrine of binding precedent as it has come to be understood effectively blurs the distinction between *law* and the judicial interpretation or application of that law.

As though recognizing this dilemma of theory, however, the common law tradition provides remedies for it. Even if a precedent is an act of judicial legislation and hence, like a legislative enactment "binding" upon the courts, the common law judge is not rigidly subservient to it. He or she may in some cases overrule a precedent, either explicitly or implicitly, or simply disregard an earlier ruling should it prove troublesome.[51] A famous

tactic for loosening the hold of precedent is that of distinguishing, whereby the present court will find that, though a precedent
is "binding," the rule stated by its predecessor was too wide or
vague, or that it does not cover the fact situation of the present
case. This reflects the reality that legal reasoning is primarily analogical in nature: the court must decide whether the present case
sufficiently resembles the precedent in order to determine
whether to apply the precedent's rule.[52] And distinguishing is
not the only intellectual tool that makes for judicial innovation
and maneuver. The American legal scholar Karl Llewellyn
devoted much research to documenting the fact that the case law
system provides judges with "leeways" as well as with constraints in dealing with precedents.[53] From his study of hundreds
of appellate opinions, he derived a long list of techniques by
which American courts construe the rulings of their predecessors, broadly or narrowly. Llewellyn noted that legal practice
regards all of these "canons of construction" as proper rules of
interpretation: that is, a judge is procedurally entitled to employ
them in deciphering the meaning of the legal texts before him or
her. Yet these rules are not all of one piece; they are diverse,
divergent, even contradictory. A judge may decide to follow,
restrict, ignore, redirect, or "kill" the holding of a precedent, all
with equal legitimacy, by utilizing these techniques. And since
the decision *which* technique to use cannot be determined by
some other, overarching set of principles, it follows that judicial
decision is not simply a matter of logical deduction from
premises (precedents) to conclusions. Rather, in the application
of precedent the court must inevitably expand or contract it, creating new legal meaning in the process. The current judge, in
other words, does not merely read precedent but rewrites it; in
every citation of a prior ruling the judge effectively determines
what that ruling shall mean in the present context. This does not
mean that judges operate without constraints upon their freedom of decision; such constraints exist, as Llewellyn took pains
to point out. It does mean, though, that these constraints take the
form of social and professional factors that determine the environment in which the craft of judging takes place.[54] They do not
operate as a conceptual straitjacket that coerces a predetermined
interpretation upon the judge, who might legitimately understand a precedential case in a variety of ways. "Later courts ...
are not content to be completely fettered by their predecessors,

and wisely so: for the development of the common law has been an empirical one proceeding step by step."[55] Or as Llewellyn himself put it: "one does not progress far into legal life without learning that there is no single right and accurate way of reading one case, or of reading a bunch of cases."[56]

At first glance, the legal theory of the Anglo-American tradition stands in stark opposition to the ideology of civil law. Common law is derived from judicial decisions, and those decisions, as precedents, create law that constrain the freedom of subsequent judges. Binding precedent deprives subsequent courts of the opportunity to reach beyond the controlling cases to some higher or background legal standard by which, as it were, to judge the judges. Yet as we have seen, the common law tradition plays host to a competing, if no longer dominant theory of precedent, which sees the judicial ruling not as law properly so called but as evidence of law, a persuasive argument that the law—a reality distinct from any particular judicial decision—is best interpreted in this particular way. It has also created, alongside its numerous precedents, a host of tools through which those precedents can be and are overruled, eliminated, re-fitted, and re-created—as well as upheld, preserved, strengthened and solidified. Thus does the common law respond to the theoretical and the practical problems that emerge from a doctrine of precedent. On the theoretical side, judges are equipped with "leeways" whereby to adjust precedents to what in their view is the correct interpretation of the law. On the practical side, judges can develop the existing so that it coheres with the demands of the contemporary scene. Common law judges are therefore endowed with considerable judicial freedom, both to arrive at what they think is the right answer and at what they think is a good and useful answer, even though they are formally bound to follow the decisions of the past. No less than judges in civil law countries, those of the common law tradition have found the means whereby to accommodate the "creative tension" between the two great conflicting needs of a legal system: to honor precedent and to overcome it.

Precedent in Jewish Law

While the civil law and the common law proceed from opposite poles on the jurisprudential spectrum—the former is primarily "legislative" in origin while the latter is at heart "judicial"—both display the sort of creative tension over the concept of precedent which I have suggested is symptomatic of legal systems. Both traditions pay deference to the rulings of the past and established judicial practices; even civil law courts cite cases and tend to follow the general thrust of judicial interpretation. And both traditions also have means of freeing the contemporary judge from the fetters of precedent when this is necessary; even common law judges (and, perhaps, *especially* the common law judges) have developed sophisticated techniques for doing so. I now want to turn to the consideration of Jewish law in the light of these realities. In what ways does the Jewish legal tradition acknowledge the power of precedent as a constraining factor upon a rabbi's freedom to decide an issue of *halakhah*? And in what ways does it accommodate the value of adherence to the authority of the past with the need for flexibility and innovation in halakhic decision?

1. *The Conventional Wisdom: There Is No Binding Precedent in Jewish Law.*

Among the scholars grouped under the rubric of *mishpat ivri*, the academic study of Jewish law, we encounter a broadly-accepted consensus that precedent exerts no binding, obligatory constraining force over the decision-maker in any case at rabbinic law. The words of Zerach Warhaftig, who has produced a major work on the subject, summarize this consensus rather well:[57]

> A decision found in the responsa literature or among a collection of court cases is a valuable source from which to learn the *halakhah* ... but the court is not constrained to follow a previous ruling. The judge's task is to render the correct decision as he sees it. He is permitted, and even obliged, to seek advice from those more knowledgeable than he, to study the sources and the precedents, but the decision is his and his alone. We therefore learn that the precedent (*takdim*) in Jewish law (*mishpat ivri*) may have a persuasive value (*mancheh*), but it is not binding (*mechayev*) upon the judge.

To these we might add the observations of Eliav Shochetman:[58]

> A rabbinical court is indeed required to consult the rules of decision-making as formulated in the halakhic literature, a literature which includes responsa based upon actual cases. Yet these

responsa are not actual cases but rather expressions of halakhic opinion. Therefore, they have the same weight and influence enjoyed by other legal sources (depending, of course, upon the reputation of the writer). A rabbinical court decision that emerges from a certain constellation of facts exerts no obligatory influence over the decision of another court, for the guiding rule has always been: "the judge must rule on the basis of what he sees."[59]

And finally, the comments of Menachem Elon, the *doyen* of *mishpat ivri* scholars:[60]

> ... the doctrine of binding precedent conflicts with the basic approach of Jewish law to decision making ... no code of Jewish law has ever been accepted which presents to the judge only a single opinion stated unqualifiedly as the law ... Within this dynamic and flexible conception of law, there is, of course, no room for the doctrine that the *ratio decidendi* of a judicial decision can bind the judicial system to reach the same result in other cases.

This conventional wisdom draws its support from a number of factors. The first of these is what we might call linguistic evidence: the legal term "precedent" does not exist in the Talmud or in the other traditional legal sources. Modern Hebrew had to invent such a term—*takdim*[61]—which serves the purposes of the Israeli legal system that has followed the doctrine of binding precedent since the period of the British mandate.[62] Traditional halakhic language does have terms which denote the judicial decision—*pesak din, ma`aseh beit din,* or simply *ma`aseh*—but these refer to the ruling of the *posek* or *dayan* in the instant case and do not carry the sense of "binding precedent." The second factor is based upon evidence drawn from Jewish judicial practice. Talmudic law does not generally require that a court explain the reasoning behind its decision,[63] and the absence of an explicitly-stated rationale—a holding or *ratio decidendi*—in turn renders it virtually impossible to draw analogies and to use the decision in one case as a precedent upon which to decide another.[64] This practice helps to explain why traditional Jewish law does not know of the appellate court:[65] the lack of arguments and explanations in the judicial ruling gives an appellate court nothing to critique and renders such an institution superfluous.[66] It helps to explain, as well, the Talmudic statement: "one should not learn the *halakhah* either from a theoretical statement (*limud*) or from a ruling in a case (*ma`aseh*)." As Rashbam explains, we do not learn from the *ma`aseh* because "one may mistake the reason upon which that particular ruling is based; indeed, this mistake is frequently made."[67] The inference is that the actual ruling was generally not accompanied by the sort of argumentation that allowed one to learn from it and to apply it as a precedent to other cases.

The third factor which diminishes the binding power of precedent in Jewish law is that of legal theory, by which I mean the understanding of the nature of law and its authority in the halakhic system. A powerful stream of rabbinic jurisprudential thought insists upon a clear and definite distinction between "law" on the one hand and applications of that law by judges on the other. The law is declared in the Torah, both written and oral, and given its authoritative literary formulation in the Babylonian Talmud and its cognates. All subsequent decisions by Jewish legal authorities are based upon the Talmud and are correct insofar as they comport with the *halakhah* as set forth in the Talmudic sources. The ruling (*pesak*) of any decisor is not to be identified as "law" but rather as an interpretation or application of the law. The decision does not make law; at best, it serves as evidence of what the law truly is. It follows, then, that on this subject Jewish legal thought parallels the dominant theory of the civil law and the declaratory theory of the common law: no prior decision can constrain a judge from ruling as he sees fit in the case before him. The duty of the *posek* is to interpret the law—that is, the Talmud—according to his own best understanding, regardless of the opinions of other judges. As the Talmud puts it: "a judge must rule on the basis of what he sees" (*ein ladayan ela mah she`einav ro'ot*).[68]

Two statements of this legal theory, both of them "classics" in the literature of Jewish jurisprudence, illustrate this point with special clarity. The first is taken from the Introduction to the *Mishneh Torah* (*Yad Hachazakah*) of Maimonides (Rambam), wherein the author spells out the guiding methodology of his massive undertaking. Rambam draws a sharp distinction between two different sets of legal materials: those interpretations, legislative enactments and other practices which are included in the Babylonian Talmud and those which arose following the Talmud's redaction. "All Israel is obliged to follow the decisions of the Babylonian Talmud ... because all Israel accepted these decisions upon themselves (*hiskimu aleyhem kol yisrael*)." By contrast, those legal materials cre-

ated following the redaction of the Talmud are binding only upon
the communities which adopted them; the *beit din* of one community cannot coerce the court of another community to follow its
interpretation or enactment. Nor can the court of one generation
expect that a successor will follow its rulings. "If one of the *geonim*
should interpret the law one way while another court concludes
that such is not the correct interpretation of the Talmud, we need
not follow the first ruling but rather whichever ruling is more persuasive (*lemi shehada`at notah*)." Two points deserve particular
mention here. First, it is the Talmud, and *not* the decisions of any
post-Talmudic authority, which determines the law, so that the
halakhic decisor may presumably overrule or ignore generations
of accumulated precedent when he believes that those rulings do
not comport with the best interpretation of the Talmudic sources.[69]
And second, there is no hierarchy among post-Talmudic scholars.
Rambam pointedly refers to them all as *geonim*—"those *geonim*
who hail from the land of Israel, or Babylonia, or Spain or
France"—a subtle indication of his rejection of the claim to special
halakhic authority on the part of the post-Talmudic Babylonian
sages were customarily designated as *geonim*.[70] No one scholar or
group of scholars deserves our legal acquiescence on the basis of
his or their position or prestige; we follow them when they are
right—that is, when their view of the law accords with the correct
interpretation of the Talmudic sources—and we dissent from them
when they are wrong. This statement, a declaration of halakhic
independence from the rulings of the past, should not blind us to
the extent to which Rambam follows those rulings in fact. The
Mishneh Torah has been called by one of its most perceptive students "a sturdy link in the great chain of Gaonic-Spanish Talmudic
commentary." Rambam's use of the *geonim* was "pervasive," as
was his reliance upon the interpretations and decisions of
Rabbenu Chananel, R. Yitzchak Alfasi and R. Yosef ibn Migash.[71]
If Maimonides is a radical in the manner in which he presents the
halakhah—in concise Hebrew, arranged in logical order, legal rules
presented without dispute or minority opinions—he is a conservative in terms of its content: the *halakhah* of the *Mishneh Torah* is
largely the *halakhah* of his predecessors. Precedent, therefore, is for
Rambam a powerful factor in the determination of the correct
legal decision. But we are dealing with "persuasive precedent"
here, precedent that teaches the student yet does not constrain him
from expressing dissent. If Maimonides is influenced by his teach-

ers, what of it? Such is the way that legal traditions in general, and the halakhic tradition in particular, develop and grow. "One naturally relies upon a crystallized and respectable tradition, knowingly or unknowingly drawing upon it."[72] So long, however, as Maimonides insists upon his freedom, and that of every other halakhic authority, to make his own decisions according to his best understanding of the Talmud, then we are safe in citing his writings on halakhic theory as evidence that Jewish law does not recognize a doctrine of binding precedent.

The second "classic" statement affirming the halakhic jurist's independence from binding precedent is that of R. Asher b.Yechiel, or Rosh (d. 1327), the author of a renowned halakhic compendium (*Sefer Hilkhot* [or *Piskey*] *Harosh*) that takes the form of a supplement or commentary to the *Halakhot* of R. Yitzchak Alfasi. Rosh, a leading student of the tosafist R. Meir of Rothenburg, emigrated from Germany and arrived in Spain in 1305, eventually settling in Toledo, where he maintained a Talmudic academy until his death. His biography plays a significant role in most estimations of his approach to halakhic decision-making. Born and bred in the halakhic traditions of Ashkenaz, Rosh expresses serious reservations over the tendency of *poskim* in his adopted land to rely uncritically upon the decisions of Rambam's *Mishneh Torah* for legal guidance. These reservations stem partly from Rosh's dissatisfaction with the literary form of the Maimonidean Code—Rambam presents the law without accompanying source citation or argumentation[73]—and partly from the fact that Rosh believes that the teachings of his own countrymen offer a superior interpretation of Talmudic law than do those of the Sefardim.[74] Rosh, moreover, exhibits a more general opposition to the reliance upon legal precedent, whether that of Maimonides or anyone else, which brings us to the "classic" statement found in his *Halakhot*.[75] His discussion relates to the Talmudic *sugya* on the two forms of judicial error, specifically the more blatant error which causes a judgment to be annulled (*hato`eh bedavar mishnah*) and the lesser error which leaves the judgment intact but which imposes a duty of compensation upon the offending judge (*hato`eh beshikul hada`at*).[76] I shall have more to say on this question; here, I want only to consider Rosh's reaction to a previous dispute, between the twelfth-century Provençal scholars R. Zerachyah Halevy (Razah) and R. Avraham b. David (Rabad). Razah[77] quotes the opinion of an unnamed sage that nowadays, when all of Jewish law has become *halakhot pesukot* ("decided law"), the second, "lesser" error no longer exists. Since the law is so clear and available to all, all judicial errors are errors over the obvious and decided truth, serious enough to annul the judge's decision and to warrant a new trial. Razah rejects this position: "blatant error" is only the ruling which can be proven beyond doubt to contradict the law as formulated in the Mishnah or the Talmud. By contrast, legal rulings of the post-Talmudic *"geonim"* do not enjoy the status of decided law. Thus, an error concerning those rulings is not the "blatant" sort of mistake which nullifies the ruling. Rabad[78] defends the opinion of the unnamed sage: the opinions of post-Talmudic authorities do carry substantial precedential weight. Indeed, he goes farther, extending the sage's words beyond the range of "error" to cover even intentional departures from the rulings of the *geonim*. He writes—uncharacteristically for him[79]—that "we do not have the authority to dispute the ruling of a *gaon* on the basis of our own opinion, neither may we interpret a text differently so as to support a legal decision that departs from that of a *gaon*, except in the case of a well-known halakhic controversy." To all this, R. Asher draws a clear distinction between "error" and "intention." If a judge, unaware of the decisions of the *geonim* on the matter before him, issues a ruling that contradicts those decisions, and if that judge would surely have ruled differently had he known of the geonic precedents, then his ruling is annulled. This applies, says the Rosh, not only to the decisions of the outstanding *geonim* of the past but even to the writings of the sages in one's own generation. This surely stands to reason: if knowledge of any decision, even a recent one, would cause a judge to alter his opinion, ignorance of that decision must qualify as the sort of "blatant error" that strips his ruling of its validity. However,

> if he knows of a geonic ruling yet finds it unconvincing, and if he can support his own view with evidence that persuade his contemporaries, then we apply the rule "Jepthah in his generation is the equal of Samuel in *his* generation." That is, you have no judge save the one who lives in your own time.[80] And that judge may depart from the decisions of his predecessors, for one is entitled to depart from, expand upon or even reject all rulings not clearly supported by the Talmud of Rav Ashi and Ravina ...

This goes beyond the somewhat more circumscribed opinion of Razah, who confines his remarks—at least here[81]—to the concept of "error": that is, whether ignorance of the opinions of post-Talmudic authorities is equivalent to a mistaken understanding of the Talmud itself. And it most certainly takes issue with Rabad's statement that the knowing departure from the rulings of past authorities constitutes "blatant error." Rosh, for his part,[82] champions the principle of judicial freedom. The test for the correctness of any halakhic decision is not its coherence with some prior judicial ruling but its agreement with the Talmudic sources of all *halakhah*. Just as the later *amoraim*, Rosh writes, permitted themselves to dissent from the rulings of the earlier *amoraim*, despite the fact that "earlier" sages tend to enjoy greater intellectual stature in our eyes, so does every *posek* possess that authority. Thus, "in a case where two prior sages disagree, let the judge not say 'I shall rule in accordance with whichever one I wish'; such is a false judgment." Rather, the judge should determine the law on his own, according to proof and evidence drawn from the texts.

In its essence, Rosh's statement parallels that of Rambam, described above, in drawing an unmistakably clear distinction between the *law* as formulated in the Babylonian Talmud and *interpretations of the law* represented by the rulings of post-Talmudic authorities. The former is binding, the latter is not; when confronted with a decision by an earlier *posek* that appears to conflict with the correct understanding of the Talmud, the later judge has the discretion to modify that ruling or to overturn it. The *law* constrains the judge's freedom; precedent, in the form of earlier judicial decisions, is not *law* and therefore does not constrain. "Precedent" does exist, to be sure, in Jewish law, since it is assumed in all these discussions that the judge will at least give careful consideration to the words of his predecessors. In this way, Jewish law reflects the tendency of all legal systems to rely heavily upon the record of past thinking and action. But this "precedent," it would seem, is not of the binding sort (*takdim mechayev*); it is a "persuasive precedent" (*takdim mancheh*) in the manner of the civil law and of the "declaratory theory" of the common law.

2. The Other Side of the Story: Precedent as a Constraining Factor in Halakhah

The evidence considered thus far, proof drawn from linguistics, legal practice, and legal theory, supports what I have called the conventional wisdom among the scholars that Jewish law does not recognize a doctrine of binding precedent. In the final analysis, the judge enjoys the discretion to rule as he sees fit on any halakhic matter, even when his ruling flies in the face of the preponderance of post-Talmudic opinion. As Joel Roth puts it, this principle of judicial independence—"a judge must rule on the basis of his own best understanding of the law"[83]— is the "systemic principle" and the "*sine qua non*" of halakhic jurisprudence, its "ultimate judicial guide."[84] The question remains, however, whether this description of the Jewish legal tradition is entirely accurate. For we can point to at least three indications which, *contra* the conventional wisdom, argue that the halakhic decisor is much more constrained by the rulings of the past than has been indicated thus far.

a. THE CONCEPT OF JUDICIAL ERROR

As noted above, *halakhah* speaks of two categories of judicial error that are causes for action by the losing party in a case at monetary law (*diney mamonot*).[85] The first is an error concerning *devar mishnah*, a matter of law that is clearly settled in the Mishnah or the Talmud.[86] Such a mistake is tantamount to deciding a case in a manner that contradicts the law itself. The decision is not "law" at all; the judgment is annulled and the case is retried.[87] The second sort of error is a mistake of *shikul hada`at*, "the weighing of opinions." In this instance, the case remains settled and the decision is a valid one. At the same time, the decision is erroneous, and the judge must compensate the losing party for the damage caused by his ruling.[88] The Talmud defines this error as a case in which a judge rules according to one side of a tanaitic or amoraic dispute ("and it is not stated that the *halakhah* accords with either view") while general judicial practice (*sugya de`alma*)[89] is to rule according to the other view.

Two points are worth special mention here. The first is that Jewish law recognizes the possibility of judicial error at all. The decision of the court is not final; it can be overturned when it is wrong, when it does not conform with the law as that law ought to be decided. As we have seen, this reversal is not enforced by a "higher" court, since Talmudic jurisprudence does not know of a system of appeals. It occurs when the court that issued the decision is made aware of its own error. The second noteworthy point is that "general judicial practice" is a criterion for discerning error. It is one thing to say that a judge's decision is "wrong" if it contradicts a settled matter of Talmudic law. Had the judge but known of that passage in the Talmud, he surely would have ruled differently; thus, we can say that his ruling is invalid on its face. It is not so obvious, however, why a decision is erroneous when it conflicts with the general tendency of judges to rule differently on the matter at issue. The decision, indeed, remains a valid one despite this error, for so long as it does not clearly run counter to settled Talmudic law we cannot declare it unequivocally to be "non-law." Still, the judge is said to be at fault, to owe compensation, because the litigants have a reasonable expectation that the judge will decide their case as most judges decide it, in accordance with the interpretations of the legal sources which prevail in their community. The judge, too, participates in this expectation. As Rambam explains the "error of *shikul hada`at*":[90]

> for example, a matter comes before the court which involves a dispute among the *tannaim* or the *amoraim*, yet the *halakhah* has not been explicitly (*beferush*) declared in accordance with either side of the dispute. The judge rules in accordance with one side, yet he does not know that the universal tendency is to rule in accordance with the other side.

The implication, of course, is that had the judge but known of that tendency, he would have followed it. Not to follow that tendency is regarded as a mistake, something resulting from his lack of knowledge of the judicial practice that constitutes precedent within his community. The judge, in other words, wishes to rule according to precedent; the community expects that he will rule according to precedent; and if he does *not* so rule, his ruling—though it is not technically in contradiction to settled Talmudic law—is nonetheless presumed to be in error.

This rule, of course, is subject to the strictures of R. Asher b. Yechiel recounted above. That is, the judge is technically permitted to dissent from the rulings of post-Talmudic authorities, inasmuch as his supreme duty is to halakhic truth—"for such is the path of Torah"[91]—rather than to precedent. Yet R. Asher explicitly limits this permit for judicial discretion to those judges who are intellectually capable of achieving the formidable task of "deciding according to one opinion or the other on the basis of clear and convincing proofs." On the other hand, if the judge cannot do this, let him not take disputed property from either litigant and award it to the other, since in every case where the law is in doubt we leave the disputed property with its current possessor. ... And if he is unable to decide according to either side of the dispute, then should he rule one way in a case where most scholars would rule the other way, this is an instance of an error of *shikul hada`at*.[92]

Even though the *posek* is free to rule in accordance with the *law* rather than with precedent, in practice this freedom is enjoyed only by those *poskim* who possess the confidence to decide the law in cases where the authorities are in dispute. As we shall see, this confidence is a precious commodity in a discipline like *halakhah* that places much weight upon the opinions of much-admired predecessors. In any event, R. Asher's words support the presumption that in most cases, where the presiding judge will not view himself as capable of declaring the law with such certainty, a departure from established precedent will be regarded as an instance of judicial error.

b. Explicit Reliance Upon Precedent

Although most judges, and surely those who do not possess extensive Talmudic training, will rule in accordance with "general judicial practice," R. Asher leaves the distinct impression that the truly knowledgeable authority may rule on questions of *halakhah* as he sees fit. So long as he decides in accordance with the *law*—that is, avoiding errors of *devar mishnah*—he is unencumbered by the constraints of precedent. Yet while this impression comports with the "conventional wisdom" that sharply distinguishes between law and judicial precedent in Jewish legal theory, it is contradicted by a powerful stream of halakhic thought and practice. I refer to those scholars and sages who by rights *ought* to declare their freedom from precedent but who in fact argue that contemporary halakhic decision should conform to the rulings of the outstanding *geonim* of the past. Taken together, their statements constitute the second counter-argument to the "conventional wisdom"; they create the contradictory impression that in almost all instances even the greatest authorities will adhere to precedent. This adherence, moreover, will not be a matter of convenience or scholarly habit. Rather, it is entirely right and proper for them to submit to the constraints of past judicial practice.

R. Yosef Karo and R. Moshe Isserles, the two preeminent halakhic authorities of the sixteenth century, illustrate this tendency quite well. Their stories, recounting the motivations and methodologies which produced the *Shulhan Arukh*, are familiar ones. They deserve retelling, however, as a means of emphasizing the fact that Jewish law is not as "precedent-free" as the conventional wisdom would have us believe and that the reliance upon precedent as an indicator of correct legal decision is a practice of great antiquity in the history of the *halakhah*.

R. Yosef b. Efraim Karo (1488-1575) is most widely known as the author of the *Shulhan Arukh*, which remains the standard "code" of Jewish law to this day. His *magnum opus*, however, is his massive compendium entitled *Beit Yosef*, cast as a commentary upon the *Arba`ah Turim* of R. Ya`akov b. Asher. The *Shulhan Arukh*, indeed, is the essence of the halakhic product of the *Beit Yosef*, the *summa* of its conclusions, "a bouquet of its choicest blossoms."[93] He wrote the *Beit Yosef*, as he tells us in the book's Introduction, to help bring order out of the halakhic chaos in which the Jewish people finds itself due to the many persecutions and dispersions that have befallen it. The prophecy of Isaiah 29:14—"the wisdom of (the people's) sages is no more"—has been fulfilled, and "the energy of the Torah and its students has been spent." The problem, ironically enough, is not that the vicissitudes of history have prevented us from studying the Torah—a theme that dominates the Introduction to the Code of Maimonides—but that, if anything, we have studied it too well. The Torah "has become not two *torot* but numberless *torot*, on account of the many books that have come into being for the purpose of explaining its laws." No great devotee of halakhic pluralism, Karo reminds the reader that the goal of every good halakhist is to arrive at the right answer to every legal question. The best way to do this, of course, is to study each issue in light of its sources in the Talmud, the commentaries, and the literature of the *poskim*. Yet working one's way through the massive halakhic literature is a daunting task, especially when it is difficult in the first place even to locate the appropriate Talmudic passages with which to begin the analysis. Accordingly, Karo will collect in one literary compendium all the information necessary to halakhic decision.[94] His work will recite[95] the Talmudic source passages for every law, the applicable commentaries to those passage by Rashi, the Tosafot and the *rishonim*, and the discussions of the issue that are found in over thirty works of *halakhah*, so that one who studies the *Beit Yosef* will possess a virtual library of Jewish law and be able to locate the materials required for legal judgment. This judgment, the determination of the *halakhah*, "is the very purpose (*takhlit*) of our work: that there should be but one Torah and one law." But how should this determination be accomplished?

> Perhaps, it occurred to me, we ought to decide among the conflicting opinions of the *poskim* on the basis of persuasive Talmudic proofs and evidence. Yet the Tosafot and the novellae (*hidushim*) of Nachmanides, R. Shelomo b. Adret and R. Nissim Gerondi are filled with evidence and proofs for every one of the conflicting opinions. It is a haughty thing to say that we can add anything of substance to these discussions. And who is arrogant enough to claim that he can intervene into the disputes of the giants of our halakhic past, refuting that which they have made clear or deciding that which they have left in doubt? For on account of our many sins, our mental capacity is insufficient to understand fully the words of our predecessors, let alone to improve upon their findings. Moreover, even were we able to take this path, it would not be advisable to do so, since it is an exceedingly long path indeed.

Karo, in this revealing passage, does not deny the existence of judicial discretion in he *halakhah*. The individual halakhic authority does enjoy the right to study the sources and to arrive at his own carefully-considered decision. It is for that very reason that the decisor ought to have at his disposal the vast collection of legal materials that the *Beit Yosef* makes available. Yet precisely because they are so vast, the individual student of Torah cannot grasp them with the confidence necessary to arrive at a sure decision. And given the multiplicity of opinions and the ubiquity of dispute within the *halakhah*, the claim that "I can arrive at a clear answer on the basis of my own understanding" is evidence of hubris rather than a healthy self-confidence. Judicial discretion, in other words, exists in theory, but in the application of the *halakhah* within the context of our real world few can adopt it as a practical means of reaching legal decisions. To resolve this dilemma, Karo declares that the *halakhah* is to be decided according to the opinions of a "banc" of leading *poskim*. As a first step, he writes, he will decide the *halakhah* in accordance with the unanimous or majority view among the three great "pillars" of the law (*amudey hahora'ah*) "upon whom rest the whole house of Israel: Alfasi, Rambam, and R. Asher b. Yechiel." He will follow that view except in those cases where the preponderance of halakhic opinion and practice diverges from it. In the event that a majority decision cannot be derived from among the "big three" *poskim*—for example, should one of them not refer to a certain matter while the other two are in dispute over it—Karo will resort to a second tier of authorities, deciding the law according to the majority view among Nachmanides, R. Shelomo b. Adret, R. Nissim Gerondi, the *Sefer Hamordekhai*, and the *Sefer Mitzvot Gadol*.

This "mathematical" method for determining the law was not without its critics.[96] Still, its existence demonstrates that the tendency toward binding precedent, to declare the *halakhah* in accordance with the opinions of particular post-Talmudic sages, was advocated by a halakhist of towering reputation. And he by no means was the innovator of this method of decision. Sefardic and "Oriental" Jewish communities had followed such a rule for centuries, adopting either by an act of communal legislation (*takanah*) or by general custom (*minhag*) the practice of establishing one or more outstanding halakhic works as the supreme legal authority.[97] Maimonides especially wore the title of supreme authority (*mara de'atra*) in Egypt, the land of Israel, and in many other localities, a fact that Karo himself recognizes as a virtually universal custom in his region[98] and which goes far in explaining the tendenz of his own *Shulhan Arukh*.[99] The custom in some Sefardic communities was to decide the *halakhah* in accordance with the opinion of R. Asher b. Yechiel. This is another of the ironies of halakhic history, since R. Asher himself opposed such an "automatic" approach to legal decision-making.[100] Yet it, like those tendencies in favor of Rambam, Alfasi, Nachmanides and others, reflected a disposition in Sefardic halakhic thought to defer in legal decision to the judgment of the great *rishonim*, the authorities of the distant past, even when one's own reasoning would lead to a different conclusion.[101] The acceptance of binding precedent thus has a long and honored history among the legal practitioners of a large segment of the Jewish community.

A similar custom emerged among the Jews in Ashkenazic lands during that period. R. Moshe Isserles (d. 1572), whose *Darkhey Moshe* commentary on the *Tur* paralleled the *Beit Yosef*, posited that the law should be decided according to "the latest authorities" (*hilkheta kevatra'ey*). This decision-making rule has a long and rather complex history. It originated in geonic times as a rule of thumb to help decide the *halakhah* in disputes among the sages of the Talmud: "even though the Rabbis may declare that 'in disputes between scholar A and scholar B the *halakhah* follows scholar A,' when later *amoraim* share the opinion of B, the law is in accord with his view."[102] During the Middle Ages, rabbinical authorities began to apply the rule to disputes among post-Talmudic *poskim*. The question which divides contemporary observers is this: when the medieval *poskim* cite the rule *hilkheta kevatra'ey*, do they refer to a particular group of authorities in the recent past, or do they include among "the latest authorities" the scholars of their own generation?[103] The difference here is significant. If *hilkheta kevatra'ey* means that the decisions of the contemporary sage take precedence over those of all previous generations, then we do not have here a rule of "precedent" at all but a rule that permits, very much in the spirit of the remarks by Maimonides and R. Asher, the individual judge to decide questions of *halakhah* on the basis of his own independent reading of the sources. If, on the other hand, "the latest authorities" are an identifiable group of relatively recent sages and books, then the demand that the *halakhah* be decided in accordance with their opinion is indeed a rule of binding precedent, albeit a different standard of precedent than that set by R. Yosef Karo and the Sefardic tradition. However other halakhic scholars defined this rule,[104] there is little doubt that R. Moshe Isserles adopted the latter definition. *We* are not the "latest authorities; the *batra'ey* are rather the most recent authorities whose *written* decisions are customarily followed in our communities.[105] These authorities, rather than the "banc" of earlier scholars (*rishonim*) assembled by Karo, are our teachers. While Isserles disagrees with Karo as to the *source* of binding halakhic precedent, the two are in accord on the notion that there *is* such a thing as binding precedent in *halakhah*, a set of past rulings which ought to determine our legal practice and cohstrain the freedom of the contemporary halakhic authority.

Like the concept of judicial error, the reliance upon precedent displayed by both Karo and Isserles is no absolute guarantee of the absence of judicial discretion in the *halakhah*. Rabbinical authorities are still entitled to rely upon their independent judgment in determining the law,[106] particularly on matters their predecessors have not adjudicated. What the examples of these scholars tell us, however, is that in theory as well as in practice the tendency to seek out and rely upon past decisions exerts considerable constraining force over the discretion of the contemporary *posek*. Facts such as these ought to give us pause before we proclaim, along with the "conventional wisdom," that Jewish law does not recognize a doctrine of binding precedent.

c. THE HALAKHIC CONSENSUS

Over time, a question that has long been a subject of lively dispute within a legal community will become settled. Though the community may have in the past entertained disagreement and divergent approaches to its solution, this multiplicity of views becomes out of place once a widely accepted answer has been arrived at. That answer now holds the status of "law," so that the burden of proof rests heavily upon those who claim that it is not in fact the only correct answer or even the best answer. This process occurs in Jewish law whenever the community of *poskim* reach a consensus as to the right answer to a previously-disputed halakhic issue. At that point, while students of the *halakhah* will continue to study the "rejected" approaches, those will be regarded as purely theoretical possibilities. The law in practice (*halakhah lema`aseh*) will be identified by most observers with the consensus view among the *poskim*. Other, conflicting views, however plausible they may be as interpretations of the halakhic sources, will be seen as incorrect.

This consensus performs a precedential function in *halakhah*, a constraint upon the freedom of rabbinic scholars to derive solutions to legal problems that differ from the consensus view. We see evidence of this consensus throughout the history of Jewish law, every time a community adopts through formal or informal processes the practice of deciding their legal issues in accordance with a single *posek* or a group of *poskim*.[107] We see it in the form of "rules" for halakhic decision-making, designed to create a uniform interpretation of legal sources that in theory could be read in two or more different ways.[108] And we see it operating on substantive halakhic questions as well, forging agreed-upon solutions to issues otherwise susceptible to a variety of approaches. In a significant sense, what we today call "Orthodox Judaism" is an example of halakhic consensus, a collective stipulation by a particular Jewish community to adhere to the particular halakhic interpretations championed by a particular set of rabbinical authorities. Consensus thus enables the Orthodox community to identify itself, to its own members and to the rest of the Jewish world. The controversy over abortion in Jewish law serves as a good example of this consensus at work. I say "controversy" because the halakhic literature supports either one of two general approaches to the permissibility of abortion. A number of authorities, including some outstanding Orthodox *poskim* of our own time, hold that a pregnancy may be terminated for a variety of reasons, including the desire to safeguard the physical and emotional health of the mother. Others, however, rule that abortion is permitted only when the procedure is necessary in order to save the life of the mother, when the fetus can be termed a "pursuer" (*rodef*) that poses a mortal danger to her. The debate has a long history; it is involved, complex, and nuanced. Yet one who reads today's Orthodox halakhic literature, particularly those writings such as compendia on "Jewish medical ethics" intended for a general audience, finds little evidence that the more lenient position remains a legitimate option under Jewish law. The more stringent position, which has now been assumed by the preponderant majority of Orthodox halakhists, has become *the* law, while the comparatively lenient alternative (which itself is far from a permit for abortion "on demand" but sets careful requirements before permitting the procedure) is treated as a deviation from the mainstream—*i.e.*, the "correct"—understanding of the *halakhah*.[109]

Consensus also operates as a constraining factor in the area of marital *halakhah*. In 1966, Rabbi Eliezer Berkovits, the well-known theologian, proposed a solution to the problem of the *agunah*, the wife unable to remarry under Jewish law because her husband either cannot or will not issue her a valid divorce document (*get peturin*). The injustice of this situation has long been evident. Under traditional *halakhah*, the wife cannot divorce the husband; he must divorce her, and if he does not she may be left with no recourse but to live alone or to accede to whatever exorbitant demands the husband will make of her as his price for issuing the *get*. Over the years, halakhists have sought to construct legal remedies that would enable the *agunah* to remarry in cases where the husband ought to but does not authorize a divorce.[110] Berkovits, for his part, suggested that prior to the wedding the bride and groom stipulate that their marriage would be annulled retroactively should the husband one day refuse to comply with the order of a valid rabbinical court (*beit din*) to issue her a *get*.[111] In support of this idea, he marshaled an impressive array of halakhic texts, from the Talmud, the codes and the responsa, from the *rishonim* and the *aharonim*, texts which he analyzed and elucidated in the customary rabbinical style. Yet none of this argumentation impressed his critics. One of these, R. Menachem M. Kasher, sternly rebuked Berkovits for his temerity in raising the idea of stipulations in marriage, given that the use of such stipulations had been unequivocally rejected by the great *poskim* of previous generations. The stature of these authorities, along with their sheer number (Kasher estimated that 1500 rabbis had explicitly rejected "conditional marriage" [*kiddushin al tenai*] under any circumstances), demonstrates that "there is no excuse to raise again a question which has already been examined and decided by all the sages of Israel. Their ruling must not be doubted."[112] The rabbinical opposition Kasher cited had been stirred by a previous proposal, floated in 1907 by an assembly of rabbis in France, that called for the use of stipulations in marriage as a remedy for the *agunah*.[113] Berkovits, too, mentioned that proposal but argued that his own plan was free of the difficulties that had led the *poskim* to reject it. Yet the halakhic consensus had been formed: "stipulations" of whatever kind are not to be entertained in Jewish marriage, no matter the Talmudic and halakhic argumentation that might be brought in their favor.

A similar fate befell Rabbi Shlomo Riskin, who called in 1989 for the rabbinical courts in Israel to coerce husbands to divorce their wives when the latter refuse conjugal rights on the claim that "he is repulsive to me" (*ma'is alay*).[114] This claim, mentioned in the Talmud, is taken by such medieval authorities as Maimonides and Rashi as grounds for coerced divorce,[115] and were the rabbis to accept it as such today, the legal position of the wife would be vastly improved. By "rebelling" against her husband—that is, by declaring him repulsive and refusing him conjugal rights—she would set into motion a chain of events that, given the power of the Israeli rabbinical courts to adjudicate divorce law and to enforce their decisions, would lead inevitably (in most cases) to her freedom. The difficulty is that the rabbis do *not* accept that claim today as grounds for coerced divorce. Riskin attributes this state of affairs to the influence of R. Ya`akov Tam, the leading Tosafist, who feared that the stability of marriage would suffer if the wife were to enjoy such easy access to divorce.[116] R. Tam's position was adopted by virtually all subsequent *rishonim,* to the point that the *Shulhan Arukh,* which frequently recites Rambam's opinion as *halakhah,* makes no mention of his position on this issue.[117] Riskin's argument for restoring the practice of coerced divorce in these cases is two-fold: Rashi and Rambam present an interpretation of the Talmudic sources that is as good as if not better than that of R. Tam; and the social concerns which seem to have led R. Tam to his ruling are far outweighed today by the need to rescue deserted wives from their status as *agunot.* We have here, again, a, apparently legitimate halakhic argument, crafted by a rabbi whose solicitude for *halakhah* is beyond reproach. Yet here again, his proposal is rejected out of hand by Orthodox commentators on the grounds that R. Tam's opinion "has been accepted into the fabric of the *Shulhan Arukh,* the basic code of practice for halakhic Jewry." Instead, Riskin is advised to join in the search for remedies for the *agunah* problem that have some chance of being accepted.[118] The halakhic consensus once more makes itself felt. The consensus having been established—in this case, it has been established for centuries—a conflicting view of the *halakhah* is rejected out of hand, despite the plausibility of that view as a matter of textual interpretation. The rejected opinion certainly retains its theoretical and historical significance, for it is of deep interest to the scholar that Rashi and Rambam read the Talmud differently on this point than do R. Tam and his successors. The "scientific" scholar, too, may want to consider the social, cultural, and other factors that might have led to these variant interpretations. But the rejected opinion is not taken seriously as an alternative approach to the real-life application of Jewish law.[119] Indeed, the very fact that it *has* been rejected by the halakhic consensus is itself a criticism against those like Riskin who might think to raise it again.

To all of this, one might respond that consensus is not a formal constraining rule in the *halakhah* but rather a social fact, the tendency within legal or religious communities to unify over time around particular resolutions to contentious issues. Once a resolution has gained wide acceptance, it may be quite natural for the community's members to "gravitate"[120] toward that resolution, affirming it as one of the accepted truths defining the community's beliefs and actions. Those who question these long-

accepted truths will be seen as dissenters, troublemakers perhaps, for raising issues that had been thought settled. But a fact
of social life should not be confused with the *theory* of law by
which the group lives. That theory may well permit the community's members to revive arguments that have lain dormant for
some time. So, too, in the *halakhah*: regardless of the tendency of
the community to coalesce around the "accepted" opinions, this
social fact does not—in theory—prevent competent scholars
from reconsidering other opinions that, though not reflected in
communal practice, still exist as plausible interpretations of the
legal sources. Against this, however, we can discern two major
reasons why the halakhic consensus operates as a precedential
force in Jewish law. First, the examples cited above show that the
existence of a consensus does constrain the decisions of rabbis,
making it much less likely that they will issue rulings that conflict with the widely-accepted view of the scholarly community.
True, this constraint may be one of practice rather than abstract
theory, but it is after all practice which decides the law. Against
this reality, theoretical possibilities may matter very little; the
halakhah that the people actually know will be the *halakhah* that is
constrained by consensus. And second, some writers do attempt
to construct theoretical justifications for the workings of the
halakhic consensus. One such theory attributes special insight,
an almost charismatic knowledge to the *gedoley hador*, the leading
halakhic sages of the day; the view that they accept should
accordingly be seen as the correct one, even if other interpretations of the sources could be advanced.[121] Another approach, that
of R. Yosef Dov Soloveitchik, derives a distinction between two
types of authoritative tradition (*masoret*) in Jewish law: a "tradition of learning," the Talmudic arguments and proofs that lead to
legal rulings; and a "tradition of practice," formed when the
community (*kelal yisrael*) adopts particular behaviors as its way
of performing the *mitzvot*. This "tradition of practice," the way in
which the *halakhah* is observed in fact, bears a strong affinity to
what I have termed the halakhic consensus, and as Soloveitchik
notes, "reasoning and proofs cannot prevail against a tradition of
practice … in such a case, it is the tradition itself and not Talmudic reasoning which determines the observance."[122] It is because
of this "tradition of practice," "which can no longer be changed
on the basis of purely intellectual considerations," that observant Jews will reject out of hand interpretations of the *halakhah*

that diverge from those that make up the consensus view shared by the recognized authorities.[123] We must conclude, therefore, that the halakhic consensus is real, that it is a factor of considerable weight in identifying the "correct" understanding of Jewish law for the observant community, and that it functions as precedent, constraining the freedom of the halakhist to derive other decisions on the basis of the sources.

The Leeways of Halakhic Precedent: A Look to the Responsa Literature

What then *is* the role of precedent in Jewish law? The answer that emerges from the halakhic writings and the academic research cited above is equivocal or, better, dichotomous, revealing an apparently deep chasm between theory and practice. The theory holds that *halakhah* does not contain a doctrine of binding precedent. The *law*, the standard of Jewish practice, is to be derived from the recognized sources of the law, primarily the Babylonian Talmud and its cognate literature. The rulings and decisions of post-Talmudic scholars are not strictly speaking "law" but interpretations of the law; possessing no inherent authority, they do not constrain the freedom of the contemporary *posek*. The individual *posek* who finds such a ruling inconsistent with the Talmudic sources is accordingly free to ignore it or to set it aside. In practice, however, the decisions of the post-Talmudic sages exert a powerful precedential force upon subsequent generations. As a matter of practice, a litigant legitimately expects that the judge will avoid judicial error, a ruling on a controversial issue that conflicts with the dominant opinion among the *poskim*. As a matter of practice, halakhists have adopted methods for deciding the law in accordance with the opinion of one post-Talmudic authority or a "banc" of such authorities. And as a matter of practice, the community will tend to identify the correct *halakhah* with the consensus view of its scholars, severely limiting thereby the likelihood that alternative points of view will enjoy a careful and considered hearing.

This theory-practice dichotomy ought to make us wary of conventional wisdoms. To put this another way: a theory is only as valid as the data it purports to explain. It is tempting to isolate a few key phrases and remarks that bob on the surface of the halakhic literary sea—"a judge must rule on the basis of his own best understanding ... ", "Jepthah in his generation is the equal of Samuel in *his* generation", among others—and to construct from them a general principle (in Joel Roth's terminology, a "systemic principle") that supposedly governs the halakhic process. It is all the more tempting to do this when such luminaries as Maimonides and R. Asher b. Yechiel make sweeping endorsements of the right of every halakhic authority to reach his own decisions on matters of Jewish law without having to pay deference to the rulings of judges who preceded him. Yet when the practice of a legal community so frequently and clearly diverges from the path set down in the theoretical statements which presume to account for that practice, then the least we can do is to consider the possibility that our theory is flawed. Perhaps the best that can be said for this particular theory is that it operates exclusively on the level of formality. That is to say, Jewish law does not insist upon a doctrine of binding precedent as an *a priori* requirement of legal correctness. Such a doctrine is lacking because halakhic theory insists upon a clear distinction between law and the interpretation of law. The rabbinical decision does not stand alone; it must in the final analysis be justified and supported by Talmudic argumentation. In that sense, Jewish law resembles both the European civil law tradition and the "declaratory" theory of Anglo-American common law in asserting that a judicial decision is *wrong* if it does not cohere with the ultimate legal sources. On the other hand, the notion that every rabbinical judge enjoys the discretion to issue whatever ruling seems correct to him, unconstrained by the opinions of past authorities, does not begin to describe the *halakhah* as it actually functions in Jewish life. It is here that I would differ from Roth: judicial discretion cannot be the *sine qua non* or the "systemic principle" of the *halakhah* because, simply put, the *halakhah* just doesn't work that way. Jewish law, as it is lived and experienced by the community in its daily life, is not so much what the Talmud says it is as what the rabbis say it is. On this level, the level of practice, the *halakhah* shares the tendency of other legal systems to pay great deference to precedent, to the accumulated weight of rabbinical legal thought and experience. The long history of *pesak* plays a role equivalent to that of precedent in other systems. True, in theory this precedent is persuasive in nature, *takdim mancheh*, formally non-binding, meant to guide but not to bind the contemporary authority. But in practice, the record of past halakhic decision can shape the legitimate expectations of the members of the community. It becomes codified; it may achieve the status of consensus among the system's practitioners. When it does so, it can exert upon the decision-maker a constraining force tantamount to that of *takdim mechayev*, binding precedent, making it exceedingly unlikely that he will stray far from the course charted by his predecessors.

Yet this portrait of the Jewish legal process is not yet complete. We saw in our analysis of the role of precedent in the two great Western legal traditions that deference to the rulings of the past is a hallmark of those systems; even civil law courts tend to follow the general thrust of judicial interpretation. We also saw, however, that these traditions have developed means to free the contemporary judge from the influence of precedent when necessary. Even common law judges, supposedly subservient to the doctrine of binding precedent, employ a set of techniques—"leeways," in Karl Llewellyn's terminology—that enable them to expand, contract, escape or re-create a precedent or a series of precedents which would otherwise prevent them from reaching the "right" answers in cases at law. Through the use of these techniques, judges exploit the "creative tension" between the respect for the past and the solicitude for judicial freedom that lies at the heart of their legal tradition. With this in mind, we turn to consider whether Jewish legal practitioners have at their disposal similar techniques for exploring the leeways of halakhic precedent. Granted that the *posek* is expected in practice to adhere to the path of halakhic tradition, to what extent does this practice grant him the flexibility, similar to that recognized in other legal systems, to turn this expectation on its head?

The only way to answer this question with accuracy is through a careful study of the rabbinical responsa literature (*she'elot uteshuvot*). This is because, far more than any other genre of halakhic writing, the responsum (*teshuvah*) conveys its author's considered answer to a specific question (*she'elah*) of Jewish law. This question might be a theoretical or hypothetical one, or it may stem from an actual case. In either event, the questioner (*sho'el*) seeks from the responsum's author (*meshiv*) an opinion as to how the issue should be decided. The *meshiv* will send his answer, almost always accompanied with a detailed discussion of the halakhic argumentation which supports it. By means of this argumentation, the responsum's reader enters as it were the author's study, catches a glimpse of the process of halakhic decision at work, watches as the *meshiv* reasons through to an answer to the question before him.[124] As opposed to a "code" of *halakhah*, which might present the legal conclusion with no accompanying argumentation, a responsum represents a sustained attempt to persuade its readers why they should understand the *halakhah* on this particular issue in this particular way and why they should reject other possible but conflicting interpretations of the law. It is in this literature that we should expect to discover just how rabbinical decisors deal with legal precedents, since in justifying his ruling the *meshiv* will have to take cognizance of those past decisions by noted scholars that either support or conflict with his opinion. Whatever might be the "general" position of Jewish law on the subject, the responsum will offer the clearest indication of how the *posek* actually deals with the authority of precedent. Does he defer to it? Does he reject it? Does he "distinguish" it and thus explain it away? Or does he find a technique, à la Llewellyn, to transform that past ruling into something new and different in the history of halakhic interpretation?

It goes without saying—though in the interests of deflecting criticism I will say it anyway—that "a careful study of the rabbinical responsa literature" lies far beyond the scope of a single article. That sort of study, by which I mean an analysis of responsa as a genre of legal literature, would fill numerous monographs; although some useful preparatory steps have already been taken,[125] the responsa literature awaits its Llewellyn. What I can try to do here is to offer but one responsum as an example of the "leeways" which a rabbinical authority can take with the legal precedents that would otherwise dictate his decision. This example, if and to the extent that it reflects a methodology that is typical among the *poskim*, may teach us much about how halakhists who honor precedent can nonetheless escape its constraining force when overriding considerations call upon them to do so.

The responsum I have chosen to study here was penned by R. Yitzchak b. Sheshet Perfet (Rivash; 1326-1408), an eminent Spanish and North African halakhist, in answer to a query from the community of Tunis.[126] The question, as rephrased by Rivash, concerns a certain Shmuel Aramah, who was to marry a ninety-

year-old woman said to be worth eighty gold doubloons. The
community leadership objected to the proposed union on the
grounds that "his goal is not marriage, but her wealth." Moreover, Shmuel did not yet have children, so that his obligation
under the commandment to "be fruitful and multiply"[127]
remained unfulfilled and manifestly could not be fulfilled by
means of the proposed marriage. Shmuel for his part rejected the
community's instruction and went promptly to the Muslim ruler
of the city, protesting that "the Jews are preventing me from taking a wife" and that Jewish law does not forbid a man from marrying a woman much older than he; "such is the custom in every
Jewish community." The community leaders responded that the
halakhah forbids a marriage of this sort until such time as a man
has fulfilled his duty of procreation. The two sides, perhaps at
the local ruler's suggestion, agreed to submit the issue to Rivash
for his opinion.

I choose this responsum in large part because the established
law on the subject, expressed in the form of Talmudic sources
and prior rulings, is apparently unambiguous. Rivash, indeed,
begins his presentation in precisely that manner:

> A man who has not yet fathered children should marry only a
> woman who is capable of bearing children. A man who has
> fathered children and has already fulfilled the *mitzvah* of procre-
> ation may if he wishes marry a woman who is not capable of bear-
> ing children. This position is stated in the Mishnah [*M.* Yevamot
> 6:6] ... and in the Talmud [*BT* Yevamot 61b]. And these are the
> words of Rambam [*Yad*, Ishut 15:7]: "A man should not marry a
> woman who is barren, or too elderly to bear children, or an *ailonit*
> [a woman with male-like features incapable of conceiving], or a
> minor girl who cannot yet bear children unless he has already ful-
> filled the *mitzvah* of procreation or has another wife with whom he
> can fulfill it."

Not only does the *halakhah* forbid this marriage; it demands that
the communal authorities take action to prevent the wedding
and, should it take place, to bring a forced end to the union.
Rivash brings several Talmudic passages to this effect, among
them *BT* Ketubot 77a: "when one has lived with his wife for ten
years and she has not given birth, he is coerced (*kofin oto*) to
divorce her." This is essential, even though the husband can
technically take a second wife, because so long as the couple live
together he will not be inclined to avail himself of that remedy

(*BT* Ketubot 64a). All of this, Rivash reminds us, is said concerning the barren wife (`akara*), whose barrenness might be temporary, the result of some illness; how much more is this the case, then, with an elderly woman who will never be able to bear children. Moreover, the Talmud cautions that a man should never stop engaging in this *mitzvah* but should always strive to marry a woman capable of bearing children (*BT* Yevamot 62b). As Rambam puts it (*Yad.* Ishut 15:16): "Although a man may have already fulfilled his obligation to procreate, it is a rabbinic commandment that he not refrain from attempting to father children so long as he is physically able, for when a person adds one more life to the Jewish people, it is as though he has built an entire world."

Rivash presents this material in a magisterial way, a narrative unbroken by controversy, disagreement, or minority opinions, one that sets forth the unchallenged, settled law. The Talmudic sources, confirmed by the rulings of Maimonides, the leading *posek* of Spain and North Africa, make clear the existence of a "halakhic consensus" on the impropriety of this proposed marriage and on the duty of the *beit din*, as the representative of Torah law, to do all in its power to frustrate this couple's intention to wed. Yet now Rivash tells us that the law, however clear and undisputed it may be, conflicts sharply with the general practice of the courts.

> The above is the formal law (*shurat hadin*). Yet what can I do? I have never seen nor heard that a *beit din* in our time has actually coerced a man to divorce his wife when she has lived with him for ten years without giving birth or if she is too old to bear children. This is true even in those cases where he has not yet fulfilled his *mitzvah* of procreation, where the law (*din*) would permit the court to compel a divorce.

This situation, too, is no coincidence. It seems that the rabbinical courts have intentionally adopted a "hands-off" policy with respect to a variety of issues in marital law.

> Likewise, I have never seen a *beit din* protest when a man seeks to marry a minor girl not yet capable of bearing children ... Even though a father is prohibited from giving his daughter in marriage until she is old enough to say that 'I wish to marry so-and-so' (*BT* Kidushin 41a), I have never seen anyone protest against this practice. (Nor do the courts interfere) in cases where the daughter of a *kohen* or of a *talmid chakham* (scholar) is to marry an ignorant man.[128]

Rivash thus sets up the sharpest kind of contrast between *halakhah* and *minhag*, between the clear and undisputed interpretation of the Talmudic sources and the actual practice of the courts. This gap, he confesses ("Yet what can I do?"), is a serious intellectual problem for the judge. The *halakhah*, in this case confirmed by the rulings of Maimonides and other *poskim*,[129] would demand that he support the Tunis authorities in their bid to prevent this marriage. Yet the practice of the courts ignores the law, and Rivash must decide whether to acquiesce in that practice. He answers this question in the affirmative, supporting the courts on strictly practical grounds.

> If the courts were to rule according to the letter of the law in all its detail in matters concerning proper marriage arrangements (*zivugim*), it would be necessary to compel divorces in all these cases. Since most of these wives would have to receive their *ketubah* and dowry, and since there is no *ketubah* which is not the subject of financial dispute, strife and contention would increase. For this reason the sages have over many generations ignored these issues. They have not sought to block these marriages from taking place, to say nothing of trying to separate the couples who marry in violation of these rules. So long as the union does not violate the laws of forbidden relationships (*ervah*) or the laws concerning prohibited marriages to priests, it is enough to leave them alone unless the couple bring a marital dispute before the judges.

This is a "practical" defense of the custom because it offers no theoretical justification for it. Rivash does not adopt here the tendency of many medieval *poskim* to reconcile the practice with the controlling halakhic standard or to show that it enjoys its own independent legal validity.[130] On the contrary: he concedes the technical correctness of the claim that these marriages do depart from the halakhic standard. Yet he invites his readers to look beyond the formality of the law to the wider purposes of the legal system, arguing that the attempt to enforce these admittedly valid halakhic requirements would lead to chaos in the administration of justice and to an increase in social discord.[131] It is to avoid these devastating consequences that the sages of many generations have wisely chosen *not* to enforce them. Rivash here sounds not unlike a twentieth-century legal pragmatist,[132] suggesting that in this instance the legal reasoning of the judges has been determined (and rightly so) by their concern for the ends and purposes of the legal system rather than by the formal logic of the law. In making this point, he cuts the legal ground from beneath the feet of the authorities of Tunis. The case, as he presents it, is no longer to be decided by "law," the interpretation of the Talmudic sources and post-Talmudic precedents, but by the practical consequences that can be predicted from the application of that law according to its clear and unambiguous understanding. The authorities cannot act upon their eminently legal desire to frustrate the wedding plans of Shmuel Aramah without creating the sort of "strife and contention" that as responsible leaders they surely wish to avoid. Since they manifestly wish to view themselves as responsible leaders, they have no real alternative but to allow the marriage to proceed.

What does this opinion tell us about precedent in Jewish law, at least in the eyes of R. Yitzchak b. Sheshet Perfet? Since he advocates that the communal authorities defer to the practices of the courts, even though these practices conflict with the Talmudic legal standard, it would seem at first glance that precedent plays an influential role in determining his decision. Indeed, we might say that his approach accords with that of the positivistic theory of the common law, the notion that law is judge-made: we follow precedent because the judicial decision *is* law, whether or not it agrees with the earlier sources upon which it is putatively based. Yet Rivash does not in fact say this; he does not make a claim for the *validity* of the courts' practice. The judges do what they do for good and practical reasons, but their *minhag* remains in conflict with the *halakhah*. It is still, in that sense, a deviation from correct law. Such a deviation cannot exist in the positivist theory, which sees the judicial decision as a self-authenticating act. Moreover, the *minhag* is itself a departure from precedent, from the consensus view of the law among *poskim* like Maimonides whose rulings have already achieved the status of precedent in this community. Deference to the past would have requited the judges to follow those rulings, but they clearly have not done this.

Nor does Rivash's decision support the opposite view, the "conventional wisdom" that binding precedent does not exist in Jewish law. True, he endorses the courts' departure from the existing legal standard, the authoritative precedent as handed down by the *poskim*, but he never rejects their ruling as the correct reading of the legal sources. It remains the law; it continues to express the *halakhah*, the legal ideal, the goal to which the community is called upon to aspire and by which it is to measure the rightness of its actions. So long as the precedent remains good law, the *minhag* of the courts—though necessary and unavoidable in practice—is legally incorrect.[133] The long introduction to the responsum, in which Rivash presents the *halakhah* in great detail, serves to underline the enduring gap between law and *minhag*, which is also a gap between legal aspiration and social reality. Such a gap represents a disappointing failure by the community to live its life in accordance with the ideals to which it purportedly pledges its allegiance.[134]

There is, however, a hint in this *teshuvah* that the *meshiv* wishes to close the gap. In a reference to a Talmudic passage that until now has not figured in his discussion, Rivash indicates a new interpretation of the "law" in support of the judicial practice.

> Therefore, in the present case, if this elderly woman desires to be known as "married,"[135] to have a husband in place of a son to be a staff in her hand and a hoe for burial (*hutra liyadah umarah lekevurah*); and if she has found this man who is willing to marry her on account of his difficult economic situation (*mipnei dohako*), even though he has no children—if you wish to avert your eyes in the way that many great and good communities, communities full of scholars and sages, have done—you may do so.

This passage is a brilliant example of legal rhetoric. I want to say more in principle about that subject below; for now, it is enough to point to several examples. First, like any good rhetorician, Rivash shifts the burden of proof from Shmuel Aramah to those who would deny him the right to marry this woman. Where the community describes Shmuel as acting out pure greed—hence, their mention of the eighty gold doubloons and their statement that "his goal is not marriage, but her wealth"—the *meshiv* now portrays him as a man suffering under severe economic pressure. We are no longer to regard him as a transgressor against accepted communal standards but as a human being like all others, seeking to make the best of his difficult lot. Second, Rivash appeals to the authority of the "great and good" communities and scholars who have permitted this sort of marriage in the past. Even though the Tunis communal leaders have the *halakhah* on their side, they surely do not imagine that they are holier and more righteous than those luminaries. In this way, the *meshiv* suggests that it is the Tunis authorities, and not Shmuel, whose conduct departs from the desired norm. Third, Rivash lets us hear the "woman's voice" in this matter. Until now, the question had been discussed solely from Shmuel's perspective, and the only relevant issue had been whether he is allowed under the law to marry a woman incapable of bearing children. Rivash asks his readers to think about the question from the woman's point of view. When we do, we realize that this is not simply a question concerning Shmuel. Both parties, *she* no less than he, wish to marry, and when we consider her desires as well as his, we are more inclined to respond positively to their (and not simply "his") intention to marry.

For our purposes, however, the most interesting feature of this passage is the phrase "a staff in her hand and a hoe for burial," taken from *BT* Yevamot 65b. The *sugya* there deals with the *mitzvah* of procreation, in particular with the rule that this obligation is incumbent upon males and not females.[136] As we have seen, it is because of this obligation that the *halakhah* can require a man to marry a woman capable of bearing children and to divorce a wife who is barren. So long as he has not fulfilled his duty under the *mitzvah* of procreation, he is entitled and even obliged to divorce his wife if she cannot give him children. It follows that the woman, who has no such obligation, enjoys no such entitlement: she cannot sue for divorce if her husband is sterile, for his condition does not frustrate her fulfillment of a *mitzvah*. As if to support this deduction, the *sugya* reports several cases involving wives who seek divorce from husbands incapable of fathering children. In each case, the rabbinical authority rejects her request on the grounds that she is not obligated by the Torah to bring children into the world and that she therefore lacks a valid claim for divorce. Yet in each case, the woman argues that her desire for children, even though it does not come to fulfill a *mitzvah*, ought nonetheless to entitle her to the freedom to find another husband. In each instance, this argument persuades the judge to grant her request.

One of these cases is reported as follows:

A woman came before the court of Rav Nachman (seeking a divorce).

He said to her: "You are not obligated (under the *mitzvah* of procreation)."[137]

She said to him: "Does this woman not require a staff in her hand and a hoe for burial?"

> Rav Nachman responded: "In a case such as this, we
> certainly require the divorce."

The woman argues that although the commandment to "be
fruitful and multiply" does not apply to her, there are other good
and legitimate reasons for her to want children. A child will
serve her as a "staff," as a support in her old age, and will see
to her burial when the time comes.[138] Rav Nachman's answer,
meanwhile, is more than just a sympathetic response to an emotional plea. By listening to the "woman's voice" in this case, he
redefines the law, re-ordering the conceptual framework within
which it adjudicates her claim. Until now, the relevant issue in
evaluating the claim for divorce in cases of childlessness was the
mitzvah of procreation. A husband may divorce an infertile wife,
because her infertility frustrates his performance of that *mitzvah*.
A wife is not entitled to a divorce from an infertile husband,
because "you are not obligated"; she has no such *mitzvah* to perform and hence cannot demand a divorce. Here, however, the
court accepts her desire for children as in and of itself a legitimate justification for divorce, even though she is under no
halakhic requirement to procreate.

Rivash, too, expands the existing law beyond its explicit
limits. Rav Nachman's ruling concerns a woman's desire for offspring; it says nothing about a woman's "right" to a husband
apart from the possibility that she may bear children from him.
The phrase "a staff for support and a hoe for burial" refers in the
Talmud to children and not to a husband. By citing that phrase
here, applying the Talmud's language to the present case, Rivash
removes it from its original context and lends it a more general
meaning. If a woman is entitled to a "staff" and a "hoe" in her
old age, it now follows that this support may come from a
spouse as well as from children. Her "right" to children now
includes her "right" to a husband, even when she is too old to
bear children from him. This "right," moreover, is sufficient to
permit the marriage even though the union will frustrate the
husband's fulfillment of the *mitzvah* of procreation. Rav Nachman's ruling, of course, says none of this, yet Rivash presents his
conclusion as a logical derivation from it. His conclusion provides a legal justification for the practice of the courts to allow
marriages such as that contemplated in our case. This marriage
is acceptable, in other words, not simply on the grounds of *min-*

hag, not simply because the courts have refrained from enforcing the Talmudic prohibition. Rather, the *halakhah*—the ruling of Rav Nachman, as re-read by R. Yitzchak b. Sheshet Perfet—positively approves of this marriage.

This re-reading is a good illustration of the ways—or, as Karl Llewellyn would say, the leeways—of precedent in Jewish law. The "precedents," the applicable Talmudic law and post-Talmudic decision on this subject, are clear. The accepted, "consensus" view of the law classifies the case of R. Shmuel Aramah and his intended bride under the *mitzvah* of procreation. The case, in other words, is "about" a man's obligation to "be fruitful and multiply" and his consequent duty to marry a woman capable of bearing children, especially if he has not yet fulfilled that obligation. These obligations have been thoroughly discussed in the halakhic tradition; the relevant Talmudic sources and post-Talmudic rulings, along with the accepted interpretations of these, are well-known. So long as it is defined in this way, the question before Rivash can have only one proper legal outcome, as he himself notes in his long introduction and discussion of the applicable *halakhah*. Now, however, Rivash invites his readers to define the question differently. He suggests that it is no longer "about" procreation but "about" a woman's legitimate need for a husband to support her in her latter years. He accomplishes this redefinition by locating a new "precedent," a text that had not previously been brought to bear on the issue, and by fitting that text to the circumstances of the present case. This tactic can be said to parallel the "leeway" Llewellyn entitles: "Enlarging the Standard Set of Sources or Techniques,"[139] introducing into the legal discussion of a question a new set of precedential material that allows the judge to issue a more innovative ruling than would otherwise be possible. Rivash thus pays deference to precedent, to the established understandings of the law, while at the same time finding the means to allow the law—using its own texts and sources—to expand beyond the boundaries of those understandings.

On Precedent, Rhetoric, and Liberal Halakhah

The argument of this paper is that Jewish law, like any other functioning legal tradition, is characterized by a healthy and creative tension between a respect for precedent and a readiness to

innovate. Respect for precedent is demonstrated by the deference that halakhists customarily pay to the established and
accepted understandings of Jewish legal texts and rules. The
readiness to innovate expresses itself in novel interpretations of
halakhic material and applications of halakhic texts. The responsa
literature awaits its Llewellyn, a researcher who will detail the
techniques by which individual *poskim* adapt their precedents to
fit the context of the *she'elot* that confront them. In the meantime,
the example of R. Yitzchak b. Sheshet Perfet indicates the sorts of
technique that are available, the potential for creative application
of precedential material that rests in the halakhist's hands.

It also suggests a more general point, namely that halakhic
reasoning, like legal reasoning in general, can be best understood
as a species of rhetoric.[140] By "rhetoric," I do not mean eloquence,
the embellishment of language. Rather, I use the term, as do a
number of contemporary scholars, to refer to the discourse of
argumentation, the methods and processes by which speakers
seek to justify claims of value to particular audiences. Rhetoric in
this sense can be defined as "a discipline for mobilizing the social
passions for the sake of belief in a contestable truth whose validity can never be demonstrated with mathematical finality."[141]
Pesak, especially in the form of a responsum, is "rhetoric" in this
sense because the *meshiv* not only lays down the law but seeks to
justify his answer to a particular reader or audience of readers.
His answer must be justified because it is not the only possible or
plausible reading of the legal sources that both he and his readers accept as authoritative. His answer is a claim of meaning, a
call to his readers that they should understand their tradition in
this manner, that they should favor this answer over the other
available readings of the sources. His answer will be judged
"correct" to the extent that he succeeds in persuading his audience to accept his interpretation and to act upon it. To the extent
that we accept this approach, we place less emphasis upon judging the "correctness" of a halakhic decision as measured against
some putatively objective standard and more emphasis upon
understanding the manner in which its author presents it.

In our example, the goal of the analysis is not to determine
whether Rivash's ruling was right or wrong but to chart the
argumentative structure by which he *justifies* his answer in terms
that his projected audience—his "ideal reader"—will presumably find convincing. This structure can be usefully divided into

three parts. First, Rivash recites the "halakhic consensus," the Talmudic sources and the precedents that so clearly prohibit the proposed marriage of Shmuel Aramah. While this would seem to be an obvious requirement of the responsa-writer, this section serves the vital rhetorical purpose of reinforcing Rivash's "ethical" appeal as a scholar of probity and integrity, one who knows the law and refuses to overlook it even though it weighs against his preferred solution.[142] Second, he portrays the legal reality, noting that Jewish courts have long refused on pragmatic grounds to enforce this and similar rules. This allows him to create in the minds of his readers a difficult dilemma between law and good legal practice. On the one hand, the "law" as constituted in the precedents prohibits the marriage, and responsible Jewish communal leaders are expected to follow the dictates of Torah and *halakhah*. On the other hand, responsible Jewish communal leaders surely wish to avoid the legal chaos and the inequities that Rivash predicts would result from an attempt to enforce the law in this instance. His readers, in other words, are expected to be torn in both directions. Loyal to both the law and to the proper functioning of their institutions of government, they will no doubt want a solution that does justice to each of these ends. Rivash provides it in the third part of his argument, in which he identifies an alternative precedent to govern the case. This, of course, is the most problematic element of his *teshuvah*: how does one establish a "new" precedent when the controlling *halakhah* is so clear and firm? The answer is two-fold. It is based, first of all, upon the logic of analogy. Rav Nachman's ruling has already determined that a woman is entitled to a "staff" and a "hoe" during her old age, and though his decision referred specifically to children as this source of future support, it is not implausible that Rav Nachman would include a husband under this rubric, particularly for a woman beyond childbearing years. Secondly, Rivash uses Rav Nachman's ruling to redefine the relevant legal situation at hand. The case is not truly "about" the male's obligation to procreate but "about" the needs of an elderly woman and, to a lesser extent, a man who seeks financial security. His sympathetic portrayal of both Shmuel Aramah and his intended bride create an alternative narrative structure[143] around the facts. The reader is now asked to judge the situation from the quite personal vantage point of two human beings who seek not to evade the law but to build lives of personal and economic security. Measuring the matter in this light, the reader is more likely to agree that the case is no longer "about" procreation at all and that, therefore, the existing precedents are no longer relevant to it.

Note that Rivash in no way challenges the correctness of the precedents. The rule set forth in the Talmud and the codes is still good law. Note, too, his recognition that the rule clearly covers the circumstances of the present case, in which a childless man seeks to marry a woman incapable of conceiving. Yet while maintaining the utmost respect for the precedent, the *posek* sets it aside, ostensibly by locating an alternative precedent in the ruling of Rav Nachman. This alternative precedent is in point of fact new law; a woman's previously-recognized "right" to children now becomes, in the hands of the fourteenth-century *posek*, a "right" to marriage. Thus, through the innovative "translation" of the language and logic of the Talmudic tradition,[144] a tradition his readers already accept as authoritative, Rivash the legal rhetorician seeks to persuade them that *halakhah* speaks with more than one voice to the situation at hand, that it offers more than one possibly correct answer to the *she'elah*, and that his own correct answer is more equitable and efficient than the other, more precedented one.

If law in general and Jewish law in particular exhibit a "creative tension" over the role of precedent, we are now in a position, I think, to better understand how that tension operates. The concept of precedent, as noted at the outset of this paper, is endemic to legal practice, and there exists a broad consensus among lawyers that precedent operates as a constraining factor upon freedom of legal decision. Yet it is the lawyers themselves, as the practitioners of the rhetorical discipline of law, who define the limits of that constraint. Precedent, like every other element of a legal tradition, is the material out of which jurists construct their discourse. It is this very discourse, the give-and-take of legal argument and the sustained effort to persuade the community of practitioners of the correctness of a particular answer, that will determine a case to be a "precedent" and precisely what that precedent means. Whatever the status of the doctrine of precedent in Jewish law, the influence of a precedent upon the ruling of a contemporary scholar is a matter to be determined by the scholar himself, operating as the practitioner/rhetorician of the *halakhah* within a community of fellow practitioners, placing that precedent in relationship to other rules, cases, and considerations. The responsum we have examined, in which the obviously controlling precedents are both honored and set aside through the *posek*'s judicial rhetoric, is a powerful example of this phenomenon.

To think of *halakhah* as a rhetorical practice, then, helps account for the ambivalent role of precedent in Jewish law. This becomes a helpful tool with which to address more general issues of legal theory. One such issue is the controversy in the academic literature surrounding what has been called the "turn to Jewish law," a scholarly motif that has emerged in response to a perceived crisis in American jurisprudence.[145] The "crisis" is the breakdown of the liberal consensus that held sway in legal practice in the United States, among practitioners as well as academicians, roughly from the 1930s to the early 1970s.[146] In place of this consensus, which had encouraged the belief of mainstream scholars in the capacity of legal reasoning to arrive at obviously correct answers to legal questions, there now exists a cacophony of theories, ideologies, and "metanarratives" that lead to radically differing conceptions of the nature of law and of legal correctness. The dilemma: can American lawyers speak of their law as a coherent system when the legal community is characterized by broad behavioral and interpretive pluralism? Some authors have suggested Jewish law as a solution, seeing in it a model of a unified legal system that at the same time tolerates *machloket* (dispute) and a plurality of interpretations of legal truth.[147] Others reject this model as a distortion of Jewish law.[148] They stress that Judaism is an essentially religious system, in which law is the product of divine revelation. Belief in the revealed status of the law acts as a firm restraint upon interpretive freedom; the predominant demand in Jewish legal practice is for uniformity rather than plurality in decision.[149] This is a fascinating controversy; unfortunately, the writers on both sides tend to base their positions upon what I would call programmatic texts: that is, statements and stories in Talmudic literature[150] that can be interpreted as providing definition or structure to Jewish law. The difficulty is that these texts are not necessarily meant to serve as essays in jurisprudential theory, nor do they operate in the world of practice as a constitution for a working Jewish legal system. They are abstract pronouncements whose applicability to the process of decision-making is, to put it mildly, ambiguous. Any attempt to define the nature of Jewish law on the basis of these texts is thus unlikely to advance beyond the realm of speculation.[151] A more promising way of measuring Jewish law's capacity for pluralism is to study its concrete *practice*, the decisions rendered by halakhic authorities in actual cases. To the extent we find these *poskim* engaging in creative interpretation and application of their legal materials—making use, we might say, of the leeways of precedent in Jewish law— then and only then might we be able to identify Jewish law as a model of a legal system that—in practice if not in theory— accommodates a variety of conceptions of legal truth.

The rhetorical conception of Jewish law also speaks to our own situation as practitioners of liberal *halakhah*. As I stated near the outset of this essay, we stand accused by the Orthodox of misunderstanding (at best) or distorting (at worst) the substance of the *halakhah* because we diverge from the path of our predecessors. This implies that liberal *halakhah* is *illegitimate*: the decisions we render and the intellectual processes by which we reach them, precisely because they defy the weight of precedent, transgress against the canons of acceptable halakhic practice. How do we respond to this charge? We might, of course, decide to ignore it completely. "Liberal *halakhah*,"we might say, "is our own business. We are the ones who determine its definitions and proper procedures; it is legitimate because we say so, contrary assertions by Orthodox critics notwithstanding." Yet however satisfying this response might be as polemic, it fails to suffice as a matter of theory and substance. The underlying assumption of our work as liberal halakhists is that what we are doing is *legitimate*, that our thinking and writing are quite at home within the halakhic tradition, and that our decisions—though they diverge from those issued by non-liberal scholars—are deeply informed by and rooted in the legal values that are the common heritage of the Jewish people. We do not imagine that we have invented an entirely new discipline and called it "*halakhah*"; rather, we call it "*halakhah*" because however new it seems it is seamlessly consistent with the discipline of Jewish law as practiced by rabbis for two millennia. Our position, indeed, is that our rulings and interpretations represent this *halakhah* at its best, that they develop the principles and insights inherent in our legal sources in a way that is compatible with our liberal Jewish values. To establish this assumption, we need a substantive answer to the contention that our work is invalid *because* we diverge from precedent.

A better response to this charge would be to announce that
Jewish law does not recognize a rule of binding precedent; we
therefore violate no standard of halakhic practice when we
depart from the interpretations of the past. This response offers
an obvious advantage, enabling us to defend our innovations
while claiming to stand well within the circle of halakhic legitimacy. Unfortunately, as we have seen, it offers an incomplete
and quite possibly misleading description of the process of Jewish law. Halakhic authorities in both theory and practice do
regard the decisions of previous authorities as exerting a constraining force over contemporary *pesak*. In this, Jewish law follows the pattern of law in general. Reliance upon precedent,
upon the accumulated wisdom of the past, is characteristic of
the activity we call law. As liberals, it is certainly in our interest
to portray the halakhic system in a manner congenial to our purposes, but that picture ought to be an honest and accurate one. If
we contend that the *halakhah* supports our interpretations of it,
the *halakhah* of which we speak should be the discipline of Jewish law as it actually is, not an idealized view of what we would
wish it to be. And that actual, real-world *halakhah* is a legal
process that respects precedent, honors it, and is suffused by it.

Our best recourse, rather, is that suggested by the title of this
paper. If we describe what are doing as *halakhah*, then the way we
do it must fit the contours of that centuries-old rabbinical practice. If there is no law—or *halakhah*—without precedent, then liberal *halakhah*, too, must take precedent seriously. This implies
more than lip service; it demands a commitment to the set of
legal values that have defined and continue to define the practice
of Jewish law. Three such values deserve mention here: constraint, language, and tradition.

Constraint is an inherent element of any legal practice that
honors precedent—which is to say, of any legal practice. The central function of precedent is to limit the discretion of judges and
other legal actors. Constraint, of course, does not operate in a
vacuum, independent of all other legal values. Another inherent
element of law is innovation, the power to develop new answers
and solutions to the problems created by an ever-changing social
reality. The co-existence of the values of precedent *and* innovation produces an unavoidable tension in legal thought, and as
we have seen, various legal systems have fashioned techniques
to accommodate that tension. Still, one cannot plausibly engage

in the activity of "law" unless one accedes to law's constraining element, an element symbolized by precedent as it operates in different legal systems. For liberal halakhists, this means we must recognize that the texts and sources of Jewish law do in fact *constrain* us; they limit what we are able to say, the claims we might reasonably make in the name of *halakhah*. I stress this point because we occasionally hear suggestions that the discipline of liberal *halakhah* be defined almost exclusively on the basis of moral principles. That is, we should identify those grand ideas and ideals in Jewish legal literature that are congenial to progressive values and make our decisions directly on that basis. For example, since one of the fundamental principles of our religious thought is social justice, and since we discern this ideal quite readily in our sources, we would say that any decision that upon serious reflection strikes us as "moral" or "just" is automatically and for that reason alone *"halakhah"* for us, regardless what the halakhic texts themselves—the Talmud and the accumulated precedents in the post-Talmudic halakhic literature— may say. While I do not doubt that a system so conceived would indeed be "liberal," I cannot call it "law." It is rather an exercise in ideological thinking, wherein decisions on specific issues are made by way of deduction from abstract "first" principles. Law, by contrast, is an exercise in *textual* thinking, which while informed by the ideologies—that is, by the general moral and political commitments—of its participants, proceeds by way of discussion and debate over the meaning of texts. And while the meaning of those texts may be contestable, equivocal, and not etched in stone, neither is it infinitely plastic. An argument over textual meaning implies that the text does mean *something* and therefore does not mean the opposite of that something; we are constrained from claiming for a text a meaning that it does not convey.[152] If we liberals are serious in saying that we are engaged in the practice of *halakhah*, we must accept the essential condition of that practice: the texts of *halakhah*—which serve as precedents—do in fact constrain the choices we can make.

The second legal value, *language*, flows directly from the first. If precedent constrains us to pay close attention to the texts of the past, it also requires that we argue over the meaning of those texts in the language of the *halakhah*. Law is a language whose vocabulary consists of texts and whose grammar is composed of the techniques by which the jurists who speak the language explain and apply these texts. The task of the lawyer is to translate the bare facts of a case, drawn from social reality, into legal language, a discourse of rules, principles, and concepts that inhabit the world of the jurist; the law can resolve the case only by working its way through these rules and principles and concepts.[153] *Halakhah*, similarly, is a discourse in which issues are talked about in a particular textual language, to the point that literary expressions that deviate from this linguistic context are not recognized as truly halakhic. Liberal halakhists have always recognized this. From the inception of the Reform movement in Europe, legal scholars associated with the cause have utilized halakhic texts and argument to explain and justify its ritual innovations.[154] Reform responsa are themselves halakhic documents; though written in the vernacular of the *sho'el* and the *meshiv*, they speak the classical rabbinic language of Talmudic text and analysis.[155] These points should be kept in mind when we hear calls for a new and different style of Reform responsa-writing that is less dependent upon halakhic text and that draws more heavily from other Jewish and non-Jewish literary genres. Taking precedent seriously requires that place ourselves firmly within the boundaries of Jewish legal practice, and that practice is conducted in the textual language that has served as the medium of expression for Jewish law for two millennia. Responsa that arrive at their conclusions without working through the texts and language of Jewish law are not *responsa* in the truest sense, precisely because they depart from that practice.

Finally, the recognition of precedent as an essential component of legal practice implies that we are working within a *tradition*. I have in mind here the concept of tradition as defined by Alisdair MacIntyre: "a living tradition then is an historically extended, socially embodied argument, and an argument precisely in part about the goods which constitute that tradition."[156] A tradition so conceived is the moral and cultural context within which the participants of any argument must stand if they hope to persuade their fellow participants of the rightness of their position or even to make themselves understood to each other.[157] A traditional discourse is rooted in the texts of the past ("historically extended"), is carried on with conversation partners who likewise participate in that tradition ("socially embodied"), and its common life is comprised largely of an argument over the precise meaning and application of those texts to questions and challenges that arise all the time. Seen in this way, a tradition is not to be identified with "stability," with "eternal verities" to be contrasted with the evanescent fads and fashions of the contemporary world. MacIntyre's tradition is rather a dynamic thing, in which a community's self-definition—that is, the understanding and interpretation of its texts—is always up for grabs, always in flux, and constantly tested in the crucible of the community's life and experience. To participate in the tradition of *halakhah* is to discover, as did Rivash, a rich and ample treasure-house of resources for argument, materials out of which new meanings are constantly proposed and frequently accepted. Liberals need not fear, therefore, that adherence to this tradition necessarily stifles their creativity. On the contrary: the halakhic tradition has long been the proving ground for creative legal thought and response. This creativity, however, does require that we see ourselves not as revolutionaries or as inventors of a new language that is all our own but as participants in the ongoing historical argument that is the language of *halakhah*.

Conclusion

Precedent, the tendency to decide disputed questions on the basis of earlier decisions, is an endemic feature of every legal system. While the precise role of precedent in Jewish law is a matter of controversy, there is no question that respect for the interpretations of the past is a central element in halakhic practice. No normative statement can make an authentic claim to the status of *halakhah* unless it pays deference to the role of precedent, unless it is characterized by the three values of constraint, language, and tradition. While those may sound like conservative values, halakhic history reveals that adherence to precedent does not deter the creative *posek* from innovating within the law, from discovering plausible alternative readings of the texts of the past. This last point is of critical importance to our liberal halakhic endeavor. If our own work is to lodge a believable claim to the status of *halakhah*, it must be truly halakhic; it must follow the path that has always defined halakhic practice. That path is not hidebound to old ways and established interpretations. It is the way of constraint *and* innovation, a respect for the past coupled with the readiness to find new meaning in old texts. We walk that path when we find new meanings in old texts and when we take precedent seriously.

Notes

1. Anthony T. Kronman, "Precedent and Tradition," *Yale Law Journal* 99 (1990), 1029-1068, at 1033.
2. This does not mean that we cannot imagine a kind of law where precedent plays no constraining role. Kronman himself (see note 1) reminds us of Max Weber's notion of "charismatic authority," which recognizes no constraint of any kind upon the right of the inspired leader to declare the law; see Anthony T. Kronman, *Max Weber* (Stanford: Stanford U. Press, 1983), 47-50. The remarks in the text refer to the other "types" of law, those Weber would term "traditional" or "legal-rational," that more accurately resemble the activity of law as we know it in the developed legal traditions.
3. It is possible to argue that precedent exerts a strong influence upon other intellectual activities besides law—one thinks here of the entire range of public social and political discourse—that relies upon argumentation rather than philosophical demonstration as its chief method for arriving at knowledge. Unlike demonstrative proof, which is equivalent to formal logic and is hence universal in its truth claims, argumentation addresses itself to particular audiences, utilizing techniques to gain their assent to a thesis presented for their approval. Precedents, understood here as the agreed-upon starting points for discussion, are absolutely crucial if coherent argument is to take place. "That is why so often the best justification of a course of conduct—the one that dispenses with the need for any other reason—consists in showing that the course is in conformity with the recognized order, that it can avail itself of unquestioned precedents"; Chaim Perelman, *The Idea of Justice and The Problem of Argument* (New York: Humanities Press, 1963), 157. This is certainly correct; however, my goal here is to distinguish law primarily from those more philosophical disciplines that do not grant the past any a priori influence over the present. Even among the public discourses, moreover, I think that Perelman would agree that precedent plays its most systematic and formal role in the discipline of law.
4. The literature is vast; the following is but a partial list. Frederick Schauer, "Precedent," *Stanford Law Review* 39 (1987), 571-605; Cass R. Sunstein, *Legal Reasoning and Political Conflict* (New York: Oxford U. Press, 1996), 76-77; Richard Wasserstrom, *The Judicial Decision* (Stanford: Stanford U. Press, 1961), 39-83; Edwin W. Patterson, *Jurisprudence: Men and Ideas of the Law* (Brooklyn: The Foundation Press, 1953), 97; Karl Llewellyn, "Case Law," *Encyclopedia of the Social Sciences* (New York: Macmillan, 1930), 3:249; Edgar Bodenheimer, "Law as Order and Justice," *Journal of Public Law* 6 (1957),

194*ff*; Edgar Bodenheimer, *Jurisprudence* (Cambridge: Harvard U. Press, 1974), 426-427; A. L. Goodhart, "Precedent in English and Continental Law," *Law Quarterly Review* 50 (1934), 40*ff*; Benjamin Cardozo, *The Nature of the Judicial Process* (New Haven: Yale U. Press, 1921), 149; Chaim Perelman, *Justice, Law, and Argument* (Dordrecht, Holland: Reidel, 1980) 132-134.

5. This argument is developed by Kronman (see note 1) at 1047*ff*., drawing primarily upon the thought of Edmund Burke.

6. I leave aside here the problem faced by the legislature in a community possessing a constitution, written or otherwise, which limits the exercise of legislative power, as well as the question of which agency is to interpret and apply the limits set forth in that constitution. My point is rather that a legislature, as the law-creating institution in a society, is not constrained in its lawmaking powers by anything save its own will. This applies to constitutions, which serve as the fundamental legislation of their communities. A constitution, that is to say, is itself a legislative act by which the community enacts limits upon the powers of future lawmakers. Judges, by contrast, according to the definition proposed in the text, do not enjoy the power to create law where none had before existed.

7. Oliver Wendell Holmes, Jr., "The Path of the Law," *Harvard Law Review* 10 (1897), 457-478, at 469.

8. Compare D. Neil MacCormick and Robert S. Summers, *Interpreting Precedents: A Comparative Study* (Aldershot, UK: Ashgate, 1997), 531-532: precedent plays a major role in the development of all major legal systems; at the same time, all systems accommodate change and evolution in precedent through judicial action.

9. The following works deserve special mention: Moshe Zemer, *Halakhah shefuyah* (Tel Aviv: Devir, 1993) / *Evolving Halakhah* (Woodstock, VT: Jewish Lights Publishing, 1999); the collected studies published by the Freehof Institute of Liberal Halakhah and edited by Walter Jacob and Moshe Zemer (*Dynamic Jewish Law*, 1991; *Rabbinic-Lay Relations in Jewish Law*, 1993; *Conversion to Judaism in Jewish Law*, 1994; *The Fetus and Fertility in Jewish Law*, 1995; *Death and Euthanasia in Jewish Law*, 1995; *Israel and the Diaspora in Jewish Law*, 1997; *Aging and the Aged in Jewish Law*, 1998); Louis Jacobs, *A Tree of Life: Diversity, Flexibility, and Creativity in Jewish Law* (Oxford: Oxford U. Press, 1984); Joel Roth, *The Halakhic Process: A Systemic Analysis* (New York: Jewish Theological Seminary of America, 1986); Eliezer Berkovits, *Hahalakhah: kochah vetafkidah* (Jerusalem: Mosad Harav Kook, 1981). And by no means should we forget the many responsa written by liberal rabbis that serve as examples of liberal *halakhah* in practice.

10. But not always; at times, it is the liberals who base their arguments upon the accepted, seemingly literal reading of the texts while the orthodox defend their position through deft and creative reinterpretation of those same texts. For an example, see Mark Washofsky, "Halakhah in Translation: The Chatam Sofer on Prayer in the Vernacular," in the forthcoming festschrift for Rabbi A. Stanley Dreyfus.

11. Following the "working definition" in Alan Watson, *The Making of the Civil Law* (Cambridge, MA: Harvard U. Press, 1981), 4: "a civil law system would be a system in which parts or the whole of Justinian's *Corpus juris civilis* have been in the past or are at present treated as the law of the land or, at the very

least, are of direct and highly persuasive force; or else it derives from any such system."

12. Mary Ann Glendon, Michael Wallace Gordon, and Christopher Osakwe, *Comparative Legal Traditions* (St. Paul: West Publishing Co., 1985), 194.

13. Roman law, of course, does not start with Justinian, whose great Code in many ways marked a departure from previous Roman jurisprudence; see below in the text. Yet even prior to Justinian, we can say that "a theory of judicial precedent comparable to that of Anglo-American law was never formally recognized at Rome." Judges (*iudices*) instead rendered decisions on a case-by-case basis. See Hans Julius Wolff, *Roman Law: An Historical Introduction* (Norman, OK: U. of Oklahoma Press, 1951), 80.

14. Wolff, 164.

15. Fritz Schultz, *History of Roman Legal Science* (Oxford: Clarendon Press, 1946), 285-286.

16. John H. Merryman, *The Civil Law Tradition* (Stanford: Stanford U. Press, 1969), 20-26. Merryman (16-17) also notes the emphasis that Enlightenment political theory placed upon the doctrine of separation of powers as essential for rational democratic government. Montesquieu's *Spirit of the Laws* is the primary citation on this point, which for our purposes provides another explanation for the tendency of the nineteenth-century legal codes to deny to judges any power to legislate.

17. Thus, those parts of pre-revolutionary France whose legal systems were dominated by Roman law were designated as *les pays du droit écrit*, while the northern and less-Latinized regions of the country were called *les pays du coutume*, since the older customary law held sway there; Gabriel Marty and Pierre Raynaud, *Droit civil* (Paris: Sirey, 1972), 1:118. France today, thanks to codification, is a "country of "written law"; *i.e.*, "legislation dominates French law"; René David, *French Law: Its Structures, Sources and Methodology* (Baton Rouge: Louisiana State Press, 1972), 155.

18. Merryman, 25; Glendon, *et al.*, 204-205. See David, 170-178. Civil law doctrine knows of three types of custom. French courts will recognize the existence of *consuetudo secundum legem* (a custom supporting the law), since this custom is regarded as the definition of the terms of the legal rule. On the other hand, *consuetudo praeter legem* (custom which precedes law), which establishes legal rules that are independent of, but not inconsistent with, legislation is recognized only in areas of the law that have not yet been codified. And the third kind of custom, *consuetudo adversus legem* (custom contrary to law), simply does not exist in a legal system dominated by legislation. When such a custom is discovered in French legal practice, it is generally reinterpreted by the courts so that it does not conflict with the authority of the code or of the relevant statute.

19. Watson, 83-84. This, he suggests, might help explain the hostility of those English philosophers concerned with legal matters, notably Hobbes and Bentham, to the common law. The common law theorists, of course, could respond with Sir Edward Coke that while "Reason is the life of the law," this was "an artificial perfection of Reason got by long study, observation, and experience"; Coke, *Institutes of the Laws of England*, ed. J. H. Thomas, Esq. (London, 1818), 1.

20. David, 179.

21. Schultz, 52-53, speaking of the "Hellenistic period" of Roman jurisprudence, when the *iudices* turned for legal advice to the great scholars (*iurisconsulti*) who would hand down learned advice (*responsa*) to them.

22. See David, 180-181, on the situation in French law: the principle of separation of powers prevents the creation of legal rules by the courts. *Cf. Code civil*, article 5: *il est défendu aux juges de prononcer par voie de disposition générale et réglementaire*.

23. ... *non exemplis sed legibus iudicandum est* (legal decisions must be based upon enacted law and not upon prior decisions in particular cases); *Code of Justinian* VII.45.13.

24. René David and John E. C. Brierley, *Major Legal Systems in the World Today* (London: Stevens and Sons, 1985), 120-121, 136.

25. See Merryman, 35-39; Glendon *et al.*, 208.

26. Merryman, 48, contrasting the "folklore" of the civil law, which ignores judicial decision as a source of law, with this reality. See also Robert A. Riegert, "The West German Code, Its Origin and Its Contract Provisions," *Tulane Law Review* 45 (1970), 69-71.

27. Glendon *et al.*, 209.

28. Michel Trope and Christophe Grzegorczyk, "Precedent in France," in D. Neil MacCormick and Robert S. Summers, *Interpreting Precedents: A Comparative Study* (Aldershot, UK: Ashgate, 1997), 115.

29. David, 180.

30. Trope and Grzegorczyk, 112-113.

31. Glendon *et al.*, 209; Riegert, 69-70. See also David, 183-184: the primary role of the *Cour de Cassation* is to enforce the uniform application of the law. "This function cannot be fulfilled if the Court of Cassation itself does not have a stable case law."

32. MacCormick and Summers, 532.

33. And see Merryman, 17: the experience in pre-revolutionary France, in particular, was that the judiciary was a conservative, anti-progressive force. Legislation, by contrast, could express the will of the people and keep the judges in check.

34. As Watson writes (p. 25): "Roman law is learned at the feet of specially appointed teachers and not from observing practitioners of all kinds." See also David and Brierley, 147-149.

35. Glendon *et al.*, 268.

36. Glendon *et al.*, 564-565. See Theodore F. T. Plucknett, *A Concise History of the Common Law* (Boston: Little, Brown, 1956), 342: since the common law developed out of the judicial custom of the king's courts, it was but natural that these courts developed regular routines of practice, which, becoming settled, could allow the people to forecast with certainty the future decisions of the judges.

37. Rupert Cross, *Precedent in English Law* (Oxford: Clarendon Press, 1977), 4.

38. The most striking example of this is the rule that prevailed in England from 1898 to 1966 whereby the House of Lords, the highest appellate body, considered itself bound to its own precedents. See Cross, 4-8.

39. Or the *ratio decidendi*, that part of the judge's ruling that is considered essential to the decision; all else in the opinion is called *dicta* and does not bind the subsequent judge. See Cross, 38*ff*.

40. See P. S. Atiyah and Robert S. Summers, *Form and Substance in Anglo-American Law* (Oxford: Clarendon Press,1987), 115, who cite the English judge Lord Patrick Devlin: "The principle of *stare decisis* does not apply only to good decisions; if it did, it would have neither value nor meaning. It is only if a (prior) decision is doubtful that the principle has to be invoked."

41. See the discussion in Cross, 12-17.

42. Atiyah and Summers, 118-127.

43. Compare Arthur L. Goodhart, *Essays in Jurisprudence and the Common Law* (Cambridge: Cambridge U. Press, 1931), 1-26, who constructs a ten-point checklist for determining the *ratio decidendi*, with the critique of Cross, 66-76. In turn, C. K. Allen, *Law in the Making* Seventh Edition (Oxford: Clarendon Press, 1964), 259, n. 3, opines that Cross's own description "is perhaps a little too complicated to be really illuminating." Allen, 260, rejects the effort to find a precise definition, proposing a pragmatic alternative: "it is for a court, of whatever degree, which is called upon to consider a precedent, to determine what the true *ratio* was."

44. Atiyah and Summers, 116*ff.* The difference between the English and American versions of *stare decisis*, they write, rests in the greater degree of formalism present in English law, as opposed to the more "substantive" approach of American courts. English judges are therefore much less likely to disregard otherwise binding precedents than are their American counterparts. American courts, too, will overrule precedents with much greater frequency than English courts. But even in America, "*stare decisis* is at least the everyday working rule of our law;" Benjamin Cardozo, *The Nature of the Judicial Process* (New Haven: Yale, 1921), 19. In the words of the U.S. Supreme Court: "it is indisputable that *stare decisis* is a basic self-governing principle within the Judicial Branch, which is entrusted with the sensitive and difficult task of fashioning and preserving a jurisprudential system that is not based upon 'an arbitrary decision'"; Patterson v. McClean Credit Union, 109 S.Ct. 2363, 2370 (1989).

45. P. J. Fitzgerald, *Salmond on Jurisprudence*, 12th ed. (London: Sweet and Maxwell, 1966), 145. See also Allen, 268-285, for examples of English judges deriving guidance from Roman or continental law. On the theory of non-authoritative precedent, see Richard Bronaugh, "Persuasive Precedent," in Laurence Goldstein, ed., *Precedent in Law* (Oxford: Clarendon Press, 1987), 217-247. Rabbinic law serves as "persuasive precedent" in the modern Israeli legal system, particularly when a court confronts a question that has no clear resolution in existing law. See Menachem Elon, *Jewish Law: History, Sources, and Principles*, translated by Bernard Auerbach and Melvin J. Sykes (Philadelphia: Jewish Publication Society, 1994), 1729-1730. See also his discussion of the Foundations of Law Act (1980), which formally requires that when a court cannot resolve a question on the basis of legislation or judicial precedent it shall look to the principles of freedom, justice, equity, and peace as expressed in the "Jewish heritage" (*moreshet yisrael*); 1827*ff.*

46. Sir Matthew Hale, *The History of the Common Law of England*, 6th ed. (London: Butterworth, 1820), 90.

47. Sir William Blackstone, *Commentaries on the Laws of England*, 1:3, 68-70.

48. On this, see Daniel J. Boorstin, *The Mysterious Science of the Law: An Essay on Blackstone's Commentaries* (Boston: Beacon Press, 1958), and H. L. A. Hart,

"The Demystification of the Law," in his *Essays on Bentham* (Oxford: Clarendon Press, 1982), 21-39.

49. A famous American expression of this idea is that of Supreme Court Justice Oliver Wendell Holmes, Jr., dissenting in case of Southern Pacific Co. v. Jensen, 244 U.S. 205, 222: "The common law is not a brooding omnipresence in the sky but the articulate voice of some sovereign or quasi-sovereign that can be identified."

50. On the decline of the declaratory theory see Cross, 26-35. Gerald Postema, "Some Roots of Our Notion of Precedent," in Goldstein, 9-33, traces the influence of Hobbes and Bentham on the changing notions of precedent in England. See as well his *Bentham and the Common Law Tradition* (Oxford: Clarendon Press, 1986), 192-196. The "school" of Anglo-American legal positivism was founded, according to all accounts, by Jeremy Bentham [see *The Limits of Jurisprudence Defined* (New York: Columbia U. Press, 1945) and *A Comment on the Commentaries*, ed. J. H. Burns and H. L. A. Hart (London: Athalone Press, 1977) and developed by his student John Austin (d. 1859; see his *The Province of Jurisprudence Determined* (Indianapolis: Hackett, 1998). Bentham and Austin hold that law must be defined as a command, an order of a sovereign; hence a judge who formulates a previously undeclared legal instruction can do so legitimately only if his ruling is understood to be a form of legislation authorized by the sovereign authority of his jurisdiction. The theory has been modified somewhat in the twentieth century by H. L. A. Hart, whose *The Concept of Law* (Oxford: Clarendon Press, 1961) presents law as a system of rules rather than individual commands.

51. Atiyah and Summers, 120-124. They follow here their general assertion that the English legal practice is more formalistic and less flexible than the American.

52. Cross, 176*ff.* On the analogical nature of legal reasoning, see Edward H. Levi, *An Introduction to Legal Reasoning* (Chicago: U. of Chicago Press, 1949), and Cass Sunstein, *Legal Reasoning and Political Conflict* (New York: Oxford U. Press, 1996).

53. See the following works of Karl Llewellyn: *The Common Law Tradition: Deciding Appeals* (Boston: Little, Brown, 1960); *The Case Law System in America*, edited and with an introduction by Paul Gewirtz, translated by Michael Ansaldi (Chicago: U. of Chicago Press, 1989); and "Remarks on the Theory of Appellate Decision," *Vanderbilt Law Review* 3 (1950), 395-406. On his life and work, see William Twining, *Karl Llewellyn and the Realist Movement* (London: Weidenfeld and Nicolson, 1973). It is my view that Llewellyn's work is a highly useful tool for the understanding of the process and realities of halakhic decision-making. I hope to expand upon this observation in a future work.

54. See Llewellyn, *The Common Law Tradition*, 19-61, for the "Major Steadying Factors in Our Appellate Courts." These "social and professional factors" do not exclude intellectual influences; among Llewellyn's steadying factors are the existence of an accepted legal doctrine and the necessity for writing an opinion that explains the decision. These are "professional," however, to the extent that a judge must justify the decision in a form that the members of the craft will find acceptable.

55. Fitzgerald, 178.

56. Llewellyn, "Remarks," 395.
57. Zerach Warhaftig, "Hatakdim bamishpat ha`ivri," *Shenaton Hamishpat Ha`ivri* 6-7 (1979-1980) 105, 119-120.
58. Eliav Shochetman, "Chovat hahanmakah bamishpat ha`ivri," *Shenaton Hamishpat Ha`ivri* 6-7 (1979-1980) 321, 395.
59. On this rule (*ein lo ladayan ela mah she`einav ro'ot*), see below.
60. Elon, *Jewish Law*, 983-985.
61. Ya`akov Canaani, *Otzar halashon ha`ivrit* (Givatayim: Massada, 1989), credits the invention to Itamar Ben-Avi (d. 1942).
62. Although there have been various bumps along this road. For the history of the doctrine of binding precedent in Israeli law, see Warhaftig, 109-113.
63. The emphasis here is on the word "generally"; the Talmud and the halakhic literature require the judge to respond positively to the litigant's request for a written record "of the legal basis upon which you rendered my judgment (*me'eizeh ta`am dantuni*)." See *BT* Sanhedrin 31b and *Yad*, Sanhedrin 6:6.
64. See Shochetman, 326-332. See also Hanina Ben-Menahem, *Judicial Deviation in Talmudic Law* (New York: Harwood, 1991), 19-40.
65. Decisions of Jewish courts are not to be reviewed by other courts, let alone "higher" tribunals exercising supervisory power; "no court may critique the ruling of another court" (*BT* Bava Batra 138b). The creation of a rabbinic appellate court (*beit din hagadol la`er`urim*) in 1921 is generally recognized as an innovation in Jewish law, brought on at the behest of the British mandatory authorities, whose own legal system, of course, is familiar with both the doctrine of binding precedent and the institution of appellate courts. See Elon, 824-825 and 1809-1818, as well as Shochetman, 355-356. On the other hand, two authors made notable attempts to demonstrate that an appellate jurisdiction is not inconsistent with Jewish law. Simcha Asaf, *Batey din vesidreyhen acharey chatimat hatalmud* (Jerusalem: Defus Hapo`alim, 1924) bases his argument upon historical examples, while R. Benzion Ouziel (*Resp. Mishpetey ouziel* 3, CM 1) utilizes traditional (though creative) halakhic reasoning.
66. Shochetman, 326.
67. Rashbam, *BT* Bava Batra 130b, *s.v. velo mipi ma`aseh*. See also *YT* Chagigah 1:8 (7b) and *Korban Ha`eidah, s.v. she'ein lemedin min hama`aseh*: "for example, when one sees his rabbi issuing a ruling, one should not declare the *halakhah* thusly, for perhaps one has erred concerning the reasoning behind the ruling in that particular case ...".
68. *BT* Bava Batra 131a.
69. And see Rambam's *Commentary to the Mishnah*, Introduction (Kafich ed.), 46: "the legal activity of all who arose after Ravina and Rav Ashi is confined to the understanding of the work they composed (*chiberu*), to which it is forbidden to add and from which it is forbidden to detract."
70. On the use of the title *gaon* to describe the *rosh yeshivah* (head of the Talmudic academy) in Babylonia from the sixth-century C.E. onward, see Robert Brody, *The Geonim of Babylonia and the Shaping of Medieval Jewish Culture* (New Haven: Yale U. Press, 1998), 49.
71. Isadore Twersky, *Introduction to the Code of Maimonides* (New Haven: Yale U. Press, 1980), 55 and 160. See, in general, Meir Havatzelet, *Harambam vehage'onim* (Jerusalem: Sura, 1967). And see Rambam's own Introduction to

his *Commentary to the Mishnah* (Kafich ed.), 47: "The *Halakhot* of our teacher R. Yitzchak (Alfasi) is the equivalent of all previous (post-Talmudic) works ... having corrected all their errors. I disagree with his rulings in no more than ten places."

72. Twersky, 160.

73. See *Resp. Harosh* 31:9 (those who cite a ruling in the *Mishneh Torah* without comparing it to its Talmudic source are likely to misunderstand or misapply that ruling) and 94:5 (Rambam "writes as does a prophet [*divrey nevu'ah*, and this is definitely *not* meant as a compliment], without accompanying argumentation").

74. See Mark Washofsky, "R. Asher b. Yehiel and the *Mishneh Torah* of Maimonides: A New Look at Some Old Evidence," in David R. Blumenthal, ed., *Approaches to Judaism in Medieval Times, Volume III* (Atlanta: Scholars Press, 1988), 147-158.

75. Hil. Harosh, Sanhedrin 4:6.

76. *BT* Sanhedrin 33a.

77. *Sefer Hameorot* to Alfasi Sanhedrin, fol. 12a.

78. In *Katuv Sham*, Rabad's *hasagot* on Razah's *Sefer Hame'orot*, ed. Jerusalem (1990), 198 (to Razah, fol. 12a).

79. It is uncharacteristic because of Rabad's reputation for creativity in halakhic thought. I say "creativity" and not "independence." The latter refers to the willingness to disagree with one's predecessors while remaining within the broad outlines of their own understanding of the *sugya*, while the former signifies new interpretations that blaze new paths in Talmudic understanding. On this view of Rabad, see Haym Soloveitchik, "Rabad of Posquières: A Programmatic Essay," in E. Etkes and Y. Salmon, eds., *Studies in the History of Jewish Society ... Presented to Professor Jacob Katz* (Jerusalem: Magnes, 1980), 7-40. The difficulty, obviously, is that Rabad made a literary career out of departing from the geonic view of the Talmud and the *halakhah*, just the sort of thing that he apparently condemns in this *hasagah*. Soloveitchik's attempt to reconcile the career with the *hasagah* (namely, that what Rabad "actually says" is that discarding geonic doctrine is virtually unheard of in halakhic circles; see at 12-13, n. 10) has much affinity with some ideas about precedent that I want to talk about in the next section of this article. It does not, however, close the gap between Rabad the creative halakhist and Rabad the conservative critic of Razah. Perhaps the best we can do is to say that the purpose Rabad set for himself in *Katuv Sham* is precisely that: to criticize Razah wherever the latter is vulnerable, even if Rabad himself would not proceed in the spirit of that critical note. On the icy personal and literary relations between the two Provençal scholars, see Y. Ya-Shema, *Rabbi zerachyah halevy ba`al hama'or uveney chugo* (Jerusalem: Mosad Harav Kook, 1992), 126-149.

80. *BT* Rosh Hashanah 25b. On the rule *yiftach bedoro keshmuel bedoro*, see Yisrael Ta-Shema, *Halakhah, minhag umetzi'ut be'ashkenaz, 1100-1350* (Jerusalem: Magnes, 1996), 67-70.

81. On the other hand, the *Sefer Hama'or* itself is characterized by its support of judicial independence and by Razah's opposition to the tendency to make the rulings of any one halakhic work (in this case, the Alfasi) the automatic standard of legal correctness within the community. See Ta-Shema, *Rabbi zerachyah halevy*, 58*ff*.

82. He is joined in this view by R. Menachem Hameiri, *Beit Habechirah*, San-
    hedrin 33a, who rejects the notion that a matter decided by the *geonim* enjoys
    the status of *davar mishnah*. This is significant in that Meiri is, in general,
    heavily influenced by the halakhic thought of Rabad, his Provençal forebear.

83. *Ein lo ladayan ela mah she`eynav ro'ot; BT* Bava Batra 131a.

84. Joel Roth, *The Halakhic Process: A Systemic Analysis* (New York: Jewish Theo-
    logical Seminary of America, 1986), 81-113. The quotations are found at 83
    and 113.

85. *BT* Sanhedrin 32a (= *M.* Sanhedrin 4:1) and 33a. The categories are intro-
    duced as part of a series of efforts to resolve a contradiction between the
    mishnah in Sanhedrin and *M.* Bekhorot 4:4. According to the former, an erro-
    neous decision at monetary law is reversed and the case retried; the latter
    declares that such a decision stands, but the judge is liable for compensation
    to the losing party.

86. So Rambam, *Yad*, Sanhedrin 6:1, following the *sugya* on *BT* Sanhedrin 33a,
    which extends the circumference of *devar mishnah* beyond the Mishnah to
    cover legal matters determined by the sages of all Talmudic generations. See
    also Meiri, *Beit Habechirah*, *BT* Sanhedrin 33a.

87. Rashi, *BT* Sanhedrin 33a, *s.v. to`eh bedevar mishnah*. See *Hil. Harosh*, Sanhedrin
    4:5: "this decision does not deserve to survive," and *Tur* CM 25: "there is no
    'ruling' when the error concerns a matter so obvious."

88. If, however, the *dayan* is a *mumcheh*, an "expert" judge, or if he has been
    appointed by a recognized Jewish political authority such as the Exilarch, or
    if the litigants agreed to abide by his ruling in all events, he is empowered to
    retry the case.

89. The text here follows the preferred reading in geonic, rishonic, and manu-
    script traditions; see *Mesoret Hashas* and *Dikdukey Soferim* (n. 6) to Sanhedrin
    33a.

90. *Yad*, Sanhedrin 6:2-3.

91. *Arukh Hashulchan*, CM 25, par. 2.

92. *Hil. Harosh*, Sanhedrin 4:6.

93. Introduction to *Shulhan Arukh*. Did Karo see the *Beit Yosef* as the indispens-
    able commentary to the *Shulhan Arukh*, in the sense that one must study the
    former in order to understand the latter and use it as a reliable code? He does
    not state this explicitly in his introduction, where he describes the *Shulchan
    Arukh* primarily as an aid to the study of the *halakhah*. On the other hand, the
    pattern of Karo's work—the creation of a large compendium containing all
    the necessary material for the understanding of the *halakhah*, followed by the
    creation of a shorter, simpler work encompassing easy-to-memorize legal
    dictasuggests to some that he might see the *Shulhan Arukh* as a sort of "horn-
    book" to be read at the conclusion of the thorough study of the *Beit Yosef*.
    Some authors, at any rate, insist on the prior study of the *Beit Yosef* before one
    declares the *halakhah* in accordance with the *Shulhan Arukh*. Among these is
    R. Yom Tov Lipmann Heller in the wonderful introduction to his *Tosafot Yom
    Tov* commentary to the Mishnah. See as well *Yad Malakhi*, Kelalei HaShulhan
    Arukh, no. 1, and *Sedei Chemed*, Kelalei Haposkim, 13:2.i

94. It is for this reason, Karo tells us, that he chose to make his *Beit Yosef* a com-
    mentary upon an existing compendium rather than a self-standing work. To
    collect all the materials by himself would have been a task without end. It is

also the reason he chose the *Tur* as the basis for the commentary rather than the *Mishneh Torah*, "the most widely-known work of *halakhah*." Since the latter presents only one opinion—that of Rambam—on each halakhic question, it would not serve to lighten Karo's workload. The *Tur*, on the other hand, already includes many of the opinions which Karo will need to cite.

95. This is meant literally. The texts Karo uses will be *sedurim*, laid out verbatim for the reader, rather than summarized.

96. See Menachem Elon, *Hamishpat ha`ivri* (Jerusalem: Magnes, 1973), 1139*ff*.

97. See R. Chaim Yosef David Azulai, *Birkey Yosef*, CM 25, no. 29, for sources on the antiquity of Karo's procedure. For a comprehensive description of this tendency, as well as lists of the various "bancs" of *poskim* that served as the ultimate halakhic authorities in these communities, see Y. Z. Kahana, *Mechkarim besifrut hateshuvot* (Jerusalem: Mosad Harav Kook, 1973), 8-88, and Ovadyah Yosef, *Sefer hayovel larav yosef dov halevy soloveitchik* (Jerusalem: Mosad Harav Kook, 1984), 267-280.

98. See *Bedek habayit*, CM 25, near the end of the chapter: "I say that in our time, the accepted *minhag* in our entire region to follow Rambam on all halakhic matters save those over which his words are difficult to understand and to reconcile." It is significant that this remark follows Karo's discussion of R. Asher's endorsement of judicial discretion (*Hil. Harosh*, Sanhedrin 4:6). That is to say, while Asher declares that a judge may interpret the law as he sees fit, even against the views of the great *poskim* of the past, Karo notes that "in our region" such is not the practice if the great *posek* in question is Maimonides.

99. See Kahana, 69-71: according to many observers, Karo's decisions in the *Shulchan Arukh* tend to follow Rambam even in cases where the other two "pillars" of the law, Alfasi and R. Asher, disagree with him.

100. Kahana, 25-28. R. Asher's opposition, as discussed above, is conveyed in *Hil. Harosh*, Sanhedrin 4:6. It is expressed as well by Asher's son Yehudah, who criticizes the city of Toledo for adopting a *takanah* after his father's death to decide the *halakhah* in accordance with Rambam except in those cases where R. Asher disagrees; *Resp. Zikhron yehudah*, no. 54.

101. See *Resp. Rashba* 2:322. I find myself in some disagreement with Joel Roth, *The Halakhic Process*, 93, on the thrust of this *teshuvah*, though this disagreement may be more a matter of emphasis than of essence. As I read him, Rashba places a much greater presumptive weight upon precedent than Roth seems willing to concede. Note that the *sho'el* who submits the question cites the Talmudic principle "a judge must rule on the basis of what he sees" (*BT Bava Batra* 131a) as an argument in favor of judicial discretion. Rashba, however, is not impressed by this, preferring to see the sages of our time—that is, the *rishonim*—as the (metaphorical, at any rate) equivalent of the ancient Sanhedrin.

102. *Seder Tanna'im Ve'amora'im*, ch. 24. See also Azulai, *Shem Hagedolim*, Sefarim, *samekh*.

103. For the two positions, respectively, see Y. Yuval, "Rishonim ve'acharonim, Antiqui et Moderni," *Zion* 57 (1992), 369-394, and Y. Ta-Shema, *Halakhah, minhag umetzi'ut beashkenaz, 1100-1350* (Jerusalem: Magnes, 1996), 58-78. Menachem Elon, *Hamishpat Ha`ivri*, 233, shares Ta-Shema's view, although he makes no mention of the stages by which the rule developed during the medieval period.

104. For example, both Ya`akov and Yehudah, the sons of R. Asher b. Yechiel, understand their father's comment in *Hil. Harosh*, Sanhedrin 4:6, as applying the rule *hilkheta kevatra'ey* to "the sages of one's own generation"; see *Resp. Zikhron yehudah*, no. 23. It should be noted however, that it is Asher's sons who use the word *batra* to refer to their father; R. Asher does not use the word *batra* to refer to himself.

105. "Little doubt?" I shudder here to disagree with the conclusions of Professor Ta-Shema (*Halakhah, minhag umetzi'ut*, 76), whose writings have earned the status of *batra* on virtually every question of scholarship concerning medieval halakhic literature; see my "Medieval Halakhic Literature and the Reform Rabbi: A Neglected Relationship," *CCAR Journal*, Fall 1993, 66-68. Yet I cannot follow him when he says that Isserles applies the rule *hilkheta kevatra'ey* to the scholars of his own generation. Isserles' formulation of this rule in *SA* CM 25:2 is nothing more than a quotation from a responsum of the fifteenth-century scholar R. Yosef Kolon (*Resp. Maharik*, no. 94). And as Yuval ("Rishonim ve'acharonim," at note 47) demonstrates by way of abundant citations from Kolon's responsa, the latter includes as *batra'ey* only those scholars who flourished during the first half of the fourteenth century in Ashkenaz, a period stretching from the redaction of the Tosafot to the calamities of 1348-1349. Ta-Shema (p. 60) recognizes this as well. And the quotation gives us no hint that Isserles reads Kolon's words any differently than did Kolon himself. Similarly, Isserles' reference to the rule *hilkheta kevatra'ey* in the Introduction to his *Darkhey Moshe*—where he criticizes Karo for not adopting that rule—also restricts its coverage to such thirteenth and fourteenth-century works as *Sefer Hamordekhai*, *Hilkhot Harosh*, and the *Tur*. As Isserles himself puts it, Karo decides the law "according to the great *geonim* Alfasi, Rambam, R. Asher, but he pays no attention to the other great scholars of Torah, even though (the ones he favors) are earlier scholars (*kama'ey*) rather than later ones (*batra'ey*)." It is scarcely imaginable that Isserles would rank his own contemporaries among the "great scholars of Torah" (*revevata adirey torah*), a designation customarily reserved for the long departed. R. Shelomo Luria, Isserles' great Polish contemporary, likewise used the term *batra'ey* to refer to scholars of the past, although he included more Sefardim within this category than did Isserles; see Yuval at note 68. The one difficulty with the position I have outlined here is the famous refusal by Isserles' teacher, R. Shalom Shakhna, to write a halakhic compendium because others would rule in accordance with that book on the grounds that *hilkheta kevatra* (*Resp. Rema*, no. 25; ed. Siev, p. 156b). This might be taken to mean that a contemporary *posek* is himself a "latest authority" under this rule. Yet I think it is more plausible that Shakhna had in mind the potential influence his book would exert upon future generations. Isserles, at any rate, gives no indication that his *own* work enjoys such status; rather, when he decides in accordance with the "latest authorities," he is referring to authorities *other* than those of his own generation.

106. Thus, in the responum cited previously (*Resp. Rema*, no. 25; ed. Siev, p. 156b), R. Shalom Shakhna refuses to write a halakhic compendium because he does not wish to have the law decided in accordance with his views; rather, quoting *BT* Bava Batra 131a, he holds that "a judge must rule on the basis of what he sees"; *i.e.*, his own reading of the law.

107. See the sources in note 97.

108. For a list of some of the works that contain these rules, see Elon, *Jewish Law*, 1540-1555. No value judgment is implied here. The establishment of some sort of regimen for determining the "correct" decision on a disputed matter may very well be a social or political necessity in a legal community; see Y. Kahana, *Mechkarim besifrut hateshuvot*, 1-8. My point is simply that this is one of the ways that a consensus view emerges out of a previously open debate over the "right" answer.

109. On the formation of this consensus see Mark Washofsky, "Abortion and the Halakhic Conversation," in Walter Jacob and Moshe Zemer, eds., *The Fetus and Fertility in Jewish Law* (Pittsburgh and Tel Aviv: The Freehof Institute of Progressive Halakhah, 1995), 39-89, especially at notes 1-9. See also the forthcoming doctoral dissertation of Daniel Schiff for a comprehensive analysis of the history of the abortion controversy in Jewish law.

110. For background see Avraham Freimann, *Seder kiddushin venisu'in* (Jerusalem: Mosad Harav Kook, 1964); Y. Z. Kahana, *Sefer ha`agunot* (Jerusalem: Mosad Harav Kook, 1954); and Mark Washofsky, "The Recalcitrant Husband," *Jewish Law Annual* 4 (1981), 144-166.

111. Eliezer Berkovits, *tenai benisu'in uveget* (Jerusalem: Mosad Harav Kook, 1966).

112. Menachem M. Kasher, "Be`inyan tenai benisu'in," *No`am* 12 (1969), 338-353.

113. The rabbinical reactions to that ill-fated proposal are collected in *Ein tenai benisu'in* (Vilna, 1930).

114. Shlomo Riskin, *Women and Jewish Divorce* (Hoboken: Ktav, 1989).

115. *BT* Ketubot 63a-b; Rashi, Ketubot 63b, *s.v. la kayafinan lah*; *Yad*, Ishut 14:8.

116. See *Tosafot*, *BT* Ketubot 63b, *s.v. aval*.

117. See *Beit Yosef*, EHE 77, fol. 115b-116a, and *SA* EHE 77:2.

118. See the review of Riskin's book by Gedalia Dov Schwartz in *Tradition* 25:2 (1990), 94-96.

119. On the other hand, some authorities are willing to consider the argument of *ma`is alay* as one of several factors—though not the exclusive factor—in persuading a rabbinical court to accept a divorce document of questionable validity. See R. Ezra Basri, "Get Me`useh," *Shenaton hamishpat ha`ivri* 16-17 (1990-1991), 535-553.

120. The word reflects Ronald Dworkin's discussion of the "gravitational force" of precedent; *Taking Rights Seriously* (Cambridge, MA: Harvard U. Press, 1977), 111*ff*.

121. Emanuel Feldman, "Trends in the American Yeshivot: A Rejoinder," in Reuven P. Bulka, *Dimensions of Orthodox Judaism* (New York: Ktav, 1983), at 334-336.

122. Yosef Dov Soloveitchik, *Shi`urim lezekher abba mari z"l* (Jerusalem: Akiva Yosef, 1983), at 428.

123. See Walter S. Wurzburger, "The Conservative View of *Halakhah* is Non-Traditional," *Judaism* 38 (1989), 377-379.

124. We should not claim too much for the responsum in this regard. The *teshuvah* does *not* necessarily render a chronological account of its author's thought processes. For example, although the responsum usually presents the question, followed by the halakhic argumentation that leads to its answer, it may well be that the *meshiv* arrived at his answer prior to his considering those

arguments, whether by way of a "hunch" or of a general impression that "this is how the question ought to be decided." Louis Jacobs suggests that this indeed is the way rabbis answer halakhic questions: they begin with a general impression drawn from their personal Judaic values and then search for legal arguments to support this preconceived conclusion. See his *A Tree of Life* (Oxford: Oxford U. Press, 1984), 11-12. Still, the reasoning as conveyed in the *teshuvah* is a vital component of the answer, for without that reasoning the *meshiv* cannot justify his decision to his readers; he cannot advocate that they adopt his view of the *halakhah* unless he shows them in some reasoned form—that is, through some pattern of argument that they might conceivably accept as "halakhic"—why they ought to adopt it.

125. Peter Haas's *Responsa: Literary History of a Rabbinic Genre* (Atlanta: Scholars Press, 1996) is an effort in this direction. What I mean by a "literary study" of the responsa is indicated in my "Responsa and Rhetoric: On Law, Literature and the Rabbinic Decision," in John C. Reeves and John Kampen, eds., *Pursuing the Text: Studies in Honor of Ben Zion Wacholder* (Sheffield: Sheffield Academic Press, 1994), 360-409. Menachem Elon, *Jewish Law*, 1453-1528, offers what is currently the best discussion of the responsa as "literary sources" of law in the Judaic tradition. And for detail and characterization of the *she'elot uteshuvot*, Solomon B. Freehof's *The Responsa Literature* (Philadelphia: Jewish Publication Society of America, 1955) is still unsurpassed.

126. *Resp. Rivash*, no. 15. See Abraham M. Hershman, *Rabbi Isaac Ben Sheshet Perfet and His Times* (New York: Jewish Theological Seminary of America, 1943), 39, who posits that this responsum was written soon after Rivash arrived in North Africa in the wake of the persecutions of 1391 in Spain.

127. The halakhic tradition derives this requirement from Gen. 1:28; see *Sefer Hachinukh*, *mitzvah* no. 1. The relevant halakhic sources are *M.* Yevamot 6:6, *BT* Yevamot 61b-62a and 65b, *Yad*, Ishut 15:2*ff.*, and *SA* EHE 1.

128. On this, see *BT* Pesachim 49a and *SA* EHE 2:8.

129. See, *e.g.*, Alfasi, Ketubot, fol. 36a, and *Hil. Harosh, M.* Ketubot 7:20 and *M.* Yevamot 6:16.

130. The classic method is to demonstrate that the apparently deviant *minhag* in fact constitutes a correct interpretation of the Talmudic sources. A good example is the defense by medieval Ashkenazic halakhists of the practice of conducting commerce with non-Jews on a Gentile religious festival, an apparently clear transgression of the prohibition laid down in *M.* Avodah Zarah 1:1. Compare the straightforward presentation of the law in Alfasi, Avodah Zarah, fol. 1a-b, with the treatment it receives in *Hilkhot Harosh*, Avodah Zarah 1:1. On the relationship between *halakhah* and *minhag* in medieval halakhic literature, see Yisrael Ta-Shema, *Minhag ashkenaz hakadmon* (Jerusalem: Magnes, 1992); Jacob Katz, *Halakhah vekabalah* (Jerusalem: Magnes, 1984); Haym Soloveitchik, "Religious Law and Change: The Medieval Ashkenazic Example," *AJS Review* 12 (1987), 205-222; and Mark Washofsky, "*Minhag* and *Halakhah*: Toward a Model of Shared Authority on Matters of Ritual," in Walter Jacob and Moshe Zemer, eds., *Rabbinic Lay Relations in Jewish Law* (Pittsburgh and Tel Aviv: The Freehof Institute of Progressive Halakhah, 1993), 99-126.

131. An unstated motivation—but one I think cannot be far from Rivash's mind— is the desire to keep the Gentile authorities from intervening into the affairs

of the Jewish community. The local ruler in this case summons the community leaders to respond to Shmuel Aramah's indictment of them, and it would seem that he is well-disposed to Aramah's claim.

132. It would be absurd to describe R. Yitzchak b. Sheshet Perfet as a philosophical pragmatist, a forerunner of Pierce, James, Dewey, and Rorty. Pragmatism as a general approach to knowledge and action involves intellectual attitudes (most notably a thoroughgoing skepticism concerning metaphysical truth claims) that would have been foreign to the mind of a fourteenth-century rabbi. My reference indicates rather that in his handling of this question, Rivash displays some of the tendencies associated with legal pragmatism, which urges that jurists apply rules of law not as formal propositions to be developed by abstract logical reasoning but as instruments serving practical purposes that lie beyond the rules themselves. The good of the legal system as a whole is just such a purpose, and Rivash cites it here as the reason for rejecting the controlling legal precedents. On legal pragmatism, see John Dewey, "Logical Method and Law," *Cornell Law Quarterly* 17 (December, 1929), 17-27; Benjamin Cardozo, *The Nature of the Judicial Process* (New Haven: Yale, 1921), 66 ("The final cause of law is the welfare of society"); Richard Posner, *Problems of Jurisprudence* (Cambridge: Harvard, 1990), especially 454-469 ("A Pragmatist Manifesto"); and the essays in M. Brint and W. Weaver, eds., *Pragmatism in Law and Society* (Boulder, CO: Westview, 1991).

133. That Rivash himself recognizes this is underlined by R. Yosef Karo, *Beit Yosef* EHE 154 (fol. 74b), who cites the beginning of this responsum as proof that a divorce *is* coerced when the wife is beyond childbearing years. See *SA* EHE 154:10 and *Beit Shmu'el*, no. 24. Significantly, Karo never mentions the *second* part of the responsum, in which Rivash notes that the practice of the courts is to refrain from coercion in these cases. R. Moshe Isserles, on the other hand, relies heavily upon this second part of the responsum for his ruling that "nowadays the custom is not to coerce on these matters" (*SA* EHE 1:3 and 154:10; and see *Darkei Moshe* EHE 1, no. 3). This method of selective citation, in which the later authority refers only to that part of the precedential source that supports his own opinion, surely belongs in the category of "leeways" that jurists enjoy with respect to precedent.

134. The language and ideas here—notably that the responsum expresses a sense of the ideal and while conceding the necessity of the failure to realize that ideal—are inspired by the observations of James Boyd White, "The Rhythms of Hope and Disappointment in the Language of Judging," *St. John's Law Review* 70 (1996), 45-50.

135. A wooden translation of Rivash's phrase *nicha lah delipuk `alah shema de'ishut.* She wishes, literally, to bear the title of "wife." This may be a delicate way to avoid stating the obvious: that no actual *ishut*—marital relations—are likely to occur in this union.

136. See the *mishnah* on the page (*M.* Yevamot 6:6); *Yad*, Ishut 15:2; *SA* EHE 1:1 and 13.

137. Thus, lacking a valid claim for divorce, if you wish to leave the marriage you will not receive your *ketubah*; Rashi, Yevamot 65b, *s.v. la mipakadat.*

138. Rashi, Yevamot 65b, *s.v. chutra leyadah.*

139. Llewellyn, *The Common Law Tradition*, 90.

140. I have argued this point elsewhere. See Mark Washofsky, "Responsa and the Art of Writing: Three Examples from the *Teshuvot* of Rabbi Moshe Feinstein," in *A Festschrift for Walter Jacob* (forthcoming), and "Responsa and Rhetoric: On Law, Literature, and the Rabbinic Decision," *Pursuing the Text: Studies in Honor of Ben Zion Wacholder*, London, Sheffield Press, 1994, pp. 360-409.

141. Anthony T. Kronman, "Rhetoric," *University of Cincinnati Law Review* 67 (1999), 677-709. The quotation is at 687.

142. On the "ethical" appeal see Aristotle, *On Rhetoric*, translated by George A. Kennedy (New York: Oxford U. Press, 1991), 1.2 (37). The reference is to *ethos*, one of the three classic *pisteis* (means of persuasion in public address, the others being *pathos* and *logos*). *Ethos* is the moral character of the speaker as presented in the speech. The point here is that Rivash, in his ample description of the established law, portrays himself as one who displays the virtues requisite of the good scholar. His readers can therefore trust him to arrive at an answer that is carefully considered and well-warranted according to the procedures of halakhic thought.

143. I have in mind here the observation of Richard Weisberg that "great [judicial] opinions, like great novels, strive to put a narrative structure around a specific and observable reality, and thus to create a more lasting universe"; "Law, Literature, and Cardozo's Judicial Poetics," *Cardozo Law Review* 1 (1979), 288. To put it somewhat more bluntly, in a judicial opinion, reality is what the judge says it is. The "great" opinion will do this with evident literary success.

144. On this notion of "translation," the creation of new meaning from old texts by placing those texts in new relationships with others, see James Boyd White, *Justice as Translation* (Chicago: U. of Chicago Press, 1990).

145. See especially Suzanne Last Stone, "In Pursuit of the Counter-Text: The Turn to the Jewish Legal Model in Contemporary American Legal Theory," *Harvard Law Review* 106 (1993), 813-894.

146. On the development of this consensus, its breakdown, and the various attempts by legal theorists to find alternative bases on which to reconstruct it, see Laura Kalman, *The Strange Career of Legal Liberalism* (New Haven: Yale U. Press, 1996).

147. The leading voice in this "turn" is that of the late Robert Cover, whose much-discussed "Forward: *Nomos* and *Narrative*," *Harvard Law Review* 97 (1984) 4*ff.*, suggests that the plurality of "metanarratives" in American culture renders problematic any attempt by the courts to speak with a unitary voice in the name of the law. Cover regards this plurality, which challenges the traditional liberal conception of a "correct" meaning of the law accessible through reason, as a positive thing, and he looks to Jewish law as the paradigm of a legal system that can tolerate a multiplicity of judicial views; see his "Obligation: A Jewish Jurisprudence of the Social Order," *Journal of Law and Religion* 5 (1987), 65-90. See also, among others, Samuel J. Levine, "*Halacha* and *Aggada*: Translating Robert Cover's '*Nomos* and *Narrative*'," *Utah Law Review* 1998 (1998), 465-504; Perry Dane, "The Maps of Sovereignty: A Meditation," *Cardozo Law Review* 12 (1991), 959-1006; Norman Lamm and Aaron Kirschenbaum, "Freedom and Constraint in the Jewish Judicial Process," *Cardozo Law Review* 1 (1979), 99-133; and Sanford Levinson, *Constitutional Faith* (Princeton: Princeton U. Press, 1988). And see David R. Dow,

"Constitutional Midrash: The Rabbis' Solution to Professor Bickel's Problem," *Houston Law Review* 29 (1992), 581: "Jewish law teaches that it is possible for competing foundational norms to reside peacefully and beneficially in a single legal system as long as the interpreters of these norms possess certain characteristics—as long as they are wise."

148. On the tendency of Jewish lawyers to exaggerate the supposed similarities between American and Jewish law—two vastly different systems, see Jerold S. Auerbach, *Rabbis and Lawyers: The Journey from Torah to Constitution* (Bloomington: Indiana U. Press, 1996), xviii.

149. See Stone, note 145.

150. These include such famous examples as the *"eilu ve'eilu"* resolution of the halakhic controversy between the schools of Hillel and Shammai in *BT* Yevamot 13b and the "oven of Akhnai" story in *BT* Bava Metzi`a 59b.

151. This scholarly controversy provokes the same observation that I apply to the arguments over the role of precedent in Jewish law: a theory is only as valid as the data it purports to explain. Or, as Justice Holmes might have put it: "General propositions do not decide concrete cases"; *Lochner v. New York*, 198 U.S. 45 (1905), Holmes, J. dissenting.

152. Here I wander dangerously close to the precipice of modern (and postmodern) literary theory, in which the question of what, if any, meaning texts and language may have is deeply and irremediably controversial. I do not wish to fall off, at least not here. A thorough analysis of this subject would demand at least a brief reference to such approaches as deconstruction, hermeneutics, reader-response theories, and the objectivity-in-interpretation school of E.D. Hirsch, Jr. Let me instead make this observation: the activity of law is a conversation in which the parties involved commit themselves to the proposition that the texts do *mean* something and that this meaning is sufficiently discernible by the parties. I cannot imagine a coherent legal conversation that does not proceed from this assumption. If texts can mean *anything*, they therefore mean *nothing*, and if they mean nothing, no point can be served by citing them as part of the conversation. Meaning can be arrived at and agreed upon even when the discussants acknowledge the semantic reality that "objective" meaning does not inhere in words. Rather, meaning is an activity of speech or writing; it can be inferred by more-or-less reliable evidence as to what the speaker or writer had in mind when saying or writing the words. See Gerald Graff, "'Keep Off the Grass,' 'Drop Dead,' and Other Indeterminacies: A Response to Sanford Levinson," *Texas Law Review* 60 (1982), 405-413.

153. For example, the bare facts of an auto accident—"he ran right into me while I was making a left turn"—are devoid of any meaning until translated into the language of tort law, which speaks of causation and negligence.

154. See, in general, Walter Jacob, *American Reform Responsa* (New York: Central Conference of American Rabbis, 1983) ,xv-xviii, and Alexander Guttmann, *The Struggle Over Reform in Rabbinic Literature* (New York: UAHC, 1976).

155. See Solomon B. Freehof's essay "Jacob Z. Lauterbach and the Halakah," *Judaism* 1 (1952), 270-273. The hundreds of *teshuvot* penned by Freehof himself, of course, are clear testimony to the halakhic language of Reform responsa.

156. Alisdair MacIntyre, *After Virtue* (Notre Dame: U. of Notre Dame Press, 1981), 207 (p. 222 in the second edition, published in 1984). In his *Whose Justice? Whose Rationality?* (Notre Dame: U. of Notre Dame Press, 1988, 12), MacIntyre expands his definition as follows: "A tradition is an argument extended through time in which certain fundamental agreements are defined and redefined in terms of two kinds of conflict: those with critics and enemies external to the tradition … and those internal, interpretive debates through which the meaning and rationale of the fundamental agreements come to be expressed and by whose progress a tradition is constituted."
157. Put differently, a tradition is "the necessary framework to rational argument"; H. Jefferson Powell, *The Moral Tradition of American Constitutionalism* (Durham, NC: Duke U. Press, 1993), 14-15. See Powell at 12-47 for a consideration of MacIntyre's theory of tradition and its relationship to law.

❖ ❖ ❖

Chapter 2

"THE LAW OF THE LAND AND JEWISH LAW"

Opposition or Concurrence?

Walter Jacob

The principle dina demalkhuta dina has and continues to define the major boundary of the halakhah, Orthodox, Reform, or Conservative, even though it is not often cited and rarely fully discussed. The modern implications of this statement need to be placed into a historic framework, which is one task of this paper. In addition it will seek to define the limits of this principle for us as Reform Jews or, for that matter, for all contemporary Jews outside the Land of Israel.[1] Within Israel the concern may be mishpat hamelekh, an ancient concept that must be rethought.

The struggle between Jewish and alien law is as old as the first occupation of the Land of Israel by a foreign conqueror in 586 B.C.E. We know virtually nothing about the relationship between the inhabitants and the occupying forces then. The law of the conqueror was the ultimate law and the ruler appointed the supreme governor whether Jewish or an outsider. It seems that conquerors permitted local autonomy to the native population, so that through Ezra, Nehemiah and their followers, Jewish leadership controlled their internal affairs and governed. This policy was continued by Egyptian, Persian, Seleudic, Ptolemaic, and Roman rulers. The only major exception came through Antiochus Epiphanes and led to the Maccabean revolt. Unrest under the Romans was caused by a harsh taxation policy and occasional insensitivity to Jewish feelings about the images of the Roman legions and not through a clash of legal systems. We know little till Roman times about the extent of outside domination aside from the payment of taxes and the restraint on wishes for independence. We have no record of any struggle between the Jewish legal system and that of the occupiers. The New Testament statement attributed to Jesus "Give unto Caesar what belongs to Caesar and to God what belongs to God" [2] was the earliest Jewish source that dealt with this issue. There was no similar statement in the rabbinic literature even later in the time of the Mishnah.

Jewish life in the Diaspora should have raised the question of competing legal systems and jurisdictions. Even if we concede that the Pharisaic system was not developed until late in this period, Jews seems to have expressed more than superficial loyalty to their Mesopotamian or Roman rulers. Even after the Pharisaic system was fully developed, no clashes between the legal system have been recorded. Although there were substantial Jewish settlements outside the Land of Israel from 586 B.C.E. onward, we hear nothing of a clash of jurisdictions in Babylonia, among the Egyptian Jewish mercenaries of Elephantine, or in the Hellenistic and Roman world. There were rebellions in Alexandria of those who wished to define the citizenship status of the Jewish group, but they sought to settle the question by force rather than legal debate. From 586 B.C.E. the majority of the Jewish population lived outside the land of Israel and any problems that arose through a clash of legal systems led to solutions which have not been recorded.

The Talmudic Sources

Samuel's famous statement dina demalkhuta dina—"The law of the land is the law"—came rather late (165-267 C.E.).[3] The four citations in the Talmud were incidental and indicated that this was not a major issue. Each citation dealt with the authority of the governmental tax or customs collectors, or the authority of governmental documents issued by a non-Jewish court or witnessed by Gentiles. Alternatives were presented in every instance and dina demalkhuta dina was never fully discussed and played virtually no role in the enormous mass of talmudic legal material. The primary expression of the ruler's power and this principle lay in his appointment of the exilarch, the head of the Jewish community; he was often appointed through consultation with the head of one of the talmudic academies, but this was a courtesy or a wise political gesture, not mandatory and the appointment itself lay outside the jurisdiction of the rabbinic authorities.

We do not know the reason for Samuel's statement or why he had to make explicit what had been implicit and de facto for many centuries. We may speculate that he sought to ingratiate himself with the ruler through this effort. Perhaps with the border tensions between the Parthian and Romans he felt the need for a declaration of loyalty. He might have sought to make the implicit more a part of the Jewish legal system, so that it could be discussed internally as Bial[4] has suggested. None of the contemporary or later decissors provided a reason for Samuel's enactment and merely stated that he was particularly close to the Persian ruler. Although this was correct, it has little bearing on a rationale for his statement.[5] As neither the Talmud nor Parthian documents shed light on this matter, speculation is futile.[6]

The statement in Gittin came from Samuel himself, while the others quoted him. In Gittin, the problem discussed was a mishnaic statement that validated documents issued by a Gentile court and witnessed by Gentiles. The only exceptions were documents of divorce and manumission of slaves. Samuel's statement agreed with this while others felt that some documents were also excluded. Samuel's statement also meant that earlier mishnaic statements that permitted the evasion of the king's taxes, were now rejected;[7] this had also troubled rabbinic authorities of the Talmud and they concluded that the Mishnah referred only to an unauthorized tax collector[8] or one who did not proceed in a legal fashion.[9] Rabba reported three rules that were given to him by Ukbas ben Nehemia, the exilarch, in which he further clarified the meaning of Samuel's rule as applying to documents that recognized the transfer of property, but not those that actually made the transfer and to various situations of taxation or royal confiscation.[10] It applied to the ruler and his agents in matters of civil law mainly in matters of property exchange, taxation and eminent domain. There was disagreement from talmudic times onward about whether the statement applied to documents that actually transferred property or that only validated such a transfer through a Gentile court, and were witnessed by Gentiles.[11] The question was settled to include only the latter.

Gaonic Period

There was also no full discussion of the principle in the Gaonic period (650-1050 C.E.) which marked the change from Sassanian to Arab rule. The ultimate Jewish authority was the exilarch, appointed by the non-Jewish ruler; he was respected and feared by the Gaonim.[12] For many centuries the exilarch appointed the Gaonim, though this was reversed by the tenth century.[13] The exilarchs through most of this period held a high position at court, were all powerful within the Jewish community and were extremely wealthy.[14] They did not need to discuss the basis of Samuel's principle. They were royal appointees who executed the mandates of the government which provided internal autonomy for the Jewish community.

During the later portion of Arab rule the Gaonim became powerful and because of the nature of the Gentile rulers dina demalkhuta dina was largely limited to matters of taxation. They excommunicated those Jews who used non-Jewish courts and made only rare exceptions.[15] In some instances they were stricter than the talmudic statement of the principle and refused to permit a transfer of property made through a non-Jewish court, witnessed by non-Jews.[16]

The limited Gaonic discussions of the statement provided some philosophical basis for it. The scholars defended it through the theory of the divine right of kings; as the Jewish or non-Jewish ruler was appointed by God, his laws had the same force as divine laws.[17] Those who held the theory of social contract felt that the popular acceptance of the ruler and his coinage meant that his laws also had to be accepted.[18]

The Sephardic Expansion of the Principle

In Islamic and Christian Spain the principle soon went beyond the authority of tax collectors and documents issued by a non-Jewish court, but was broadened to include a series of other matters. Jews often preferred to use non-Jewish courts to settle their affairs and quarrels with other Jews and with Gentiles. We should remember the Talmudic and Gaonic objections to this,[19] but the later ruling of R. Tam was generally accepted. He opposed a Jew forcing another into the secular courts, but if both agreed to use them, then it was permissible. A further development in the early Middle Ages led to dina demalkhuta dina becoming part of Jewish law and not merely law for the Jewish population. Rabbenu Tam did this by utilizing the principle of hefker bet din hefker.[20] Slightly earlier the same effect was brought to the principle through inclusion in the code of Maimonides.[21]

In twelfth-century Spain the transfer of any property (sale, gift, will, etc.) through a Gentile court was recognized. [22] This was so despite the fact that other authorities considered wills and ketubot outside the realm of Gentile courts[23] and excluded them from dina demalkhuta dina. Later others also considered such documents within the power of the ruler, and valid if written in the language of the land[24]; and even when the marriage was done under Gentile auspices, the document was not considered invalid.[25] So we see a case in which Isaac b. Sheshet (Barfat) invalidated a Gentile marriage, but upheld the ketubah issued with it;[26] sometimes Gentile practices were accepted into the Jewish court system.

In Aragon we have the curious example of a ruler demanding that his court decide an issue between two Jews in accordance with Jewish law, as the bet din had been unable to reach a timely decision.[27] Still later Joseph Caro provided an interesting twist by making a distinction between a ketubah issued in a Christian land where the king made no such demands, and a Moslem land where such documents were subject to royal decrees.[28] Concerns were also expressed about the fairness of the courts and whether they were influenced by bribes.[29]

The most bitterly debated issue was the appointment of communal leaders through royal decree. Did dina demalkhuta dina permit this? As we have seen, this had occurred without question throughout the talmudic period in Persia. The Exilarch was a royal appointee; this had continued to be accepted without question through the entire Gaonic period. As mentioned earlier, the rabbinic academies vied with each other over the right to propose candidates and for a long time Pumpedita was dominant; however, the ruler had the power to ignore such nominations and proceed on his own.[30] The appointment of Isaac b. Sheshet as the leader of the Algerian community without consultation led to a bitter struggle, which was only resolved after his appointment was modified by the king.[31]

The Sephardic community until modern times, as far as one can ascertain through a brief review of the responsa, continued along this path and accepted a rather wide-ranging interpretation of dina demalkhuta dina. This comported with the reality that Jews preferred to settle their fiscal affairs in the general courts and usually trusted them. Appointments made by the ruler with consultation were accepted even if reluctantly. One may well say that dina demalkhuta dina became customary and so was accepted into the halakhah as occurred with other customs, too, despite its lack of any biblical authority.[32]

The Ashkenazic Application of the Principle

The smaller and more compact Ashkenazic communities of early Central Europe were unwilling to go so far and saw all but the most necessary compliance with royal decree as a violation of Jewish law. If a choice between Jewish law and the king's law existed, then Jewish law was to be followed. Although they agreed with the Tosafists—who considered that the king's power stemmed from his ownership of the land he ruled,[33] and recognized the principle that any litigants could decide whether to use the non-Jewish or Jewish courts—it was strongly discouraged[34] but continued to be reported frequently.

These Ashkenazic as well as some Sephardic authorities sought to place restrictions on the effect of Samuel's law and to limit the king's law, but that was a procedure of doubtful value and seemed intended more for internal consumption.[35] An effort was also made to restrict impositions and taxes of the king to those placed on all citizens, not Jews alone; although this was a nice thought, it could often not be carried into practice.[36] Some sought to limit dina demalkhuta dina to new ordinances which were in the spirit of earlier ones; others were considered invalid.[37] Of course even these authorities understood the royal need for additional revenue.[38]

The Ashkenazic community faced the same problem as the Sephardim as royal appointees to positions of communal leadership or to the communal rabbinate, but they fought it with partial success through takanot.[39] The smaller size of the community and their compact nature made this possible. The appointee might not be removed and his power of taxation remained, but otherwise, no one paid any attention to him. In fact unfit individuals regularly applied to the king for such positions and then had to be accepted by the communities. The practice of recognizing the power of the government to appoint continued and we find individuals from Isserles to the nineteenth century Hatam Sofer accepting it, albeit reluctantly.[40] On the other hand, in the German lands communal autonomy nevertheless prevailed.[41]

In Poland, Lithuania, as well as some other lands, the communities began to cooperate by the middle of the sixteenth century; they formed national tribunals, organized synods and governing councils. This was encouraged by the rulers as it simplified the collection of taxes. In turn they provided a higher degree of autonomy for the Jewish community and so dina demalkhuta dina played a smaller role than elsewhere for several centuries.[42]

In the main, Samuel's principle was limited to civil law outside the realm of family law as it had been codified by Maimonides.[43] The boundaries became vaguer from the seventeenth century onward, so we find purely Gentile witnesses to a death, or the state's declaration of death in the case of a soldier accepted for purposes of releasing an agunah; similarly dina demalkhuta dina was also invoked in the commercial aspects of the redemption of the first born, the sale of leavened items, Gentile wine, etc.[44]

The Gentile governments were often not trusted, so we find contradicting decisions and interpretations of dina demalkhuta dina: it was possible for a scholar to decide that it was not permitted to hide a Jew sought by the government, but one could advise him and presumably not turn him in when one knew where he was.[45]

The parameters provided by earlier times were interpreted restrictively and this succeeded in the Ashkenazic lands until the nature of the state changed. The ancient stability began to disappear by the middle of the eighteenth century. Jews along with others became restless and sought to eliminate old disabilities, but this also meant taking on new responsibilities which came with such privileges. The boundaries of dina demalkhuta dina would need to be altered. Jewish corporate existence in the Ashkenazic lands had meant that Jews governed themselves and the areas of possible friction existed only on the periphery in dealings with Gentiles, disputes among "Court Jews," and those who sought to use Gentile courts. All of this was about to change.

Emancipation

The late-eighteenth and early-nineteenth centuries saw the emergence of larger, more powerful, national entities in central Europe. This meant a change in the status of various classes and groups in society. For Jews this brought a glimmer of hope for more rights. In the lands of Eastern Europe all of this was to take longer and the unified character of Ashkenazic Jewry was about to change. This meant that questions from the West addressed by rabbinic authorities in Eastern European lands rarely dealt with the realities of life of the questioner, but with the facts as seen from a distance and in totally different circumstances. The western rabbis eventually had to face the onrush of modernity: they were challenged by the new merchant class and its large enterprises, the financial transactions of corporations, a much larger involvement with the non-Jewish world, and the demands of the state in matters of marriage, divorce, as well as compulsory school attendance. The world had changed drastically and dina demalkhuta dina, whose scope the Ashkenazic community had limited, now had to be considered anew.

The governments sought broader national authority through curbing the power of the cities, the clergy, and guilds. None of this was easy; it was simpler to limit the autonomy of the Jewish community and its leaders. Various privileges often had a long history, but they could be abrogated by the ruler.[46] The new charter given by Frederick II of Prussia in 1750 reflected this change and limited rabbinic jurisdiction to ritual and synagogal matters.[47] Moses Mendelssohn placed all of this into a philosophical context through his division of Judaism into "eternal truths," available to all human beings and "revealed law," which was particular to Jews.[48] As significant for our purposes, he understood that the modern state derived its authority from all of its inhabitants including Jews. Furthermore, only the state had the right to coerce, which in Judaism had been accomplished through the herem; it was now eliminated and with it the chief power of the rabbinic court. The major effect of this charter would take a while to be felt; it was seen as progress by the Jewish communities as a number of restrictions were lifted.

A more difficult situation arose through Joseph II of Austria's Ehepatent (1783) which provided state regulation for marriages.[49] The rabbinic authorities needed to deal with this immediately. The best way to face this new demand was through a takanah which obligated the communities involved to observe the secular law. Dina demalkhuta dina was not mentioned as this was a matter of marriage. The process of Emancipation went further in France even under the old regime; a commission to look into the status of Jews was established in 1788 by Louis XVI; in 1791 the National Assembly provided equal rights to Jews, but contemporary political events made that meaningless.

The status of the Jewish community was forcefully raised by Napoleon through the Assembly of Jewish Notables (the Assembly) and the Sanhedrin which he called. Napoleon had imposed restrictions on both the Catholic and Protestant churches and made them subservient through regulating the appointment of religious leaders, the system of education, and church governance;[50] he wanted to proceed similarly with the Jewish community; the process began through the Assembly which gathered on 10 July, 1806. Napoleon provided twelve questions which the assembled delegates were to answer. He insisted that the group begin its deliberations on a shabbat, an initial challenge. The delegates understood that they needed to please Napoleon and to achieve the rights which the Jews of France desired. On the other hand they did not wish to violate tradition or to anger the rabbinic authorities in the East European lands untouched by modernity. The general principle was to indicate the validity of dina demalkhuta dina in all matters where it did not specifically contradict Jewish obligations. In the area of marriage and divorce, dina demalkhuta dina was carefully cited and extended into the field of family law. Other citations were also used to create the necessary compliance. As a get was not considered valid if any bond between husband and wife remained and as the lack of a civil divorce created such a bond, a get was not valid until a civil divorce had been given .[51] Civil marriage and civil divorce were added to the Jewish requirements in the Western lands. Various rabbinic authorities added their voice to this decision.[52]

Dina demalkhuta dina was also cited in connection with military service (Napolean's question 6). The questions and answers to 7, 8, and 9 dealt with the authority of the rabbinate, and clearly signalled that the Jewish corporate entity had vanished. Dina demalkhuta dina had been used to reconcile Jewish law and the demands of the state; it had now been used to incorporate the state's legal system into Jewish law[53] and to allow it to dominate Jewish law.

The decisions of the Assembly were to be carried out through a Sanhedrin established by Napoleon; it began to meet on 4 February, 1807. The group worded its decisions with care, so that they would avoid violations of Jewish law whenever possible; however, the very fact that this body and its predecessor was called into being through Napoleon indicated clearly where power lay. Judaism was now a religious confession rather than a corporate identity. After Napoleon's defeat, the discussions diminished everywhere except in Germany where the new nationalism came into conflict with traditional corporate Judaism.

The Reform Movement

The new Jewish scholarship, which included many reformers, sought a historic understanding of every facet of Judaism, including dina demalkhuta dina. Abraham Geiger (1810-1874), Zacharias Frankel (1801-1875), Samuel Holdheim (1806-1860) and others participated in this effort. Geiger and Frankel understood it to be used principally with criminal and civil law, and not family and ritual law. Holdheim went a step further and suggested that the ketubah was primarily an economic document, so it applied there too.[54] This became controversial and most rabbis rejected his view. Another area of potential conflict was military service. Jews wished to participate in the defense of the lands in which they lived; many were very patriotic. Not as clear were the obligations in an offensive war or peace time military service but Tiktin, Rabbi of Breslau, and Weil of Berlin, among others, insisted that those obligations stood also.[55] These scholarly excursions were interesting, but in reality the people had already decided that the borders were looser. Civil marriage and civil divorce followed by appropriate Jewish rites rapidly became the norm as did acceptance of Gentile witnesses to the death of an individual, particularly in wartime. The rabbis could exercise some authority there, but nothing akin to what they had possessed as long as the Jewish community was an autonomous unit. Now Jews could simply walk away from a decision which they did not like.

Despite some semblance of centralization, the Jewish communities were independent, as was clearly indicated by the numerous local prayer book editions which appeared during the nineteenth century throughout Central Europe. The Jewish citizen may have paid his religious taxes to the Jewish community, supported it and tacitly acknowledged its existence, but he did not need to follow its dictates. Communal pressure existed and was a factor, but not for those who truly wished to rebel. For those who were more traditional, the Jewish communities and the rabbinate of the lands of Eastern Europe in which Emancipation did not take place or only to a limited degree, remained a pressure point. Yet the Eastern European rabbinate was less effective as the rabbinic pronouncements usually appeared in Hebrew and in closely argued legalistic writings neither seen nor understood by the general Jewish public.

The Reform movement took dina demalkhuta dina into a new sphere mainly through Abraham Geiger's efforts to deal with the issues raised by divorce. Compliance with the state's regulations had already been agreed since the Austrian Ehepatent of 1782, now Geiger carried matters further and stated that civil divorce alone should be recognized.[56] Abraham Geiger understood divorce as a purely civil act without any moral content; in Judaism it was not accompanied by any religious ceremony, so it had no religious standing.[57] In America a decision was reached at the Philadelphia Conference of the American Rabbis in 1869 [58] whereas in Germany a religious divorce which acknowledged the equality of men and women and prevented the man from withholding the divorce, was adopted in 1912 at a conference in Posen.[59] Family law was now included in dina demalkhuta dina, as were some ritual laws, so Jewish children were permitted to attend school on Saturday.

As we look at the development of Reform Judaism through its pronouncements as various European assemblies and later in America, we see that dina demalkhuta dina was rarely mentioned, however, it was tacitly accepted. So at the Braunschweig Conference of 1844, they declared that "They acted in the sense of the Talmud, making the civil law supreme in all circumstances." The Conference then dealt with mixed marriage and stated that it would be considered valid only if the ensuing children were "educated in the Jewish faith." This was followed by a rather vague statement that "Judaism will never yield up the right of independence, within its specific compass and emphatically declines to tolerate all further interference on the part of the state in its inner development and its own religious affairs."[60] "Jews must observe those civil laws regarding marriage in the respective states to which they are subject. ... The Jew is obligated to regard as his native country the one to which he belongs by birth and through civic conditions. He must defend and obey all its laws."[61] "The Rabbi has no ecclesiastical powers, he has only such rights as the State and the congregation / invests in him."[62]

The meeting in Frankfurt of 1845 declared: "We know but one fatherland, the one in which we live and aim to strike root deeper and deeper."[63] Breslau in 1846 brought no new resolutions. The Cleveland Conference of 1855 which included all groups of Judaism declared: "Statutes and ordinances contrary to the laws of the land are invalid."[64]

The meetings in Leipzig of 1869 stated: "Judaism is in harmony with the principle of the unity of the human race; of the equality of all before the law; of the equality of all in duties and rights to the country and to the State; and with the principle of full liberty of the individual in his religious convictions and in the confession of the same."[65] As soon as a court of law had declared a person dead, such declaration holds good and is considered legal in ritual cases. A woman without a get may marry after a year.[66] Civil marriage was fully recognized though the religious ceremony was to be encouraged; it was not considered indispensable. Despite all of these statements, the assembly also passed a resolution which said: "The autonomy, independence and self-government of Judaism in all religious matters must be most sacredly preserved."[67] In this much narrowed sphere, they sought to retain some autonomy.

In Augsburg in 1871 those assembled reiterated that civil marriage would be accepted, but an additional religious cere-mony was encouraged. The assembly in Philadelphia in 1869 declared that only civil divorce was necessary as is purely civil matter. The law of the land prevailed in cases of doubtful death.[68] Pittsburgh in 1885, Columbus in 1935, and Pittsburgh in 1999 added nothing on the subject and did not mention dina demalkhuta dina. In an effort to add a religious element to divorce and to be egalitarian, various suggestions were made in the nineteenth and twentieth century. This led to the Seder Peri-dah, now observed by some Reform congregations.[69]

As we look at the development of Reform halakhah in the twentieth century, we find dina demalkuta dina was implied frequently, but rarely cited directly.[70] In the Solomon B. Freehof volumes, Reform Jewish Practice, and the parallel but less widely known volume by David Polish and Jacob Doppelt "A Guide for Reform Jews, " no need was felt to cite dina dem-lakhuta dina as both dealt with the practices of the synagogue and home. Even when it could have been discussed, it was avoided and other issues connected with the matter at hand were emphasized. In the question of the remarriage of a Jew and a non-Jew after a civil ceremony, Freehof might have dis-cussed it. Instead the brief discussion focused on whether it was possible to conduct a religious ceremony after the couple had already cohabited.[71] If we examine the responsa written under the auspices of the Responsa Committee, the five hundred writ-ten by Solomon B. Freehof, five hundred by me, and those of Gunther Plaut and Mark Washofsky, we see dina demalkhuta dina appears only peripherally with rare exceptions. The role of the state was taken for granted and not discussed. So marriages performed by lay people or cantors were discussed without ref-erence to the state. Only when a very specific issue was at stake, did this change, as in the question of whether a wedding might take place without a license, addressed to Freehof in 1974.[72] In a question about defective material used in construction dina demalhuta dina was mentioned,[73] as in a responsum on the gar-nishing of wages.[74] Julius Rappaport in his responsum on the use of wine for ritual purposes during the Prohibition dealt with all the ceremonies in which wine is used, but did not mention dina demalkhuta dina.[75]

It was taken for granted that the civil government and courts have the power, are just, and must be obeyed. This is true whether the discussion was about some one lost at sea,[76] collecting pledges made to the synagogue,[77] or dealing honestly with the Social Security.[78] During previous ages of mistrust of the secular government, the responses might have been different, or at least somewhat guarded. Different times zones and their implication for Jewish observances were accepted without hesitation.[79] When questions dealt with an area about which the state had not made up its mind, as, for example, the marriage of transsexuals,[80] the responsas stated that they would ultimately depend upon the state's position.

In the case of Jews testifying against fellow Jews in a civil suit, dina demalkhuta dina was actually cited and discussed. In this responsum, which summarized the instances in which dina demalkhuta dina applied, Freehof stated that "it certainly is incontrovertible that the laws of Medicare, of income tax, and of Social Security are the decisions of a just government applying equally to all citizens. Therefore it is our religious duty to obey those laws. Those who violate these laws violate a mandate of Jewish law thereby and are not to be protected."[81] Freehof then goes further and stated that the witnesses were not merely invited to testify, but ordered to do, so they are moser b'ones and must testify to protect themselves. In addition these individuals pose a danger to the Jewish community and one should testify against them on those grounds (Shulhan Arukh, Hoshen Mishpat, 388.11).[82] A similar line of reasoning was followed in questions about Social Security, Alzheimer's care,[83] and other government programs such as support for homes for the aged.[84] The sancta of the civil authorities were recognized so that Jews would participate in national celebrations.[85]

In matters of marriage and divorce, the power of the state's laws was acknowledged [86] as in the discussion of consanguinity in 1978. Concubinage, which existed in Judaism in various periods, could only be discussed in a historical and theoretical context as it is illegal in North America. When the Responsa Committee was asked about the morality of bringing a suit in a civil court, the issue was the morality of the action, not whether it was sanctioned by halakhah and should, perhaps be taken to a bet din.[87]

In the period since the Emancipation all groups within Judaism have acknowledged the state's interest in matters related to marriage. It meant, as previously cited, that a Jewish marriage would not be performed if it were prohibited by the state. Similarly no get would be issued unless it had been preceded by civil divorce. Through these acts, the principle of dina demalkhuta dina was extended beyond civil law. Reform Judaism, particularly in Germany and America, has gone one step further by recognizing civil divorce without an accompanying get and by ceasing any pretense that Jewish civil or criminal law is to be followed. Its adherents may choose arbitration by a bet din, but this continues to be rare.

Conservative and Reconstructionist Judaism

The way in which Conservative Judaism has treated dina demalkhuta dina may be seen through the actions of its Commitee On Law and Standards as well as the writing of its scholars. The Conservative movement has followed the same process as the Reform movement by issuing responsa through its Committee on Law and Standards. The published proceedings of the Committee on Jewish Law And Standards contains references to dina demalkhuta dina, but no detailed discussion. This has been equally true of some of its leading scholars who have written widely on many aspects of the halakhah.[88] As with the Reform movement, dina demalkhuta dina has been taken for granted as the background in a large number of debates. Elliot Dorff and Arthur Rosett have presented a full discussion of dina demalkhuta dina along with its historical background. They indicated that the movement recognizes civil marriage although not happily. Civil divorce, on the other hand, has not been recognized. The problems of the woman who may become an agunah are then fully discussed and various possible solutions presented.[89] In other words, it exists in the background and has been taken for granted.

The Reconstructionist movement has followed the pattern of the Reform movement and understood dina demalkhuta dina broadly. Mordecai Kaplan dealt with it only peripherally in an attack on modern orthodoxy.[90]

Orthodox Judaism

As the Ashkenazic tradition was dominant in the countries of the West, its attitude of resistance rather than accommodation was the path chosen by the Orthodox community. The statements limiting dina demalkhuta dina of previous ages were quoted with little added to them. This naturally led to a clash between rabbinic pronouncements and the realities of communal life. Accommodations were made by some, as for example David Hoffmann, especially in matters relating to the laws on public school attendance on shabbat.[90] Many other issues also had to be faced especially those connected with business relationships with non-Jews.[91] In a sense Samson Raphael Hirsch accepted some accomodation through his philosophy of torah im derekh ereetz, but its practical application was limited. Although Orthodox rabbis lamented the general use of secular courts and the many other areas in which they were no longer consulted, they rarely tried to place dina demlakhuta dina into a new framework and did their best to enforce an acceptance of early limits.

Conclusion

If we take a retrospective view of dina demalkhuta dina we must see it as the natural result of living as a minority, large or small, in many lands and civilizations. Without it we would not have survived or been able to function. As long as the Jewish corporate existence was recognized alongside other corporate bodies, there were large areas in which the secular authorities did not wish to enter. This changed with the advent of the modern state and Judaism changed, without a murmur. Except in the matter of divorce we have not moved further than the rest of Judaism.

The Orthodox community has also almost totally abandoned the codes of civil law, considered divine. A bet din may arbitrate and the civil authorities, naturally, do not care if a dispute is settled amicably through other means, but it is rarely used. In fact it is so rare that it makes the newspaper headlines when utilized outside the tight-knit New York traditional communities.

It is ironic that Judaism, which is so free and far removed from persecution and even prejudice, finds itself almost completely subject to the state. Although free, it is more controlled than in virtually any previous generation. That is one way of viewing this situation. On the other hand we may well claim that we now have the ideal situation in which Jews can subject themselves completely to Jewish law (halakhah) as long as they do so voluntarily and add this observance to that claimed by the state.

Is our modern expansion of dina demalkhuta dina permanent or only a temporary accomodation? The long history of the adjustment of this principle should teach us that nothing is permanent. Our view of it and the way in which Judaism uses it will surely change Modern times have taken it further than ever before.

Notes

1. The law of the Land of Israel is an amalgam of Turkish, British, American, and Jewish law; this and the division of legal authority between secular and rabbinic courts would make this an interesting topic for an additional paper. As the State of Israel is esentially a secular state, in some ways the conflict of dina demalkhuta dina exists there too though theoretically this should not be so. The general problem of dina demalkhuta dina has been treated from a different point of view by Leo Landman, Jewish Law in the Diaspora: Confrontation and Accommodation (Dropsie College Press), Philadelphia, 1968; and by Samuel Shilo, Dina d'Malkhuta Dina, Jerusalem, 1974.
2. Matthew 22.21; Mark 12.17; the New Testament also contains various statements of loyalty to Caesar (John 19.15; Acts 17.7; 25.8, etc.). The meaning of these statements in their context is not entirely clear. The topic has been discussed both in its New Testament setting as well as its later ramifications, especially after Martin Luther.
3. Gittin 10b; Nedarim 28a; Baba Kama 113a; Baba Batra 54b.
4. Biale, Power and Powerlessness in Jewish History, (Schocken), New York, 1986, pp. 54 ff.
5. An example of closeness was provided through the citation that Samuel did not order mourning for Jews fighting on the Roman side against the Parthians in their siege of Caesarea as this did not involve the majority of Jews. It simply indicated that he would not mourn for those who allied themselves with the enemy forces (Moed Katan 26a).
6. Bial, op. cit., pp. 54ff.; Jacob Neusner, A History of the Jews in Babylonia, II The Early Sassanian Period, (E.J. Brill, Leiden), 1966.
7. M. Nedarim 3.3.
8. Nedarim 28a.

9. Baba Kama 113b.
10. Baba Batra 55a.
11. Gittin 10b.
12. Erubin 11b.
13. Letter of Sherira Gaon (ed.) N.D. Rabinowich, (Jacob Joseph Press), Jerusalem, 1988.
14. Salo W. Baron, The Jewish Community, (Jewish Publication Society), Philadelphia, 1945, Vol. 1, pp. 175 ff.
15. Lewin, Baba Kama, p. 99; Harkavy, Teshuvot Hagaonim, p. 440.
16. Simcha Asaf, Teshuvat Hagaonim, p. 75.
17. Simcha Asaf, ibid., vol. 2, p. 75.
18. amuel b. Meir (Rashbam), Baba Batra 54b; Hayim ben Isaac, Or Zarua 34; Solomon Ibn Adret, Responsa Vol. 6 # 149; Shulhan Arukh, Hoshen Mishpat, 369.2. The effect of new coinage issued by the king on a debt previously incurred raised the question of royal prerogative (Solomon ibn Adret, Responsa, III 34, 40, V 198).
19. Gittin 88b; Harkavy, Teshuvot Hagaonim 278.
20. I. Agus, Teshuvot Baalei Tosfot.
21. Hil. Gezelah 5.12-18; Hil. Sekhiyah Umatan 1.15.
22. Asher, 18.2; Solomon b. Adret, Responsa III 15, 16, 79; VII1 48; Barfat, Responsa 51.
23. R. Yerucham, Sefer Mesharim; Samuel de Medine, Hoshen Mishpat, 350; Barfat, Responsa 51;Caro, Bet Joseph to Tur, Hoshen Mishpat, 26.
24. For the text and a discussion of its meaning see Louis Finkelstein, Jewish Self-Government in the Middle Ages, (Philipp Feldheim), New York, 1964, pp. 350 ff.
25. Barfat, Responsa, 5 and 6; though Joseph Caro disagreed with this decision (Abkat Rachel, 81); he made a distinction between Islamic lands where such documents were part of the royal prerogative and Christian lands where they were not.
26. Isaac b. Sheshet (Barfat), Responsa 5 and 6.
27. Isaac b. Sheshet (Barfat), Responsa, 305.
28. Joseph Caro, Abkat Rachel 81.
29. Solomon ibn Adret, Responsa, II, 244, V 287; Asher, Responsa, 89.8; Mishneh Torah, Hil, Malveh velaveh 27.1; etc.
30. Appointments occurred often without consultation and aroused storms of protest. See Salo W. Baron, The Jewish Community, vol. 1, pp. 285 ff.
31. Isaac b. Sheshet (Barfat), Responsa 271; Samuel b. Simon of Duran, Responsa, I, 158; 533; Solomon ibn Adret, Responsa I, 475; A Neuman, Jews in Spain, Jewish Publication Society, Philadelphia, 1946, p. 114.
32. An interesting modern Israeli discussion of the place of custom and dina demalkhuta dina may be found in Nahum Rakover, Modern Applications of Jewish Law, Jewish Heritage Society, Jerusalem 1992, pp. 103 ff.
33. See Note 21.
34. This principle stated that every person had the right to decide how to dispose of his financial affairs. However, the authorities understood the use of non-Jewish courts to be destructive to communal cohesion.
35. In the eighteenth century Moses Sofer tried to keep the financial issues of ketubot outside the range of the king's law by stating that, after all, they were

intended for women only and so of no significance. (Hatam Sofer, commentary to Even Haezer 126).

36. Mishneh Torah, Hil. Gezelah 5.14; Solomon b. Adret, Responsa, 5.198.
37. Solomon Ibn Adret, Responsa 6.254; Asher ben Yehiel, Responsa 86.9; Solomon ben Simon of Duran, Responsa 212; etc.
38. Shulhan Arukh, Hoshen Mishpat 369.
39. Finkelstein, op. Cit., pp. 357 f.
40. Isserles, Responsa, 123; also Hatam Sofer.
41. L. Finkelstein, op. cit., p. 154.
42. Baron, op. cit., pp. 323 ff.
43. Mishneh Torah, Hil. Zekhiya umatanah 1.15; Hil. Gezelah 5.12-18; Solomon ibn Adret, Torat Habayit III
44. Hatam Sofer, Even Haezer 43;Joseph Saul Nathanson, Shoel Emeshiv, etc.
45. air Hayyim Bachrach , Havat Yair, 176.
46. Jacob Katz, Tradition and Crisis,(Schocken Books), New York, 1993.
47. J. R. Marcus, The Jew in the Medieval World, (ebrew Union CollegePress), Cincinnati, 1938, p. 96.
48. M. Mendelssohn, Jerusalem and Other Jewish Writings, (Bloch Publishing), New York, 1969, pp. 102ff.
49. Freiman, Seder Kiduishin Venisuin, (Mosad Harav Kook), Jerusalem, 1964, pp. 312f.
50. Gil Graff, Separation of Church and State, pp. 73ff.
51. Tama, Transactions of the Parisian Sanhedrin, (tr. F. D. Kirwan), (Charles Taylor), London, 1807; Shulhan Arukh, Even Haezer 137, 143.
52. Ibid.; Jacob Reischer, Shevut Yaakov, Orah Hayyim 1.20.
53. Ibid., p. 197.
54. Samuel Holdheim, Ueber die Autonomie der Rabbinen, (Kurschner), Schwerin, 1843, pp. 59 ff., 137-165 and L. Loew, Gesammelte Schriften, (Alexander Baba), Szegedin, pp. 348-352.
55. Mishneh Torah, Hil. Shabbat 2.23; etc.; A. J. Frankel, Literaturblatt des Orients, 1842 in which he quoted Abraham Tiktin and Meyer Weil.
56. Wissenschaftliche Zeitschrift fur judische Theologie Vol. 1 (1837) pp. 1–14.
57. Abraham Geiger, Zeitschrift fur Wissenschaft und Leben, Vol. VIII.
58. W. Gunther Plaut, The Rise of Reform Judaism, (WUPJ), New York, 1963, pp. 222 f.; W. Gunther Plaut, The Growth of Reform Judaism, (WUPJ), New York, 1965, pp. 259 f.
59. W. Gunther Plaut, The Growth of Reform Judaism, New York, 1965, pp. 69
60. "Prottokolle," CCAR Yearbook I, (Bloch Publishing), Cincinnati, 1891, p. 82
61. Ibid., p. 82.
62. Ibid., p. 83.
63. Ibid., p. 88.
64. Ibid., p. 124.
65. Ibid., p. 101.
66. Ibid., p. 106.
67. Ibid., p. 108.
68. Ibid., p. 119.
69. Rabbi's Manual, Central Conference of American Rabbis, (CCAR Press), New York, 1988, pp. 97ff.

70. A responsum by Kaufmann Kohler issued in 1914 dealt with a marriage problem and concluded that the Conference had to debate the issue of the extent of the State's dominance in this matter (Walter Jacob, American Reform Responsa, Central Conference of American Rabbis, New York, 1983, p. 436). Another by Gotthard Deutsch on "Divorce of an Insane Husband" provided a lengthy discussion of various Jewish legal principles involved in this question, but not dina demalkhuta dina, although he mentioned national civil law at the conclusion of the responsum. (Ibid., 514 ff).

71. Solomon B. Freehof, Reform Jewish Practice, (UAHC), New York, 1944, Vol. 2, pp. 83 ff.

72. Solomon B. Freehof, Contemporary Reform Responsa,(Hebrew Union College Press), Cincinnati, 1974, pp. 98 ff.

73. Contemporary American Reform Responsa, (Central Conference of American Rabbis), New York, 1987, p. 16.

74. Ibid., 263.

75. Walter Jacob, American Reform Responsa, pp. 123 ff.

76. Solomon B. Freehof, Recent Reform Responsa, (Hebrew Union College Press), Cincinnati, 1963, no. 22.

77. Ibid. no. 44.

78. Solomon B. Freehof, Current Reform Responsa, (Hebrew Union College Press), Cincinnati, 1969, no. 52.

79. Solomon B. Freehof, Modern Reform Responsa,(Hebrew Union College Press), Cincinnati, 1971, no. 43.

80. Solomon B. Freehof, Responsa for Our Time, (Hebrew Union College Press), Cincinnati, 1977, no. 42.

81. Solomon B. Freehof, Ibid., no. 54.

82. Walter Jacob, Contemporary American Reform Responsa, (CCAR Press), New York, 1987, no. 6.

83. Walter Jacob, Contemporary American Reform Responsa, no. 86.

84. Walter Jacob, Questions and Reform Jewish Answers, (CCAR Press), New York, 1992, no. 91.

85. W. Gunther Plaut and Mark Washofsky, Teshuvot for the Nineties, (CCAR Press), New York, 1997, pp. 159.

86. Walter Jacob, American Reform Responsa, no. 129.

87. Walter Jacob, Contemporary American Reform Responsa, no. 11.

88. David Golinkin,ed., Proceedings of the Committee on Jewish Law and Standards of the Conservative Movement 1927-1970, (Rabbinbical Assembly), Jerusalem, 1997, 3 vols. Similarly Joel Roth's The Halakhic Process, A Systemic Analysis, (Jewish Theological Seminary), New York, 1986 did not deal with this question; David Golinkin (ed.), The Responsa of Professor Louis Ginzberg, (Jewish Theological Seminary), New York, 1996.

89. Elliot N. Dorff and Arthur Rosett, A Living Tree, the Roots and Growth of Jewish Law, (State University of New York), Albany, 1988, 515 ff.

90. Mordecai Kaplan, Judaism as a Civilization, (MacMillan), New York, 1934, p. 158.

91. David Hoffmann, Melamed Lehoil, (Hermon Verlag), Frankfurt a M., 1926, 1927, 1932, vol. 1, p. 65-67, 75.

92. Ibid.,vol. 1, pp. 49 ff, 108 ff., vol. 3 pp. 22 ff, 32 f.

Chapter 3

❖ ❖ ❖

Asu Seyag LaTorah
Make a Fence to Protect the Torah

Rabbi Richard S. Rheins

At the inaugural conference of the Institute of Liberal Halakhah, my teacher and friend Mark Washofsky addressed the question of whether "liberal *halakhah*" was a contradiction in terms. He asked "Can the system of rabbinic law accommodate contemporary values of justice, morality and progress?"[1] In developing his answer, Washofsky brilliantly laid the groundwork for a dialogue between liberal *halakhists* and those of the Orthodox community. As he stated, the "ultimate goal of liberal *halakhic* writing is to encourage among the observant community an openness to alternative interpretations of law."[2] While I share the hope of my mentor for a future era of respectful dialogue and intellectual exchange between Orthodox and Liberal *halakhists*, a more pressing and immediate problem is establishing the legitimacy of Liberal/Progressive *halakhah* among our own non-Orthodox laity and rabbinic colleagues.

Notes for this section begin on page 107.

Those of us who support the continuing development of Progressive *Halakhah* face major challenges.[3] Too many Jews misunderstand the word *"halakhah"* as "Jewish Law," an imposing body of ancient and inflexible statutes and restrictions. But *halakhah* does not mean "law." Rather, it is derived from the Hebrew root *h-l-kh* "to go." *Halakhah* expresses less a concept of law and legalism than a "method," a "Jewish way of doing things."

Many Jews affiliated with Reform and Conservative congregations do not live lives informed by *halakhah*, yet it provides a documented record of the evolution and development of Judaism's cherished traditions. It also preserves evidence of the many variations of how those rituals were and are practiced from place to place and era to era. Judaism's growth and flexibility are clearly demonstrated in *halakhic* literature. Ultimately, *Halakhah* provides both the "how to" and the "why," and explanations that help Jews see how, through the fulfillment of *mitzvot*, they are linked to the continuum of Jewish expression through thousands of years.

Without adequate explanations, Jewish rituals and observances may appear to some as bewildering anachronisms. I am not suggesting, nor does Progressive *halakhah* advocate, uniformity of practice and blind obedience to specific rituals. Liberal and secularly educated Jews are quick to protest against mindless and rote "performance" of rituals. The very birth of the Reform movement was due to the agitation of emancipated Jews who longed for a meaningful and refined expression of Judaism. "Reformers" of the nineteenth century researched and reconsidered the origins of old traditions and they reserved the right to reject those rituals that seemed outdated, superstitious, wrongheaded, or simply lacking edifying values. They felt fully empowered to modify rituals in order to make them more relevant to the contemporary Jewish community. They accompanied those changes with carefully argued responsa that demonstrated how their modifications were in keeping with the essential principles of Judaism and *halakhah*.[4] Significantly, many of those changes, which were considered "radical," eventually became widespread among Jews, regardless of denomination. Prayer in the vernacular, formal religious school education for females, and placing the *bimah* in front of the congregation were all Reform innovations. They became widespread both because they addressed the will of the laity and because they were shown to be in keeping with the spirit of *halakhic* development.

Progressive *halakhah* has made remarkable advances during the last fifty years. Interest in Talmud and *halakhah* among Reform and Conservative laity continues to accelerate. Dozens of volumes of Reform responsa and other works on *halakhah* have been published.[5] The Freehof Institute of Progressive Halakhah has taken root and flourishes. In 1988, the Conservative movement began to publish its collections of responsa in order to foster the study and observance of *halakhah* by its members.[6]

There are many areas of growing cooperation and partnership between Conservative rabbis and those Reform rabbis who are committed to *halakhic* standards. Reform and Conservative *halakhic* methodologies are remarkably similar, even if we reach different conclusions.[7] I believe that the term "Progressive *halakhah*"properly refers to both efforts. Both are seeking to offer a logical and vital alternative to the unacceptable extremes that plague the Jewish people: on the one hand, unrestrained autonomy with no communal standards, and on the other hand, repressive fundamentalism that champions medieval sensibility.

Progressive *Halakhah* does not aim to promote "neo-Orthodoxy," as some of its more assimilated critics charge. Nor is Progressive *halakhah* seeking to water down or trivialize Jewish tradition, as some of the uncompromising purists charge. In a nut- shell, Progressive *halakhah*, because it is a reflection of non-fundamentalist ideology, is far more willing to innovate and explore unique responses to the challenges that face modern Judaism. This paper seeks to provide a brief outline of the phenomenon of rabbinic legislation, the power to deviate from the literal word of the Torah, and the limits of that power.

Progressive Halakhahs vis-à-vis Orthodox *Halakhah*

Progressive *halakhah* openly embraces the scientific discoveries and inquiries that present such a grave intellectual indictment of Orthodoxy's fundamentalism. We may confidently claim that Progressive *Halakhah* is the truest vehicle for maintaining and continuing the spirit and genius of Jewish thought and practice. Progressive *halakhah* is, however, a work in progress (much like the Jewish people). Before it will win the attention and respect of

Reform and Conservative Jews, we must state more clearly its authenticity vis-à-vis the Orthodox model.

Robert Gordis eloquently expressed the frustration many of us feel toward the extremist *halakhic* methodology of the Orthodox. In *The Dynamics of Judaism* he wrote

> "It is ironic that in our day when the doctrine of papal infallibility is being challenged even in the Catholic Church, a novel doctrine of rabbinic infallibility is being advanced in fundamentalist Jewish circles. In order to suppress any movement for change in the *halakhah*, we are told that it is forbidden to question, let alone disagree with, the views of a given scholar or group of scholars, because they represent *da-at Torah*, "the true meaning of Torah." This gift has been vouchsafed to them because they are the mystical embodiment of divine truth. Such a doctrine, designed to stifle discussion and controversy, was never advanced in the past by any of the thousands of Talmudic Sages, by Saadia or his adversaries in the tenth century, by the advocates and opponents of Maimonides in the thirteenth, or even by the adherents of the *Shulhan Arukh* and its rabbinic opponents in the sixteenth and seventeenth centuries.[8]

Halakhic literature is replete with inspiring models of dynamic flexibility that demonstrate rabbinic creativity. The long and proud history of Judaism's spiritual and intellectual development was due in no small part to the courageous innovations and accommodations established and promoted by *halakhic* authorities (*poskim*) in every generation. Progressive *halakhah* strives to learn from these models and emulate them.[9]

While traditional *halakhic* methodology can be quite flexible, and in the hands of enlightened authorities throughout Jewish history has proven to be a most creative tool, most current Orthodox *poskim* are emphasizing the preservative and conservative properties of *halakhah*, not its progressive qualities.[10] Moshe Sofer (*Hatam Sofer*) was a harsh critic of Reform—not only the Reform movement, but of the very idea that Judaism can change and evolve. He wrote: *"Hadash assur min ha-Torah"* (anything new is forbidden by the Torah!)[11] For him even local custom took on the urgency and importance of the Torah itself. As one Orthodox rabbi described him, the Hatam Sofer "would brook no deviation from the custom of his country that women cover their heads so that not even a single strand of hair be visible, a custom based upon a teaching of the Zohar."[12]

Notwithstanding the prevailing trend among Orthodox authorities toward ever-greater restrictions and conservative readings of *halakhic* sources, it is a mistake to confuse their intransigence for religious piety. The late great historian Jacob Katz taught that the current Orthodox attitude of inflexibility is itself a reform (!)—a reaction to sociological and political influences and not a natural result of pure *halakhic* reasoning.[13] In numerous case studies, Katz has demonstrated that *halakhah*'s role has historically been one of reacting to the changing needs and realities of the Jewish people.[14]

It is essential to emphasize that radical innovations, unique interpretations, and bold contradictions to the literal instructions of the Torah text are not the inventions of Reform Judaism. They are the legacy of sages of the Mishnah and Gemara!

Rabbinic authorities have claimed the right, even the obligation, to make rulings that will help strengthen the Jewish people. When the sages of the *Kenesset HaGedolah*, (the Great Assembly), instructed us: *va'asu seyag laTorah*, (make a fence to protect the Torah), they did not mean to fossilize Jewish life and thought—just the opposite! Throughout rabbinic literature the principle of *seyag laTorah* is a shorthand way of guaranteeing the right of contemporary Jewish authorities to legislate even radical innovations to help the Jewish people survive and fulfill the Divine will as they could best determine. As Maimonides wrote in his commentary to the Mishnah:

> The fourth [of the five divisions of Oral Law]: These are *gezerot*, laws the prophets and Sages decreed in every generation in order *la-asot seyag laTorah*—to erect a fence around the laws of the Torah. The-Holy-One-Blessed-Be-He commanded us in general terms to create such legislation when He said: "You shall protect my safeguards." (Leviticus 18:30) This is explained by tradition to mean: 'Make safeguards for my safeguards'" (*Yevomot* 21a)[15]

Rabbinic sages revered the Torah as divinely inspired and yet they realized the importance of developing legislation that was distinct from the letter of the law as it appeared in the Torah. Early Jewish philosophers apparently shared this conviction. So it has been argued that the first-century Jewish philosopher Philo promoted the importance of Oral law. In his *De Specialibu Legibus* (The Special Laws), he offers a fascinating commentary on Deuteronomy 19:14: "You shall not remove your neighbor's landmarks which were set up by earlier generations." Philo understood this verse as protecting the authority of ancestral customs.

> For customs are unwritten laws, the decisions approved by men of
> old, not inscribed on monuments nor on leaves of paper which the
> moth destroys, but on the souls of those who are partners in the same
> citizenship.... Praise cannot be duly given to one who obeys the writ-
> ten law, since he acts under the admonition of restraint and fear of
> punishment. But he who faithfully observes the unwritten deserves
> commendation, since the virtue which he displays is freely willed.[16]

Philo's thought was echoed in *Pirkei Avot* (3:17): "*Masoret
seyag laTorah ...*" (*Tradition is a protective fence for the Torah*). Scholars and sages two thousand years ago knew that if the Torah
were to have a meaningful, ongoing and just impact on the lives
of contemporary Jews, it had to be accompanied by commentary, interpretation and creative legislation. As Maimonides
wrote in his introduction to the *Mishnah*:

> Know that every *mitzvah* the Holy One Blessed Be He gave our
> teacher Moses, peace be upon him, was given to him with detailed
> explanations. First He gave him the *mitzvah*, then He told him the
> explanation and details and all wisdom contained in the Torah
> verses. ... When a situation arose on which no explanation had
> been heard from the prophet (Moses), they determined a response
> by means of deduction, logical argument guided by the thirteen
> methods of Torah interpretation[17]. ... Whenever a disagreement
> developed, they followed the majority opinion, as the Torah pre-
> scribes (Exodus 23:2): "to decide according to the majority."[18]

The Torah required commentary, interpretation and creative
application that met popular approval among the sages and no
doubt from the general population as well. Indeed, the ascen-
dancy of the Pharisees and their heirs, the rabbis, was due in
large part because of the popular support they earned by demon-
strating a mastery and creative approach to Scripture. Our best
first-century eyewitness Josephus maintained that the popular
support and influence of the Pharisees was due to the reputation
they had for excellence in their interpretation of the Torah (*A.J.*
17.41; *B.J.* 1.110; 2.162; *Vita* 191) as well as for *the customs they
introduced* and transmitted (*A.J.* 13.296, 297, 408).[19]

For the early Sages, protecting the Torah meant safeguarding
the Jewish people and promoting the continuance of the ancestral
faith, not by slavish obedience to the literal words of the Torah,
but through various forms of legislation that could enhance the
essence of the Torah's message and intent. This legislative activity was the beginning of the classic rabbinic *halakhic* process.

What are the principles of flexibility and limitations inherent in the *halakhic* process? How did the sages of the Mishnah and Gemara establish their right to challenge the literal teachings of the Torah text? If radical innovation was and is possible, what principles constrain rabbis (both past and present)? What are the origins of rabbinic authority, our self-proclaimed mission to build a *seyag laTorah*, a protective fence around the Torah, by means of *takkanot* and *gezerot*? *Takkanot* and *gezerot* are forms of rabbinic legislation. Though the terms are frequently used interchangeably, some authorities use the term *takkanah* when the rabbis mandate a new action or observance and *gezerah* when the rabbis make a ruling that extends or limits an existing observance. [20] These principles enabled rabbis of every generation to legislate and even to contradict a law from the Torah. How could they claim such discretionary power?

From Torah to Legislation

New interpretations, applications and radical changes to law as it appears in the Torah can be traced to biblical times.[21] The Torah itself provides clear examples of challenges to law and subsequent changes. The daughters of Zelophechad complained to Moses that just because their father had no son, the family inheritance should not be lost. Rather, it should be given to the daughters (Numbers 27:1-11): "Let not our father's name be lost to his clan just because he had no son! Give us a holding among our father's kinsmen." Moses sought divine help to adjudicate this case. And the Lord said to Moses, "The plea of Zelophechad's daughters is just. ..." After this challenge, daughters were included in the line of inheritance. A little later, a new challenge arose. What happens if the daughters of Zelophechad do not marry one who is of the tribe of Manasseh? Will not the land, promised by the Torah to the tribe Manasseh, be transferred by means of marriage to another tribe? Once again Moses turned to God and the law was further amended: "This is what the Lord has commanded concerning the daughters of Zelophechad: They may marry anyone they wish, provided they marry into a clan of their father's tribe. No inheritance of the Israelites may pass over from one tribe to another, but the Israelites must remain bound each to the ancestral portion of his tribe"

(Numbers 36:1-9). Thus we can see the evolution of *halakhah* occurred in the Torah itself!

Ezra the scribe was also a noted biblical legislator. He enacted new laws against intermarriage (Ezra 9:1–10:44). He was credited with a number of *takanot*, including: the public reading of the Torah at the *Minhah* service on Shabbat and on Mondays and Thursdays; and other matters (*Baba Kama* 82a).

Tellingly, Ezra was credited with revolutionary changes to the very fundamental elements of the Torah: its script. *Sanhedrin* 21b stated: "Originally, the Torah was presented to Israel in Hebrew script and in the Holy Tongue (*bikh-tav iv-ri uleshon ha-kodesh*). It (the Torah) was presented to them again in the days of Ezra in Assyrian script and the Aramaic tongue (*bikh-tav ashurit uleshon arami*)." A *Baraita* then continued: "Rabbi Yosi says, Ezra was worthy of having the Torah presented to Israel through him had Moses not preceded him (*Sanhedrin* 21b)."

What compelled Ezra to institute (legislate) such radical changes? The Book of Nehemiah explained that Ezra and Nehemiah were faced with Jews who were unfamiliar with the Torah. They apparently were unable to understand Hebrew. "They read from the scroll of the Teaching of God (*va-yikreu va-Sefer beTorah ha-Elohim*), translating it and giving the sense; so they understood the reading (Nehemiah 8:18). Ezra decided that if a language barrier prevented Jews from understanding the Torah, then then tradition and form should not stand in the way of essential principles and integrity.

Another ancient example of legislation that altered the literal reading of a Torah law can be found in I Maccabees. Early in the war against the Seleucids, many Jews were unwilling to violate the laws of Shabbat even to defend themselves. The Seleucids therefore attacked on the Sabbath and the defenseless Jews were slaughtered.[22] Shortly thereafter, Mattathias, the leader of the Jewish revolt, proposed a *takkanah*:

> When Mattathias and his friends heard this, they mourned greatly over them, each one saying to the other, "If all of us do as our brothers have done, and do not fight against the heathen for our lives and our laws, they will soon destroy us from off the earth." They then made the following decision, "If any man attack us in battle on the Sabbath day, let us oppose him, that we may not all die as our brothers did in the hiding places"(2:39-41).

Again, the preservation of the Jewish people and their faith took precedence over scrupulous observance to the laws of the Torah, even those as significant as Sabbath prohibitions. Jews in later days could cite these important precedents for legislative activity. In fact, on first glance it appears that the Talmudic sages simply assumed that they were empowered to legislate for *Pirkei Avot* taught:

> Moses received the Torah at Sinai and transmitted it to Joshua, Joshua to the elders, and the elders to the prophets, and the prophets to the men of the great synagogue. The latter used to say three things: be patient in [the administration of] justice, rear many disciples and *make a fence around the Torah (va-asu seyag laTorah)*.

What *hutzpah* for the earliest sages to claim the right to legislate! Did not the Torah explicitly warn against altering the laws of Moses? *"Lo tosifu al hadevar asher Anokhi metzaveh etkhem ve-lo tigre-u mimenu"* (Do not add anything to that which I have commanded you and do not subtract from it"(Deuteronomy 4:2).[23]

To overcome this imposing obstacle, the sages understood *lo toseif* and *lo tigre-u* narrowly. Rashi interpreted *lo tosifu* (do not add) as a prohibition against adding to the prescribed elements of a commandment. For instance, we are prohibited from adding a fifth species to the four species of the *lulav* and *etrog*. Likewise, we are forbidden to add a fourth blessing to the threefold priestly blessing (*birkat Kohanim*) found in the Torah.[24] Nachmanides noted that the addition of the reading of the Scroll of Esther on Purim was an early challenge to the above prohibition.[25] By what right did our ancestors add the festival of Purim to the Jewish calendar of observances when it celebrates an event that happened centuries after the canonization of the Torah? In the words of Nachmanides, Purim and other rabbinically legislated observances are permitted as long as: "one realizes that these *takanot* (ordinances of the sages) were enacted as a fence [to protect the Torah] and are not the actual words of the Holy One Blessed by He of the Torah."[26]

A thirteenth century contemporary of Nachmanides, Rabbi Hizkiyah Hizkuni (Hazekuni) of Provence, had another ingenious way of limiting the effect of Deuteronomy. 4:2. Quite logically, he understands that the injunction not to add or subtract is in specific reference to the Torah's prohibition against the worship of other gods and idol worship.[27] Thus, the Torah's intent was simply to preserve the absolute ban on idolatry, not to limit the later generations from adding legislation.

Tradition has established that the Torah text contains 613 commandments (*mitzvot*) that are explicitly divine in origin. Though there is some variation about which are the specific 613 commandments from the Torah, they are generally divided into two categories: 248 affirmative commandments (*mitzvot aseh*) and 365 negative commandments (*mitzvot lo ta-aseh*).[28] The rabbis understood Deuteronomy 4:2 as prohibiting them from adding to the 613 Torah laws (*de-oraita*), but that verse did not restrict them from legislating rabbinic laws (*de-rabbanan*).

Having overcome the restrictions of Deuteronomy 4:2, the rabbis still had to find the textual support in the Torah for the authority to add laws that would help shape and define Jewish practice. They grounded the right to legislate on Deuteronomy 17:11: "According to the sentence of the Torah which they shall teach you, and according to the judgment which they shall tell you, you shall do; *you shall not deviate ('lo tasur') from that which they instruct you either to the right or to the left.*"

The operative verse is Deuteronomy 17:11, *Al pi hatorah asher yorukha ve-al hamishpat asher yomru lekha ta-aseh* lo tasur *min hadevar asher yageedu lekha yamin usmol.* The Torah specifically referred to the Levitical priests (*Kohanim*) and the local judge (*Shofet*) as the authorities which must be obeyed. Naturally, the rabbis saw themselves as the rightful heirs to judge, guide and instruct the Jewish people in the post-Temple era. This crucial verse helped to establish rabbinic authority and the right to legislate. But it also taught that their words must be obeyed. As the Talmud taught: "All the ordinances of the Rabbis were based by them on the prohibition *lo tasur* (you shall not deviate)."[29]

Interestingly, the above proof-text was an important argument in the arsenal the medieval Rabbis marshaled during the infamous Disputations organized by the Catholic Church.[30] The church's persecutors charged that Jews had abandoned the Bible in favor of the Talmud. They cited as evidence the rabbinic teaching that the Talmud (*Torah she-b'al peh*) was divine. Christian doctrine, according to Augustine, based its "tolerance" of Jews on the predica-tion of Jewish adherence to the divinity of the Bible. If it could be proven that Jews had abandoned the Bible (in favor of the Talmud), Christians no longer needed to tolerate Jews in Europe.[31] The rabbinic defenders in the *Disputations* had to demonstrate the indispensability of the talmudic interpretation and application of the Bible. They also had to demonstrate the rabbinic right to legislate. Rabbi Moses of Coucy provided such a defense in his *Sefer Mitzvot Gadol*. He described how rabbinic sages, disciples of the prophets, were the rightful heirs to carry out the Biblical injunction: "You must not deviate from that which they instruct you either to the right or to the left" (Deut. 17:11). He then wrote: "And whosoever should examine this book [i.e., the Talmud] will see how they made a fence for the Torah (*asu seyag latorah*) and on their authority enacted [ordinances] to create a buffer that will prevent Jews from violating a Biblical prohibition."[32]

The rabbinic legislative powers were developed throughout the Talmudic era. A comprehensive review of the major principles and guidelines for legislative activity by the *halakhic* authorities can be found in Menachem Elon's monumental four-volume work: *Jewish Law: History Sources, Principles*. In it, Elon identified several major methodological principles of rabbinic legislation,[33] including[33] *Shev ve-al ta-aseh*[34] "Sit and do not perform," a positive *mitzvah* from the Torah. A rabbinic court may legislate that a precept of the Torah should not be carried out. For instance, the Rabbis prohibited the sounding of a *shofar* when Rosh HaShanah fell on Shabbat even though the Torah commanded that the *shofar* to be sounded,[35] and they extended the Biblical law against boiling meat in its mother's milk to include poultry.[36]

The converse of the first principle listed above (sit and do not do) is *kum va-aseh*[37] (get up and do). Specifically, this concept established the Rabbinic right to issue decrees that compel us *to do that which the Torah has commanded us not to do*. This is the most controversial of the principles of rabbinic legislation. It is hardly surprising that not all rabbis agreed that they had this authority. The Talmud recorded a debate between the third-century *amoraim* Hisdah and Rabbah on this issue.[38] Rabbah did not believe that rabbis possessed the authority to permit an act prohibited by the Torah. Hisdah thought they did.

This debate in *Yevamot 90b* involved an exegesis of Deuteronomy 18:15 ("The Lord your God will raise up for you a prophet from among your own people, like myself; unto him you shall hearken."):

> Come and hear: "Unto him you shall hearken (Deut. 18:15)," even if he tells you to transgress any of the commandments of the Torah. For instance, Elijah on Mount Carmel—obey him in every respect

in accordance with the needs of the hour! There it is different, for it
is written, Unto him shall you hearken—Then let [rabbinic law] be
deduced from it! The safeguarding of a cause is different ...

"Unto him you shall hearken" refers to the power of the
prophets to legislate. Rabbi Chisda maintained that, like the
prophets, rabbinic courts could legislate even to the extent of
permitting an act that the Torah prohibits. Rabbah disputes
Hisda on this point. *Yevamot* 90b explored the difference between
the extraordinary acts of Elijah and the acts of rabbis to amend or
even abrogate laws of Torah in order to establish a *seyag letorah*.

Elijah violated the Torah's ban against sacrificing in a place
other than Jerusalem when he made his great sacrificial confrontation with the priests of Baal on Mount Carmel (I Kings
18:31ff). Rabbah maintained that there was a substantial difference between Elijah's heroic act and the rabbinic right to legislate. Elijah's was a desperate act to save the day and not an
attempt to establish a precedent.

The Tosafists asked, "How can a prophet, like Elijah, who
delivers a divine message, be analogous to a *halakhic* authority
whose enactment is not of divine origin?" Nachmanides and
others understood that when a prophet abrogated Torah, he did
so not by divine command but on his own authority. Likewise,
the rabbis legislate on their own authority and not with the pre-
tension of divine command.[39]

Though the dispute of *Yevamot* 90b was decided in favor of
Rabbah, the Talmud established three important exceptions,
which, in effect, granted the rabbis sweeping power in accordance with Chisda's position. The three exceptions are:

Hefker bet din hefker[40] (what the rabbinic court nullifies is nulli-
fied). In a property dispute, the rabbis have the right to declare an
individual's property forfeited. This principle became a doctrine
that permitted legislation to both nullify existing legal rights
(granted by the Torah) and to create new rights (not conferred by
the Torah). This was the principle upon which Hillel based his
famous *takkanah* known as the *prosbul* that gave creditors the right
to collect debts even after the end of a sabbatical year.[41]

Le-migdar milta (to safeguard the matter). The Rabbis have the
authority to issue *takkanot*, protective measures even in criminal
and capital cases, during times of dire necessity.

Hora'at sha'ah[42] (a decision for the hour, that is an emergency enactment) and *ha-sha-ah tzerikhah le-khakh* (the extraordinary needs of the hour). The Rabbis established the right to enact temporary legislation to protect the health and faith of the Jewish people even if it meant contradicting a commandment from the Torah. In these emergency situations the Rabbis frequently evoked the phrase from Psalm 119:126: *et la-asot* (it is time for the Lord to word, they have made void Your law).[43]

The exceptions to Rabbah's rejection of the Rabbinic authority to declare *kum va-aseh*, seem to be reserved for emergency situations. The exceptions were, in theory, only (*lefi sha'ah*) temporary measures that did not establish precedent, but practically many "emergency" decrees established by the rabbis during times of crisis became permanent. For example, the prohibition against memorizing the "written Torah" or writing the "oral Torah." The Talmudic sages understood this law to be *de-oraita*, based on a law from the Torah. The scriptural citation was Exodus 34:27:[44] "And the Lord said to Moses: 'Write (*ketav-lekha et-hadevarim ha-eileh*) down these commandments, for in accordance with these commandments (*ki al pi hadevarim*) I make a covenant with you and Israel.'"

This verse was interpreted to mean that teachings that were handed down to Moses in writing (i.e., the Torah) must not be transmitted orally.[45] Likewise, teachings that were given orally (i.e., Mishnayot and Beraitot) must not be written down.[46] But the Mishnah was written down! In writing it down, did not the Rabbis violate a prohibition from the Torah? However, as Rashi and the Rambam explained, the Mishnah was written down in violation of the Torah only because of the terrible crisis the Jewish people faced after the destruction of the Second Temple.[47] The sages cited the emergency authority inferred from Psalm 119:126: *"Et la-asot"* (When it is time to act for the Lord, you may even nullify your Torah!). This "emergency decree" has now been in effect one thousand nine hundred years.

Ultimately, Joseph Karo, the great codifier of Jewish law, understood that the Talmudic debate between Rabbah and Hisdah was won by Hisdah (Yevamot 90b). The Rabbis had the authority to permit that which the Torah prohibits.

> ... for we say *kum aseh*, (rise up and do that which the Torah prohibited)...because we conclude that in order to "safeguard the mat-

ter" (*le-migdar milta*), the Sages are empowered to abrogate a law of
the Torah even by directing the performance of an act the Torah
prohibits. The reinforcement of Rabbinic enactments even in those
cases that do not, strictly speaking, involve *safeguarding* will lead to
the better observance of those measures designed to create such a
safeguard, because if people fail to respect one Rabbinic enactment,
they will ultimately lose respect for all of them. Therefore, anything
that reinforces a Rabbinic enactment comes within the application
of the principle *safeguarding the matter*.[48]

Rabbinic legislation which contradicted the Torah may be
enacted in order to protect the spiritual and physical well being of
the Jewish people and Judaism. Still, no one should infer from
this that the rabbis assumed the power to speak with the same
eternal authority as the Torah. The rabbis have been obligated to
make it clear that their enactments are not additions to the Torah.
Rabbis are not empowered to add or subtract from the Torah, they
are empowered to declare *takkanot* and *gezerot* that strengthen
Judaism and the Jewish people. As Maimonides wrote in *Mishneh
Torah, Hilkhot Mamrim* 2.4:

> If in order to bring back the multitudes to religion and save them
> from general religious laxity, the court deems it necessary to set
> aside temporarily a positive or a negative command, it may do so,
> taking into account the need of the hour. Even as a physician will
> amputate the hand or the foot of a patient in order to save his life,
> so the court may advocate, when an emergency arises, the tempo-
> rary disregard of some of the commandment, so that the whole of
> the commandments may be preserved. This is in keeping with
> what the early Sages said: "*Desecrate on His account one Sabbath that
> many Sabbaths will be observed*" (*Yoma* 85b).[49]

Limits To Rabbinic Legislation

Despite the authority to legislate, there have always been stringent limits; their dominance has always been obvious. Were
innovation and radical reform easy, Judaism today would be
very different. Judaism has evolved. Most observances and
beliefs that dominate modern Judaism (monotheism, Shabbat,
festivals, daily prayer, *tzedakah*, dietary restrictions, Torah study,
the Hebrew language, *Brit Milah*, etc.) can all be traced to the
Biblical period.[50] The "conservative" nature of Judaism has preserved a link to our ancestors and fostered bonds among Jews of

every denomination. It may be inaccurate to speak of *Am Echad*, nevertheless, a large degree of homogeneity remains among our major denominations. This is the direct result of the strict limits the rabbis placed upon their legislative authority. Radical innovations, eclectic expressions and individual autonomy lead to more sectarian divisions.[51]

Some liberal Rabbis seem far too eager to experiment and create without reflection on the long-term effect on Jewish continuity. While my colleagues and I are quick to criticize our Orthodox brethren for not taking advantage of the flexibility inherent in *halakhah*, we Progressive Jews must answer to the charge that we play too fast and loose with tradition and *halakhic* process. Therefore, let me review the major principles that limit *halakhic* legislation: rabbis were criticized for issuing excessively restrictive decrees. rabbis were not permitted to impose a *takkanah* or *gezerah* that the majority of Jews would not heed. Rabbis were forbidden to issue a decree against the will of the majority of Jews. Criticism was especially unleashed against those who promulgated excessive restriction (*gezerot*) that burdened the people. In *Avot d'R. Natan* the author warned that such burdens are more likely to lead the people to abandon the law than to achieve levels of super-piety.[52] A sage of the *Yerushalmi* stated: "Is it not enough for you what the Torah has forbidden, that you go and prohibit additional things!"[53]

The prohibition against a *gezerah* or *takkanah* that the majority of the people will not obey was clearly stated in *Avodah Zarah* 36a:

> Our sages relied upon the dictum of Rabban Simeon b. Gamaliel and R. Eliezer b. Zadok who declared: "We make no decree upon the community unless the majority are able to abide by it." R. Adda b. Ahaba said: "What Scriptural verse supports this rule? You are cursed with the curse; for you rob Me, even this whole nation (Malachi 3:9). When the whole nation has [accepted an ordinance, then the curse which is the penalty of its infraction] does apply, otherwise it does not."

Maimonides codified this limitation in his *Mishneh Torah*: "Before instituting a *gezerah* or enacting a *takkanah* or introducing a *minhag* which it deems necessary, the rabbinic court (*Beit Din*) should calmly deliberate and make sure that the majority of the community can live up to it. At no time is a decree to be imposed upon the public which the majority cannot endure (*Hilkhot Mamrim*, 2.5)."

Religious authorities always encouraged greater observance and piety. To combat assimilation, laxity, superstition and ignorance, Rabbis have issued countless *gezerot* and *takkanot*. In addition, *minhagim* (customs) have been promoted, but rabbis may not issue mandates that are contrary to the popular will. Sometimes Rabbis have tried to eliminate a popular custom that they find inconsistent with the Jewish ideal.

The refusal of the majority of Jews to accept an ordinance not only prevents the new decree from taking effect, it also nullifies a longstanding rabbinic prohibition. As Rambam wrote:

> If the court has issued a *gezerah* in the belief that the majority of the community could endure it, and after the enactment thereof the people made light of it and it was not accepted by the majority, the decree is void and the court is denied the right to coerce the people to abide by it. If after a decree had been promulgated, the court was of the opinion that it was universally accepted by Israel and nothing was done about it for years, and after the lapse of a long period a later court investigates the doings of Israel and finds that the decree is not generally accepted, the latter court, even if it is inferior to the former in wisdom and number, is authorized to abrogate it (*Mamrim* 2.6-7).

Just as the Rabbis were restricted by popular will from issuing overly burdensome *gezerot*, so, too, they werecautioned against being overly permissive: "Any court that permits two things that have been declared forbidden should hesitate about permitting a third thing (*Mamrim* 2.8)."

Practical Applications of Progressive *Halakhah*

From this brief review of *halakhic* legislation, it is clear that Progressive *halakhah* has an important and valid mission in the struggle against assimilation and secularism. Liberal Judaism can serve the masses of Israeli Jews caught between an oppressive medieval ultra-Orthodoxy and the crass emptiness of secularism. Progressive *halakhah* must follow the lead of our ancestral sages and find innovations, interpretations and applications that preserve essential Jewish principles while renewing Judaism's vitality and relevancy. *Asu seyag laTorah* is a mandate to change when necessary. The changes must be in consonance with the majority.

The awesome authority of *halakhic* legislation must be utilized judiciously. Legislative powers are best saved for true emergencies and untenable situations. Progressive *halakhah* must continue to develop methodologies that incorporate critical scholarship and modern ethical values in the decision-making process. Those methodologies must acknowledge the dramatic differences between liberal Jews and fundamentalist Jews.[54]

The role of Progressive Halakhah is not to impose its authority on Jews. It is a much needed tool that enables liberal Jews to teach the why and how to of modern Jewish practice and ethics. It establishes parameters that are most important.

Notes

1. Mark Washofsky, "The Search for Liberal Halakhah," *Dynamic Jewish Law*, (Freehof Institute of Progressive Halakhah, Rodef Shalom Press), Pittsburgh, 1991, pp. 25ff.
2. Ibid., p. 45.
3. This article is based on a lecture I delivered at a regional rabbinic conference in 1999. It seeks to provide a short aid to Jews interested in the development of *halakhic* principles (both traditional and progressive). My teachers and colleagues, Mark Washofsky and Moshe Zemer, have recently published books that offer more comprehensive and authoritative explanations of the same. Moshe Zemer's *Halakha Shefuyah*, has been revised and translated: *Evolving Halakhah: A Progressive Approach to Traditional Jewish Law*, (Jewish Lights), Vermont, 1999. Mark Washofsky has just published *Jewish Living: A Guide To Contemporary Reform Practice*, (UAHC Press), New York, 2001.
4. See *The Struggle over Reform in Rabbinic Literature*, Alexander Guttman, (WUPJ), New York, 1977.
5. In addition to the above-mentioned books (*Evolving Halakhah* by Moshe Zemer, and *Jewish Living* by Mark Washofsky), for an excellent review of Progressive Halakhah's ideals and methodology see *Dynamic Jewish Law, Progressive Halakhah*, edited by Walter Jacob and Moshe Zemer; and Mark Washofsky's introduction *Responsa and the "Reform Rabbinate"* published in *Teshuvot for the Nineties*, CCAR, 1997, pp. xiii-xxix.
6. *Proceedings of the Committee on Jewish Law and Standards of the Conservative Movement*, 4 Vols: *1927-1970* and *1980-1985*, Jerusalem, 1997.
7. See *Emet Ve-Emunah, Statement of Principles of Conservative Judaism*, (Jewish Theological Seminary of America, 1988), pp. 21-24. For an example of progressive halakhah as practiced by the Conservative movement, see *The Ordi-*

nation of Women as Rabbis, edited by Simon Greenberg, Jewish Theological Seminary of America, 1988. See note 1 for references about the Reform movement's version of Progressive Halakhah.

8. Robert Gordis, *The Dynamics of Judaism,* (Indiana University Press), Bloomington, 1990. P. 82.

9. Zemer's *Evolving Halakhah* is especially valuable for this purpose.

10. Fortunately, there are exceptions. For a good example of a modern Orthodox Rabbi striving to incorporate modern ideals (such as egalitarianism) into Orthodoxy, see the recent article by Rabbi Adam Mintz, "Secularism, Spirituality, and the Future of American Jewry," edited by Elliot Abrams and David G. Dalin, Ethics and Public Policy Center, 1999. Rabbi Mintz, spiritual leader of the Lincoln Square Synagogue in New York City, concludes: "Education is really the great equalizer. Men and women, young and old—everybody is able to study Torah and reach the highest level he or she can achieve. In this respect there is no difference between men and women. If we are somehow able to incorporate the notion of equality of education into the Shabbat morning service without disturbing the traditions of that service, we will be continuing the process that was begun a century ago of allowing the Orthodox synagogue to meet the needs of a changing Orthodox community, while at the same time remaining faithful to our tradition" (p. 59).

11. Chatam Sofer, Responsa *Orach Chayyim,* number 28.

12. Mendell Lewittes, *Principles and Development of Jewish Law,* Bloch Publishing, 1987, p. 186. See Chatam Sofer's Responsa, *Orach Chayiim,* number 36.

13. Jacob Katz, *The Shabbes Goy, A Study in Halakhic Flexibility,* (JPS), Philadelphia, 1989, especially pp. 144-156 and 235-241.

14. In addition to the above-mentioned *Shabbes Goy,* see Katz's *Divine Law in Human Hands, Case Studies in Halakhic Flexibility,* The Magnes Press, The Hebrew University, Jerusalem, 1998.

15. Maimonides' *Introduction to the Mishnah,* chapter four.

16. *De Specialibus Legibus,* 4.149-150 in the Loeb series and following the translation of F.H. Colson. According to Martin Goodman in *JJS* Vol. 1, Spring 1999, p. 18, Naomi G. Cohen maintains that Philo was referring specifically to Oral Law in her *Philo Judaeus: His Universe of Discourse* (1993).

17. The thirteen methods of Torah interpretation are found in the introduction to *Sifra* and are reprinted in some traditional prayer books, including Birnbaum's , pp. 42-43.

18. Rambam's Introduction to the Mishnah is found in traditional editions of tractate *Berakhot* and is titled *Rambam's Introduction to (the Mishnaic) Order of Zeraim* (seeds).

19. Cf. Goodman, *JJS,* Spring 1999, pp.17-20.

20. For example: Rabbennu Gershom's ban against polygamy (which is permitted by the Torah) is a *gezerah* because it limits an existing observance. When Rabban Gemaliel mandated a new arrangement of the *shemoneh esreh* for the post-Temple era, his declaration was a *takkanah.* See Mendell Lewittes, *Principles and Development of Jewish Law,* pp. 93ff.; Menachem Elon, *Jewish Law,* pp. 490ff.

21. See Ephraim E. Urbach, *The Halakhah, Its Sources and Development,* (Massada Ltd.), Jerusalem, 1986, pp. 3-6.

22. I Maccabees 2: 29-38.

23. This prohibition is repeated in Deuteronomy 13:1 *"...lo toseif alav velo tigra mimenu."*

24. See Rashi to Deut. 4:2, *s.v. Lo tosifu;* also, Rashi to Deut 13:1, *s.v. Lo toseif alav.*

25. *Megillah*14a-b; *Yerushalmi Megillah* 1, #7.

26. See Nachmanides to Deut 4:2, *s.v. Lo tosifu.*

27. See Tigay's commentary to Deut. 4:2 in the *JPS Torah Commentary,* (JPS), Philadelphia, 1987, pp. 43-44.

28. Two popular lists of the *mitzvot* are those of Moses Maimanides (Rambam) and the Chafetz Chayim (Rabbi Yisrael Meir haKohen). Rambam's list is found in the first volume of his *Mishneh Torah* and Chafetz Chayim wrote *Sefer ha-Mitzvot ha-qatzar* (*The Concise Book of Mitzvot*) translated and published by Feldheim, 1990. Of course, one would be remiss not to mention *Sefer haHinnukh,* the thirteenth century classic that lists each of the 613 *mitzvot* in the order and context in which they appear in the Torah. The five volume Hebrew-English edition by Feldheim is highly recommended.

29. *Berakhot* 19b.

30. *Polemics in Sefer Miswot Gadol of Rabbi Moses of Coucy,* Jeffrey R. Woolf, Jewish Quarterly Review, LXXXIX, Nos. 1-2 (July-October 1998), pp. 85-94.

31. *Ibid.,* pp. 85-86.

32. *Ha-Smag ha-Shalem,* pp. 5-6.

33. Menachem Elon, *Jewish Law,* Vol. II, pp. 495 ff. The following list can be found in its full treatment on pp. 505-533.

34. Elon, *Jewish Law,* pp. 505-506.

35. *Rosh HaShanah* 29b. This *gezerah* is a perfect example of the dynamism of *halakhah.* The original decree forbade the sounding of the shofar when *Rosh HaShanah* fell on Shabbat in any place except the Temple. The reason for this *gezerah* was to build a fence around the Torah that would prevent Jews from mistakenly violating Shabbat on *Rosh HaShanah.* The concern was that some Jews might be tempted to carry their *shofar* in public or have it repaired and thereby violate Shabbat. After the destruction of the Temple, Rabban Yohanan ben Zakhai favored annulling this *gezerah.* He permitted the sounding of the shofar when *Rosh HaShanah* fell on Shabbat in every town where there was a *beit din.* Despite Yohanan's opinion, traditional *Halakhah* prohibits the *shofar* when *Rosh HaShanah* falls on Shabbat (see Rambam's *Hilkhot Shofar* 2.6).

36. See Rambam's *Hilkhot Mamrim* 2.9 on the issue of including fowl in the prohibition of mixing meat and milk. Our late, beloved teacher Jakob Petuchowski wrote a marvelous essay on the same subject that is now reprinted in a new collection: *Studies in Modern Theology and Prayer,* JPS, 1998, pp. 61-73. What mostly fascinated Petuchowski was the evidence of pluralism as demonstrated by the fact that not every community accepted the expansion of the prohibition against mixing milk and meat to include poultry.

37. Elon, *Jewish Law,* pp. 521-533. Also see Joel Roth, *The Halakhic Process,* pp.190-204.

38. Yevamot 89b-90b. Elon, *Jewish Law,* p. 506; Roth, *The Halakhic Process,* pp. 190ff.

39. Tosafot: to Yevamot 90b *s.v. Ve-ligmar mineih* and Sanhedrin 89b (*Eliyahu be-har haCarmel*). Cf. Nachmanides in his novella to *Yevamot;* Menachem Elon, *Jewish Law,* pp. 519-20 and note 117.

40. Elon, *Jewish Law,* pp. 507-514.

41. *Mishhah Shevi'it* 10:3-4.
42. Elon, *Jewish Law*, pp. 533-536.
43. For instance, Terumah 14b; Berakhot 63a.
44. Gittin 60b.
45. According to tradition, the written Torah conveys hidden meanings through the use of spellings and symbols that would be missed if one only heard the Torah.
46. It was believed that certain profound thoughts should be conveyed orally so they could be fully explained. If the profound thought is written down and is read without instruction or commentary, the true meaning may be missed.
47. Rashi to *Gittin* 60a, *s.v. Et la-asot*; Rambam in his introduction to *Mishneh Torah*.
48. *Kesef Mishneh* to Rambam's *Mishneh Torah, Nedarim* 3.9, *s.v. U-le-inyan*.
49. See also, *Mishneh Torah, Shabbat* 2.3.
50. Many Reform congregations during the "classical period" (approximately 1880-1960) de-emphasized *kashrut* and promoted the vernacular. Nevertheless, Hebrew and to a far lesser extent Jewish dietary laws (especially during Passover) were still very much in evidence in Reform congregations. Today, most Reform congregations use a much greater percentage of Hebrew in their services and "Biblical Kashrut" (i.e., no pork or shell fish may be served) has become the norm.
51. Protestant Christianity is an instructive paradigm for what happens when localized groups of religious leaders are free to legislate and innovate without limits. Today there are thousands of Protestant denominations. Most of those communities have splintered off from other denominations in a dispute over liturgy or doctrine. Most of these denominations were established within the last 150 years in the United States. In contrast, over the past two thousand years, notwithstanding the distance between Jewish communities (both culturally and geographically) in the Diaspora, and the horrible ordeals that these far-flung communities have endured, there is remarkable unity of spirit and practice and there have been but a handful of different Jewish denominations.
52. *Avot d'R. Natan* 1:5.
53. JT*Nedarim* 9:1. A case in point is the promulgation of restrictions added by Eastern European Ashkenazim on what is permitted during Passover. One finds Rabbis of every generation and of every denomination who have voiced concern that excluding *kitniyot* (e.g., rice, legumes, corn), as if they were *hametz*, imposes such a hardship on the diet of Jews that many would despair of trying to keep any form of *pesadik*. For a wonderful review of the *halakhic* opinions on both sides of the *kitniyot* issue, see S.Y. Zevin, *The Festivals in Halachah*, vol. III, pp. 111-127.
54. In general, Reform Jews insist on a clear demarcation between issues of Communal Religious/Ritual concern and their personal lifestyle decisions. For example, a Rabbi and/or synagogue's authority to set the time, date, and standards of services is generally accepted. But the decision concerning a family's degree of *kashrut* is zealously guarded by the individuals.

Chapter 4

❖ ❖ ❖

A CRITIQUE OF SOLOMON B. FREEHOF'S CONCEPT OF *MINHAG* AND REFORM JEWISH PRACTICE

Joan S. Friedman

In 1944 Solomon B. Freehof was, to all appearances, at the height of his rabbinic career. Ordained at Hebrew Union College in 1915 after an outstanding academic performance, he had served as a chaplain with the American Expeditionary Forces in France and with the army of occupation in Germany,[1] as a faculty member at HUC, as rabbi of KAM Congregation in Chicago, and since 1934, as senior rabbi of Rodef Shalom Congregation in Pittsburgh. He was about to complete four years as vice-president and then president of the Central Conference of American Rabbis, during which time he was actively involved in the struggles over Zionism within the CCAR and the UAHC and its member congregations which resulted in the emergence of the American Council for Judaism.[2] He had over 20 years of experience on the CCAR Liturgy Committee and had served as its chairman since 1930; under his leadership the Conference produced its revised *Union*

Notes for this section begin on page 129.

Prayer Book. During the war years he also served as chairman of the CCAR Emergency Committee on Placement, which worked to provide chaplains for the military while not denying the people at home some rabbinic presence,[3] and as chairman of the Responsa Committee of the Jewish Welfare Board's Committee on Army and Navy Religious Activities,[4] which resolved questions of Jewish practice for the military.

In 1944, however, Freehof published a volume, which, in retrospect, must be seen as the theoretical and practical foundation for what would become his life's crowning achievement: the Reform responsa. This work, to which he added a second volume in 1952, was titled *Reform Jewish Practice and its Rabbinic Background*. Its "chief purpose," as he stated in the introduction, was "to describe present-day Reform Jewish practices and the traditional rabbinic laws from which they are derived."[5]

It was a work without precedent. Other giants of Reform scholarship had produced essays and responsa on individual questions, of course, but no one had written such a systematic survey. The body of the work displays Freehof's textual erudition and confirms his emergence as the successor to Kaufmann Kohler and especially Jacob Z. Lauterbach, both of whose responsa he cites repeatedly. But Freehof goes further than Kohler or Lauterbach by presenting in his introduction an original theory concerning the relationship of Reform Judaism to traditional Jewish law. It is his desire to demonstrate not only that specific Reform practices are rooted in traditional practices, but that the very process by which Reform Judaism has developed its distinctive practice is itself grounded in—indeed, identical to—the actual process by which Jewish practice has always developed.

Since Judaism has always been a religion in which "deed" came first, changes in Jewish practice are also "religious revolutions," according to Freehof.[6] The destruction of the Temple in the year 70 C.E. and the subsequent growth of the Diaspora occasioned two such revolutions in ancient times.[7] At these times, Jewish law required massive readjustment. But the law itself was incapable of such readjustment because without the Sanhedrin,[8] there was no way for Jewish law to have the requisite flexibility. Thus problems such as the *agunah* remain unsolvable in Jewish law. Whatever flexibility and adaptability were present in the past in Jewish law was due to the "creative power" of the people, not the rabbis. Freehof identifies this creative power as *minhag*, "the raw material which the law took up and shifted, rearranged, justified, and embodied as the legal practice. The law itself did not create. The people created and the law organized."[9]

In modern times, too, argues Freehof, historical change has necessitated a religious revolution in Judaism. Emancipation, the end of Jewish corporate existence, destroyed the community for which Jewish law was developed and intended. In the modern world most Jews ignore most of Jewish law, and even "the small percentage who still observe the dietary laws, the Sabbath and Jewish marriage laws, even for them, loyal, self-sacrificing Orthodox Jews in a bewildering modern world, the whole Jewish civil law code, the Choshen Mishpot, no longer exists."[10] Once again, the people's creativity is stepping into the breach, creating new *minhagim.* Reform Judaism is the oldest of such coping attempts and it has succeeded in retaining many Jews within Judaism for several generations. In Reform Judaism,

> [t]he rabbis have expressed certain principles, certain theological ideals, but the people by themselves by their rejections and their acceptances, by their neglects and their observances have largely determined their own religious practices. Reform Jewish practice is not fixed. It is still changing. But by this time it has fairly well crystallized. It has arrived for the present at least at a definite form. It must therefore be of interest to all who are concerned with the problem of the adjustment of Jewish life to the modern world to study how this group of Jews has adjusted itself.[11]

Freehof will therefore describe contemporary Reform practice in his book and, wherever applicable, illustrate its roots in older Jewish practice. He notes, however, that he will include

> [o]nly those traditional laws and customs ... which are connected with actual prevalent Reform practice. Thus, those branches of traditional law which have left very little mark upon present-day life of the Reform Jew are not dealt with. To put it bluntly, there is, unfortunately, as little observance of the dietary laws among Reform Jews as there is among millions of other modern Jews and also as little observance of the traditional laws of Sabbath rest. Hence, these branches of Orthodox law are not dealt with.[12]

Freehof's theory is an attractive one for Reform Jews in that it conceptualizes Reform not as a radical innovation in Jewish life, but as the latest manifestation of a venerable Jewish response to changes in the historical circumstances of the Jewish people. On

both halakhic and historical grounds, however, it is highly sus-
pect. This article is an initial critique of his theory. "The law itself
did not create. The people created and the law organized."

While it is clear that the process of halakhic change involves
extensive interplay between the rabbinate and the people, to
state categorically that the true creativity in the process comes
from the people and not from the rabbinate is a radical assertion.
In fact, Freehof's very first example of popular creativity in
response to changed circumstances is none other than the para-
digmatic model of *rabbinic* creativity taught to every elementary
school student of Jewish history, namely, the story of Rabban
Yohanan ben Zakkai and the sages of Yavneh who, by their dar-
ing and creative halakhic activity, saved Judaism in the wake of
the destruction of the Temple. No less a historian than Salo Baron
refers to R. Yohanan as "the rebuilder of national life during the
great crisis"[13] to underscore the importance of his leadership and
that of his colleagues and the innovations in law and practice
with which they are credited. More recent historians tend toward
the view that the phenomenon we know as "rabbinic Judaism"
was, in fact, the creation of a small group and only very gradually (with great help from the Abbasid caliphate's support for the
Gaonate and the Exilarchate) did it become the normative way of
life for the vast majority of Jews.[14]

Whether one views the rabbis as representing the will of the
majority of the people or as a small minority whose form of
Judaism was only gradually accepted, neither opinion, however,
validates Freehof's view of the development of rabbinic Judaism
after 70 C.E. as primarily a grass roots phenomenon.

We may adduce numerous other examples of rabbinic
authorities who issued drastic decisions in response to the needs
of the hour: Hillel's *prosbul,* Rabbenu Gershom's *taqqanot,* and
the Polish rabbis' decisions after the Cossack uprising[15] come
readily to mind. In fact, the very phrase `*et la'asot lashem heferu
toratekha* underscores both the ability and the obligation of the
rabbinate to initiate change. Why, then, is Freehof so insistent
that change comes from the bottom?

The notion that Jewish practice evolves among the people
and is then regularized and codified by the rabbinic leadership is,
indeed, reflected in the history of at least one significant Jewish
movement: Reform Judaism, particularly in the United States.[16]
Although there were many instances of rabbinically instituted

reforms prior to the formation of the CCAR, the rapidity of change, the paucity of rabbis in the second half of the nineteenth century, and the great variety of practice gives the impression that the initial impetus for religious reform among American Jews, as among German Jews earlier, came from the people. Yearbooks from the early decades of the CCAR's existence reveal the rabbis' urgent desire to systematize the practice of American Reform Jews—rarely to cancel, retract, or oppose the changes that had manifested themselves in their synagogues and personal lives, but to order them, and to reorganize Jewish religious practice on a basis that reflected the people's actual practice. During Kaufmann Kohler's tenure as president of the Hebrew Union College (1903-1926) and as a dominant personality within the CCAR, he labored mightily to produce unity of thought and practice in the movement. "Classical" Reform Judaism, which owed its shape more to him than to any other single individual, remained largely unchanged in outward form throughout the interwar period.

Solomon B. Freehof was ordained at HUC in 1915 and served on its faculty until 1924. The evidence before Freehof's eyes in Reform Judaism was that the people initiated or desired change as circumstances changed, and the rabbinate organized and regularized the changes. The rabbinate did not lead the way in making change (except, as he notes, "[t]he rabbis have expressed certain principles, certain theological ideals ..."[17]). What Freehof learned and saw of Reform in his years as a student and as a rabbi up to the time he wrote this book conforms precisely to the model he presents here.[18] "The doctors of the law understood ... that they depended upon the creative imagination of the people."[19]

As proof of his theory that Reform is simply continuing the time-honored process of creating new *minhagim*, Freehof cites six passages: two each from the two Talmuds and the *Shulhan Arukh*. A closer examination of these passages, however, will reveal that their support for his argument is problematic.

1. Berakhot 45b

M. Berakhot 6:8 reads: "If one drinks water to quench one's thirst, one should say [beforehand the blessing], ... by whose word all things exist." R. Tarfon says: [one should say] "... who creates many living beings." The Gemara explains: R. Tarfon says: [He should say] "… who creates many living beings. Rabba bar Rav Hanan said to Abaye, and some say [he said it] to R. Yosef: What is the law? He said to him: Go and see what the people do".[20]

The Mishnah gives two opinions regarding the correct blessing to recite before drinking water, that of the anonymous Mishnah and that of Rabbi Tarfon. The Amora Rabba bar Rav Hanan asks which is the proper procedure. This is a logical question, because the Mishnah here gives two individual opinions[21] and does not decide between them or offer a more authoritative statement from the Sages. Abaye (or Rav Yosef) responds, "Go and see what the people do." In other words, the people's actual practice will determine what the *halakhah* should be in this case. Their actual practice was, presumably, the way in which the *halakhah* was eventually fixed: one recites Rabbi Meir's version before drinking water and Rabbi Tarfon's version after—even though Rabbi Tarfon was of the opinion that this was the blessing *before* drinking, and neither Tannaitic opinion says anything about a blessing *after* drinking. In this case, the "normative practice" of the people was apparently the source of the rabbinic law as it was eventually codified.[22]

Is this a case of *minhag* creating *halakhah*? It is to the extent that "custom determines which view is to be accepted when the halakhic authorities disagree as to what the law is with regard to a particular matter."[23] It is impossible to see this, however, as an example of Freehof's "people's creativity." "The people" did not formulate either of these blessings. The rabbis did. Nor did the people even originate the idea that one must recite a blessing before and after consuming food. The rabbis did, through their exegesis of Torah. The people, in other words, were already operating within parameters defined for them by rabbinic scholarship.

2. Pesahim 66a

The question at hand is how to offer the Pesah offering when Pesah begins at the conclusion of Shabbat. The offering has to be slaughtered on the fourteenth of Nisan, that is, on Shabbat. How are the people supposed to carry their slaughtering knives to the Temple?

> They said to [Hillel]: Master, If one forgot and did not bring a knife before Shabbat, then what? He said to them: I learned this halakhah and forgot it. But leave it to Israel [to show you the answer]—if they

are not prophets, they are the children of prophets. On the next day, whoever had a lamb for the pesah had stuck the knife in the wool; whoever had a kid had stuck the knife in between the horns [so that the animals were carrying the knives, and no one was violating Shabbat by carrying]. [Hillel] saw what they were doing and remembered the halakha, and said: This is the very tradition I received from Shemaya and Avtalyon.

In this passage Hillel says that there already is a law to answer the question put to him, but that he has forgotten it. When he sees what the people actually do, he recognizes their practice as being exactly what the rabbinic legislation prescribed. So what is the weight of the people's practice in this case?

The significance of this passage is far from clear to later rabbinic authorities. The narrower, minority view is that the people's custom merely proved that there was a prior law and is valid only for that reason. The majority view, however, is broader: "[T]he people can create law through custom, and ... custom does more than merely prove the existence of a law created by some other means."[24] For Elon, this *baraita* is an example of "the creative force of custom."[25]

The reason why the people's custom can be relied on to create law in this and similar instances is "because there is a presumption that the people ... base their conduct on the *halakhah* [and] intend their practices to be true to its spirit.[26] In other words, the people's conduct in the absence of rabbinic guidance is valid because it is assumed that the people are acting out of devotion to Torah.

Freehof, like all committed Reform Jews, sees in the Reform modification of traditional practices not rejection of Judaism, but rather clear evidence of the people's desire to remain Jews under greatly changed historical circumstances. Therefore, the changes made by the movement in liturgical and other practices meet this criterion of devotion to Torah in his estimation and constitute examples of popularly generated *minhag*. *Pesahim* 66a implies that the people's devotion to Torah makes them a reliable source of Jewish practice. But is this true in every instance? What about, for example, Freehof's own brief acknowledgement that the observance of the Sabbath is virtually absent from the lives of Reform Jews? "Of course, not every custom of the people could be permitted to abrogate any law. ... [C]ustom abrogates the law only if it is the custom of respected people."[27] Contrary to his sweeping endorsement of popular creativity, there is, in fact, a limit to his enthusiasm for it. The customs he will describe as *Reform Jewish Practice* are not the sum total of what Reform Jews do; rather, they are only those parts of the behavior of Reform Jews to which he and the rest of the CCAR have given their approval. In other words, the rabbis do not merely "organize"; they actively approve and disapprove and shape Jewish behavior. On the whole, then, while *Pesahim* 66a does justify at least some authority for popular creativity, Freehof's own life's work indicates that that authority is not without limits.

3. Y. Yevamot 12:1 (12c)

M. Yevamot 12:1 reads: "*Halitzah* takes place before a court of three judges, even if all three are laypeople. If he released her with a shoe made of leather, it is valid; with a shoe made of cloth, it is invalid; with a sandal with a heel, it is valid; but without a heel it is invalid."

The relevant passage for Freehof is:

> R. Ba b. Judah [said] in the name of Rav: If Elijah should come and say that they perform *halitzah* with a leather shoe, they listen to him. If he should say that they do not perform *halitzah* with a sandal, they do not listen to him. For the community is accustomed to perform *halitzah* with a sandal, and custom overrides the law. R. Zeira [and] R. Jeremiah [said] in the name of Rav: If Elijah should come and say that they do not perform *halitzah* with a leather shoe, they listen to him. If he should say that they do not perform *halitzah* with a sandal, they do not listen to him. For the community is accustomed to perform the rites of *halitzah* with a sandal, and custom overrides the law.[28]

In both versions of this slightly garbled Amoraic pronouncement, the first supposed decision from Elijah relates to the shoe which the community does not use. Whether he tells them it may be used or it may not be used, this statement is to be regarded as authoritative. In the former case, he would be confirming the Mishnah and, in the latter case he has the halakhic standing to forbid that which the Mishnah permits. In both versions, however, his second supposed decision would prohibit that which the community customarily practices. Nevertheless, Elijah does not have the halakhic standing to force the community to alter its custom. The community's custom is authoritative even over a suprahuman authority.

This is not, however, an issue of popular creativity, either in an area not addressed by law or in terms of established law; rather, it is the right of a community to continue to engage in a halakhically sanctioned practice in the face of new law mandated by another halakhic authority.[29] This citation neither proves nor disproves Freehof's theory.

4. Y. Bava Metzia 7:1 (11b)

M. Bava Metzia 7:1: "One who hires workers and tells them to start early and finish late—in a place where it is not the custom to start early and finish late, he may not compel them to do so. In a place where customarily they provide [the workers with] food, he must provide food; [where they] supply a sweet, he must supply a sweet. Everything is according to the custom of the province."[30]

The Gemara says:

> Rav Hoshaiah said: This means that custom overrides the law. Rav Imi said: In every case but this, the burden of proof rests on the one who seeks to receive something from his fellow. In Tiberias they do not begin work early or leave late; in Bet Maon they do. Tiberians who go up to hire workers from Bet Maon [must follow the custom of] Bet Maon; Bet Maonians who go down to hire workers in Tiberias [must follow the custom of] Tiberias. ... What about a place where there is no fixed custom? R. Judah b. Boni, R. Ammi, and Rav Judah say: The court has stipulated that the starting time is determined by the workers and the end time is determined by the employer. What is the reason [i.e., scriptural basis]? "You bring on darkness and it is night, / when all the beasts of the forests stir. / The lions roar for prey, / seeking their food from God. / When the sun rises, they come home / and couch in their dens. / Man then goes out to his work, to his labor until the evening." (Ps. 104:20-23).[31]

Once again, the issue at hand is not one of new practices changing accepted usage. Here, existing custom is invoked as the explicitly stated, valid halakhic basis for certain conduct and, when there is no existing custom, one falls back on *halakhah* and not popular creativity.[32]

5. *Shulhan Arukh* OH 690:17

"It is the custom of all Israel that the [*megilla*] reader spreads the scroll out as he reads, like a letter, in order to show the miracle. And when he finishes, then he goes back and rolls it all up and recites the blessing. [Isserles:] Some have written that people are accustomed to say the four verses of redemption aloud [with the reader], namely: Esther 2:5, 8:15, 8:16, 10:3, and such is the custom in these lands (*Hagahot Maimuniot* 8; *Kol Bo*; *Abudharam*), and then the *chazan* repeats them. They have also written that the children are accustomed to draw the likeness of Haman, or write his name, on pieces of wood and stones, and to strike them against each other in order that the name of Haman be blotted out, as in 'You shall wipe out the memory of Amalek' (Deut. 25:19)17 and 'the name of the wicked will rot.' (Prov. 10:7) From this the custom got mixed up and turned into the practice of striking Haman when they read the *megilla* in the synagogue (*Abudharam*). But one should not abrogate a single custom or mock it, for they were not established for nothing (*Bet Yosef* in the name of *Orhot Hayim*)."33

In the enumeration of the many and varied customs associated with the reading of the *megillah*, we do, indeed, see an example in which the people's creativity leads to the diffusion of practices which are then recognized as *halakhah* and codified by the rabbinic authorities, who explicitly acknowledge that what they are recognizing is *minhag*. The same is true in the following passage.

6. Shulhan Arukh YD 376:4

"At present it is the custom that after the grave is filled with earth (or after the mourner turns his face from the grave), they remove their shoes and sandals, go some little distance away from the cemetery, and recite the burial Kaddish. After that they pull up dirt and grasses and throw them behind their backs, and wash their hands with water. [Isserles:] Some say that they sit down seven times, because the spirits are accompanying him, and each time they sit, the spirits flee (Maharil, resp. No.23, in the name of "some say"). But in these provinces they are only accustomed to sit three times, after they wash their hands, and each time they say [Ps. 90:17 and Ps. 91:1]. When the deceased is buried on a festival, they may sit these three times as on a week-day (No.20 in *Hagahot Minhagim*). The same is true if the burial took place just before Shabbat: They may do this on Shabbat. People are accustomed to be very careful not to enter a house before washing and sitting three times, and the custom of our ancestors is Torah (Maharil, ibid.). ... "[34]

According to Freehof, these two and the hundreds of other appeals to the durability of custom by Isserles are evidence that "the rabbinical authorities appreciated the fact that the creative material in Jewish law which the official law could only analyze, sift and organize, was the true basis of the continued vitality of Judaism." The great emphasis on custom, he asserts, proves that practice was not a "mood" imposed on the community by the rabbinate, "but ... a mass reaction, a mass creativity which produced practice and observance whenever Judaism needed to readjust itself to new conditions."[35]

Freehof is certainly correct in seeing in Isserles' comments evidence for flourishing popular creativity, but his argument has a serious weakness. In the halakhic system, the power of *minhag* to create, change, or overrule *halakhah* varies widely depending on what sort of *halakhah* is in question. Custom does not carry equal weight in all realms of the law.

Menachem Elon's halakhic taxonomy divides the *halakhah* into two realms, *mammon* and *issur*. "Although all parts of the *halakhah* are rooted in the same source, share the same principles and methods of analysis, and provide and receive reciprocal support, nevertheless, study of the halakhic sources reveals that the *halakhah* did make very fundamental distinctions between its two major categories, namely, monetary matters (that part of the *halakhah* included in the concept of *mamon*) and non-monetary matters (that part of the *halakhah* included in the concept of *issur*)."[36] One of the significant differences between these two areas of *halakhah* concerns the force of *minhag*. "The distinction between *issur* and *mamon* is also an important factor in regard to the binding authority and the creative power of custom, particularly with regard to the fundamental principle in this field that 'custom overrides the law' (*minhag mevattel halakhah*), which applies exclusively to matters of *mamon* but not at all to matters of *isur*."[37]

In matters of *mammon* parties may agree between themselves "to contract out of a law contained in the Torah," so long as no prohibition is violated. Two individuals may agree to conduct their business by Torah law, by any customary procedure developed over the centuries and recognized by the halakhic authorities, or by some new procedure they themselves develop or adopt. This principle allowed for maximum flexibility to meet changing commercial conditions. Over the centuries, vast structures of *halakhah* dealing with commercial transactions, communal taxation, and other "civil" matters were thus constructed and reconstructed, virtually all based on *minhag*. *Minhag* easily outweighs *halakhah* in the entire realm of *mamon*.

The reason why the same flexibility cannot apply in "'religious' law," as Elon's translators render the term, is evident. In the words of R. Simeon ben Solomon Duran: "Obviously, if we may repeal a prohibition on the basis of custom, then all prohibitions may be repealed one by one; and the Torah, God forbid, will be abrogated."[38] In other words, from the perspective of *halakhah*, no matter how normative in any Jewish community civil divorces and eating lobster may be, such "customs" can never override the laws which regard that woman as *eshet ish* and which declare that food to be *treif*.

Elon notes one great exception to this rule in the realm of *issur*. *Minhag* plays an enormous and highly valued role in the area of liturgy and ritual practice. "[T]he principle 'custom overrides the law' was used to establish various rules that relate neither to *mamon* nor to *issur*, such as laws relating to prayer ..."[39] Indeed, even a very casual perusal of the halakhic literature through the marvel of computerized databases bears this out: The phrase from Berakhot 45b, "Go and see what the people do," occurs overwhelmingly in *mamon* or in matters of ritual and liturgical practice. By contrast, there are few if any instances where *minhag* determines practice in matters of *ishut, gerut, kashrut*, or other questions of *issur*.

What, then, are we to make of Freehof's misrepresentation of the meaning of several halakhic texts? From a halakhic perspective he has made an egregious error in using proofs from *mamon* and liturgical and ritual practice to justify changes in *issur*. Yet given his prodigious scholarship, it is impossible to believe that he simply erred. The even more dismaying alternative, however, is that he deliberately blurred the meaning of his sources to buttress his argument—a disturbing tendentiousness that would fatally weaken his case and certainly would do him no credit.

There is a third alternative: We must recognize that although Freehof was a prodigious scholar of the *halakhah* and knew its categories and its distinctions, in this introduction he is not writing as a halakhist but as a Reform ideologue. He is reading the *halakhah* through a Reform lens, but he confuses the reader because he does not explicitly admit this.

"Reform practice," as Freehof candidly admits, is limited almost entirely to the realm of liturgy and ritual (primarily life cycle ritual)—areas of *halakhah* in which *minhag* historically played a crucial role. *Reform Jewish Practice* reflects the reality that for most Reform Jews, "Judaism" meant (means?) going to the temple on holidays and perhaps Friday nights, and life cycle events, and no more.[40] It happens that these fall within an area of *halakhah* in which *minhag* has traditionally been given an important voice. In particular, a fascination with *minhag* was a hallmark of the Ashkenazic rabbinic culture which produced R. Moses Isserles.[41] Isserles' glosses to Karo's *Shulhan Arukh* not only delineated the differences in *halakhah* between Ashkenazim and Sefardim but, as we have seen above, they painstakingly preserved and codified the customary practices of the Ashkenazim in liturgy, ritual, and daily life. In writing this book Freehof thought he was doing for twentieth century Reform Jews what Isserles had done for sixteenth century Polish Jews—using the tools of the rabbinic tradition itself to justify and validate the distinctive religious culture of a particular Jewish community. That is why the two citations from Isserles were excellent sources for him to cite.

Nevertheless, although Freehof knows and uses halakhic sources, he does not approach them from a halakhic perspective but from a classical Reform perspective in which no Jewish *practice*, however beloved or important, can ever rise above the level of "ceremony."[42] The essential truths of ethical monotheism are distinct from "ceremonies." "Indispensable" and valued though the latter may be, they are only human attempts to express divinely revealed truths.[43] Thus, though the halakhic sources themselves accord very different weights to different "practices" (*de-oraita, de-rabbanan, halakhah le-moshe mi-sinai, halakhah, minhag,* etc.) for Freehof it is all the same: Everything his Jews do is "practice" and carries equal weight, whether it is conversion without *milah* and *tevilah*, changes in the order of the weekly Torah reading, or having flowers at a funeral. Freehof can claim continuity with tradition for Reform on the basis of the power of *minhag* only because he has tacitly collapsed the distinction between *minhag* and *halakhah*. It is all merely "practice" or "custom."

For example, in describing Reform practice around the public reading of the Torah, Freehof uses the terms "custom" or "customary" to refer to the traditional annual and triennial cycles, the modern Reform use of a combination of the two, the practice of calling up two members of the congregation to unroll and roll up the Torah, raising the Torah, reading the Haftarah, and calling a certain number of men to the Torah on Sabbaths and other days.[44] These matters fall within the realm of liturgical and ritual practice, the area of greatest flexibility with regard to minhag, yet even so, not everything is reducible to *minhag* from the point of view of the *halakhah*. Calling seven to the Torah on Shabbat morning is mandated by the Mishnah without discussion or alternative, and is properly understood as law, not mere custom.

Realizing that Freehof is writing about *halakhah* through a classical Reform perspective also explains why, in a book which is essentially a *sefer minhagim*, he can include without further distinction questions of *issur* such as the rejection of special marriage laws relating to *kohanim*,[45] conversion without *milah* or *tevilah*,[46] elimination of "legal" aspects of Jewish marriage in favor of civil guarantees and replacing the *ketubah* with "an ethical homily,"[47] replacement of the *get* with civil divorce[48] attendance by *kohanim* at funerals, and the permissibility of cremation.[50] From a halakhic perspective none of these is subject to change on the basis of *minhag*.

One other tacit assumption, also a hallmark of the classical Reform era, also undergirds Freehof's thought: the conviction that Orthodoxy is a system of the past, that it is inevitably doomed to disappear in the modern world, and that Reform Judaism is the next stage of Judaism's evolution and the form in which it will survive into the future. Freehof's invocation of the post 1970 changes in Judaism as precedent for contemporary changes initiated by Reformers, his assertion that traditional practice was for a world that has now completely disappeared, his description of Orthodoxy as "an ideal, an heroic self-discipline"—honored more in the breach than the observance[51]: all these reflect the certainty that Reform would eventually become the Judaism of all religious Jews, not merely one movement among several. In this context the following passage becomes intelligible and sheds further light on his use of his chosen halakhic sources:

> Certainly even for the small percentage who observe the dietary laws, the Sabbath and Jewish marriage laws, even for them, loyal, self-sacrificing Orthodox Jews in a bewildering modern world, the whole Jewish civil law code, the Choshen Mishpot no longer exists. They no longer, except in rare instances, resort to rabbinical law for the settlement of their business matters....They go to the civil law courts. Scholars, of course, still study Jewish civil law....It is as the introduction to the Even Haezer of the Shulhan Arukh puts it: "There are many laws in this book which are not customary in Israel these days ... but he who studies these matters ... nevertheless fulfills the commandment of learning the Law." A few generations ago the law governed life. Now the study of the law is intellectual exercise and pious self-absorption.[52]

Freehof's point, implicit here but far more explicit in subsequent writings, is that the Orthodox resort to secular courts in matters of *mamon* constitutes an abandonment of Jewish law different only in degree but not in kind from the Reform abandonment of Jewish law.[53] The autonomy of the corporate Jewish community made it possible for Jewish civil law to exist; now that there is no more autonomy, that part of the law has no purpose. Freehof implies that those who still adhere to Jewish law in the other three sections of the *Shulhan Arukh* are fighting a losing battle. Like the Reformers, they, too, will eventually give in to the inevitable tide of history and will begin to "practice" Judaism in the way which is suitable to the modern world.

Freehof is correct, strictly speaking, in asserting that by turning to the civil courts even Orthodox Jews are violating Jewish law. There are numerous halakhic pronouncements warning of dire consequences to any Jew who turns to the Gentile courts for redress against a fellow Jew.[54] But a scholarly examination of the issue of Jewish use of non-Jewish courts to adjudicate matters of *mamon* cannot overlook the crucial historical question, namely, the extent of Jewish self-adjudication allowed and enforced by non-Jewish rulers. As Elon notes, the rabbinic prohibition against use of non-Jewish courts "was promulgated at a time when the Jewish legal system was about to set out on the long and difficult course of maintaining juridical autonomy without a sovereign state; and this pronouncement established one of the sturdiest bulwarks protecting the continuous existence and development of the Jewish court in all the periods of the exile."[55] Jewish "civil law" was not necessarily distinctive, as were the practices governed by Jewish "religious law," but the broader the scope allowed to Jewish civil law, the more distinctive the Jewish polity was as a whole. Maintaining juridical autonomy was therefore desirable. It was difficult, however, to maintain the authority of Jewish courts when they lacked powers of enforcement. The inescapable historical observation is that Jewish courts adjudicated matters of *mamon* when the Gentile government allowed and enforced such jurisdiction or when Jews voluntarily submitted to their jurisdiction (which usually meant only until A or B realized s/he could obtain a more favorable verdict by going to the Gentile courts). Yet even when Jewish civil jurisdiction was minimal, as it was in many early modern German communities,[56] Jews did not conclude from that, as Freehof does here, that they would or should abandon "religious" law as a corollary.[57]

Here we see revealed yet another element of Freehof's Reform lens. For Reform Judaism, the end of separate Jewish status and the integration of the Jews into western societies as a religious group was an unmixed blessing. Emancipation brought the abrogation of Jewish "civil law" and made it possible for Reformers to create a new definition of Judaism-as-religion-only using a western, Protestant paradigm of "religion" in which *dinei mammonot* were ipso facto defined as not "religious" because the very category of law had no place in religion, other than the divinely revealed moral law. For traditionalists it was not an unmixed blessing, because it removed the communal structure within which Jewish life had always existed.[58] Thus in conflating the post-Emancipation non-functioning of *halakhah* in the realm of *mamon* with the abandonment of ritual practices, Freehof offers an ideological historiography to complement his ideological reading of *halakha*.

But if, as Freehof has it, the abandonment of Jewish civil law is only the first step on an inevitable continuum of change in "practice," if all realms of Jewish law are alike in that they are equally subject to the transformatory winds of modernity and the people's decision to abandon them or change them, then they were also alike in the past, in the people's decision to create them. Hence, for Freehof, there is no contradiction in using *J. Bava Metzia*, which deals with *mamon*, as justification for changes in ritual or "religious" practice. Elon's taxonomy and the conceptual approach of *mishpat ivri* are irrelevant, as are the historical realities that mitigated for or against the existence of a functioning Jewish legal system beyond the realm of *issur*.

To be sure, he realized that there are problems with such an approach, chief among them the vexing question of Shabbat. He certainly did not want to say that the fact that Reform Jews largely ignore Shabbat means that the ongoing process of *minhag* has eliminated the day of rest from Judaism, though in print its absence is merely "unfortunate."[59] But in truth, his collapse of the entire halakhic system into the amorphous category of *minhag*/practice leaves him no consistent way to criticize that non-observance. For Freehof, vox populi may not be *vox dei*, since "ceremonies" are not in any case divinely ordained,[60] but essentially, Jewish practice is whatever Jewish people want to practice at any given historical juncture.[61]

Conclusion

Freehof's Introduction to *Reform Jewish Practice* employs halakhic sources to justify an argument which is not halakhic but ideological. Freehof understands Reform Judaism to be, as a result of the Emancipation, the successor to Orthodoxy. Its succession is demonstrated and legitimated through the concept of *minhag*, a halakhic concept which Freehof tacitly redefines in order to equate it with what he labels Reform "practice." However, this equation is flawed, as is his historical analysis, rendering his entire approach problematic.

Postscript:In his Introduction to *Reform Jewish Practice* Freehof wrote, "Reform Jewish practice is not fixed. It is still changing. But by this time it has fairly well crystallized. It has arrived for the present at least at a definite form. ... [A]ll the Reform practices together form a fairly harmonious unity ..."[62] This passage reflects the essential unity of form which still marked Reform Judaism at mid-century. When that status quo began, however, to change in subsequent decades—id est, when the process of *minhag*, as Freehof had defined it, threatened to undermine the practice he regarded as normative, his response was not always positive. He was no longer as open to "popular creativity." Although in his published work he struggled toward a consistent accommodation to the ongoing process of *minhag* within

Reform Judaism, his private responsa correspondence frequently revealed criticism of popular practice and a resistance to change. For example, in reply to an inquiry concerning the wearing of a *tallit* but not a head covering, he wrote:

> A case could be made for wearing the tallis and not the hat, the tallis being originally with fringes and the fringes commanded by the Bible, for everybody, whereas the wearing of the hat is of dubious origin, as you know. However, this would be artificial. In actual Jewish life for the last ten centuries, a hat was as sacred as a tallis. I cannot understand why we have the tallis altogether and not the hat, and why any of them, but there we are in the realm of sentiment. Why do our people shudder at pork chops and eat ham and bacon? What is the principle? ... Someone ought to make a study of the psychological basis for the strange choice of the people, and this applies to Orthodox Jews too in America, as to what they will observe and what they will not observe. I suppose that to our people the putting on of the hat would sound like a reversion to Orthodoxy, while the wearing of the talllis does not seem quite that Orthodox. *However, all I can say to you is that this is a choice based upon popular feeling, and I can see no more logic in it than you can.*[63] [Emphasis added]

Freehof's evident distaste for the "illogi" of popular practice belies his earlier enthusiasm for "popular creativity." Clearly, another limit to popular creativity is when it concerns ritual practices already declared meaningless and discarded by the classical Reform rabbinate.

Or consider the irony in his response to an inquiry concerning changing from Ashkenazic to Sefardic pronunciation of Hebrew:

> It is almost a consensus that it is wrong to change an inherited minhag. ... There is a strong feeling in the legal literature that a minhag, especially an old one, is a very precious thing, a source of devotion which binds the generations together. Our Ashkenazic pronunciation is, first of all, *ours,* and also has an honored history. ... To discard it means to discard an unbroken mode of Hebrew pronunciation (with some small variation) in which our Ashkenazic ancestors have prayed for a millenium and a half. Practically speaking, it means destroying the sense of familiarity of whatever Hebrew sentences our worshipers have, and making the entire service strange to them, especially nowadays, when our Reform Movement in America is growing and for many of our new members the English part of the service and the singing of the choir are already strange. ... It is, of course, praiseworthy to express our solidarity with Israel. Let us do it with our contributions, with [our] visits, and with our contact with

Israeli art. As for our *religious* life, based upon our own traditions, this should remain *ours*.[64]

This passage and many others like it reveal the fundamental paradox inherent in *minhag:* at some point, every *minhag* is a new behavior, and while some people welcome the new, some are still deeply attached to the old. In upholding the Reform Judaism of *Reform Jewish Practice* against subsequent change, Freehof is merely articulating his own version of the Hatam Sofer's famous dictum, *hadash asur mi-d'oraita.*

Notes

1. Lee Levinger, A Jewish Chaplin in France, (New York, 1921), pp. Pp. 86-87.
2. See Howard Greenstein, *Turning Point: Zionism and Reform Judaism*, Chico, CA, 1981, pp. 37ff. and pp. 66ff. Freehof was known to sympathize with the Zionists (in a personal conversation June 20, 1999, Rabbi Theodore H. Gordon stated that Freehof's sympathies were common knowledge in the CCAR, because in conversations on other subjects he would make offhand allusions) but was always a moderate by nature and had a great aversion to public controversy. He had friends on both sides of the divide and it was natural for him to attempt a mediating role.
3. The committee also struggled to oversee pulpit changes on the home front so that those rabbis who had volunteered for the military would not feel that they were sacrificing their postwar careers. They were not always successful.
4. His Conservative and Orthodox colleagues on the committee were Milton Steinberg and Leo Jung. (*Responsa in War Time*, New York, 1947, p.i).
5. Solomon B. Freehof, *Reform Jewish Practice and its Rabbinic Background*, combined edition. New York, 1963, p. 15.
6. Freehof, p. 5.
7. Here Freehof characteristically avoids controversy through masterful circumlocution: "When the Jewish community in Palestine grew smaller and smaller, the Jewish community all over the world grew correspondingly larger and Jewry became primarily a Diaspora people." (P. 5) His readers could decide for themselves whether this change in geographical circumstances constituted "exile" or a God-given opportunity for Israel to fulfill its "mission ."
8. The question of the historicity of the Sanhedrin and how Freehof presents it is a thorny issue which we need not enter into for purposes of this discussion.
9. Freehof, p. 7. Menachem Elon defines *minhag* as "a particular normative behavior that has been continuous and unquestioned" Menachem Elon, Jew-

ish Law: History Sources. Principles, trans. Bernard Auerbach and Melvin Sykes, Philadelphia, 1994, vol. II, p.885.

10. Freehof, p. 11..

11. Freehof, pp. 13.

12. Freehof, pp. 14-15.

13. Salo W. Baron, *A Social and Religious History of the Jews*, New York, 1958, vol. II, p. 277.

14. See e.g. Shaye J.D. Cohen, "Roman Domination," in Shanks, ed., *Ancient Israel*, Washington, DC, 1988, p. 235: "The absence of other organized groups in post-70 Judea] does not of course mean that all Jews everywhere instantly became pious followers of the rabbis. The contrary was the case. In Second Temple times most Jews did not belong to any sect or group but were content to serve God in their own folk way This pattern continued in the rabbinic period as well, as the rabbinic texts themselves make abundantly clear But in the end the masses recognized the rabbis as the leaders and shapers of Judaism." Neusner's work underscores the extent to which the rabbi' view of a proper Jewish life did not match the people's view see, e.g., ch. 1, "The People and the Law," in *Jacob Neuser, The Wonder- Working Lawyers of Talmudic Babylonia*, Lanham, MD, 1987, but his perspective only further undermines Freehof's argument, since in the end the rabbis succeeded in imposing their form of Judaism on the entire Jewish people. Shmuel Safrai offers a more conventional picture in which the rabbis and their institutions quickly emerge as the "backbone" of Jewish existence after 70, but he also states that "the people [were] led by the sages." S. Safra, "The Era of the Mishnah and Talmud" in H. H. Ben-Sasson, ed., *A History of the Jewish People*, Cambridge, 1976, pp. 309-311.

15. In the wake of the Chmielnicki uprising a rabbinical synod met in Lublin in 1650 and found ways to free many *agunot* and otherwise regularize devastated Jewish family life. Heinrich Graetz, *Geschichte der Juden*, Leipzig, 1882, vol. 10, p. 75.

16. "When religious leaders, familiar with the theory as well as the practice of the Reform movement in Germany, came to America they found a lay impetus for religious reform already present. The task the laymen assigned them—and they to themselves—was to give it an intellectual foundation and to direct its course." Michael Meyer, *Response to Modernity: A History of the Reform Movement in Judaism*, New York, 1988, p. 236. See also Leon Jick, *The Americanization of the Synagogue*, Hanover, NH, 1976.

17. Freehof, p. 13.

18. Whether and to what extent Freehof's model of popularity initiated change in fact holds true for any other peiod of "religious crisis" in Jewish history, or whether he was grossly overgeneralizing on the basis of his own time and exerience, is a worthwhile inqiry for another time.

19. Freehof, p. 7.

20. See also Eruvin 14b and Menahot 35b.

21. Sanhedrin 86b.

22. *Mishnah Torah*. H. Berakhot 8:1; *Shulhan Arukh* OH 204:7. Note that even Alfasi does not resolve it. See Rashi *ad loc.*

23. Elon, vol. II, p. 896.

24. Elon, vol. II, p. 884, n. 14.

25. Elon, vol. II, pp. 901-902.
26. Elon, vol. II, p. 882.
27. Freehof, p. 8, citing Tractate Sofrim 14:16.
28. J. Yevamot 12:1 (12c).
29. This is also Elon's conclusion, Vol. II, pp. 907-909 and notes *ad loc.*
30. M. Bava Metzia 7:1.
31. J. Bava Metzia 7:1 (11b).
32. Tosefta Bava Metzia 11:23 (Lieberman, ed.) explicitly states that the residents of a city are free to determine local wages and working conditions.
33. *Bet Yosef* 690. In other words, Karo first cited the customs and their importance and their base, however tenuous, in Scripture. Then in the *Shulhan Arukh* he eliminated them. Isserles supplemented the *Shulhan Arukh* with Karo's own words, but eliminated the reference to a scriptural basis.
34. Yoreh Deah 376:4.
35. Freehof, p. 9. The notion that there is an entity called "Judaism" which "needs readjustment" at certain specific times requires a separate critique.
36. Elon, vol. I, pp. 122ff.
37. Ibid, p. 131.
38. Elon, vol. II, p. 910, citing Resp. Rashbash #419.
39. Ibid, p. 903, n. 27.
40. The first volume contains chapters on Public Worship, Marriage and Divorce, Naming of Children and Circumcision, and Burial and Mourning; the second volume adds chapters of The Synagogue Building, The Synagogue Service, Marriage and Conversion, and Death, Burial and Mourning.
41. See the brief overview by I. Ta-Shma, "Minhagim Books," *Encyclopedia Judaica*, Jerusalem, 1972, Vol. 12, col. 27-29.
42. On September 1, 1978, in an interview recorded by Rabbi Kenneth J. Weiss, Dr. Freehof stated: "The Reform movement was born on the world of enlightenment, of culture and science, in which things were judged by what sense and what logic and what proper justification they had. And if a ceremony seemed to have no logical meaning it could be dropped, it would be dropped, without any [unintelligible]. We moved out of the age of philosophy into the age of psychology. That means now, things are judged, not by what they make sense, but what they do to you. Once, I would say, 'I can believe in this.' Now I say, 'It sends me.' So therefore, ceremonies which had no justification in the past still don't have justification but have appeal in the present. So [because of this change] there is a different attitude toward the meaning of ceremonialism. But we can adopt whatever sends us—provided we know that *we* are adopting it. And if we know that we are adopting it, and if it ceases to have meaning we can again drop it, then we are Reform Jews. Not by what ceremonies we observe or don't observe, but what we think of the ceremonies that we observe. ... If we believe that we have the right when they cease to have meaning to us ... So our congregation never had bar mitzvah, now has bar mitzvah. The spirit has changed. Our congregation never had a chuppah, our ladies have embroidered a magnificent chuppah. Our congregation that never had a chazzan now has a Reform chazzan, a lady chazzan. We call it, however, with a self-satisfying name, a cantorial soloist, so we feel more Reform at it. In other words, we're in a period where we need pictorialization of Judaism again and it might as well

be the old ones. But only if we understand that we have adopted them, and not that it's Torah mi-Sinai." (AJA C-229)

43. In the words of Kaufmann Kohler: "For the pagan mind in general the ceremonies constitute religion, which is viewed as a mode of worship void of ethical purposes. In the course of time, however, the original object of these ceremonies is forgotten, and they become empty forms until upon a higher stage they are invested with new meaning and made to convey higher thoughts. There is, consequently, a singular affinity noticeable between the ceremonies of various peoples and classes, since, as a rule, they have a common origin in primitive life. Ceremonies are never the creations of individuals; they grow and change like languages. ... Each ceremony may thus be traced to its origin in primitive time. ... We, who behold in religion an ever-progressive force working through the inner consciousness of man, first collectively and afterwards individually, must ascertain the origin and purpose of each and every ceremony in order to find out whether by appealing to our minds and hearts it fulfills a religious function or whether it has become an empty shell with the kernel gone. ... In thus reviewing the entire system of Jewish observances as they have come down to us through the centuries, we find them to be indispensable forms of expressing the religious feelings prompted by the various events of life. As we advance in culture, enlightenment, and refinement, these various ceremonies may appear to us as empty shells void of meaning, but we must never forget that nothing grows on the tree or in the soil without shielding leaf and husk. Abstract truth and ethical practice fail to satisfy the religious craving of man. He needs ceremonies that impress him with the nearness and the holiness of the divine." Kaufmann Kohler, "The Origin and Function of Ceremonies in Judaism," *CCAR Yearbook*, Vol. 17, 1907, pp. 208, 210, 221.

44. Freehof, pp. 31ff.

45. Freehof, p. 56.

46. Freehof, p. 71.

47. Freehof, pp. 88-89. Although he does not explicitly mention it here, the Reform decision to rely on "the legal safeguards" of the "law of the state" and to regard the religious dimension as the marriage's "spiritual and moral side" has been frequently justified by appeal to the halakhic principle of *dina de-malkhuta dina*. Halakhically, however, this principle, however, does not function in the realm of *issur*. Elon, vol. I, pp. 132ff.

48. Freehof, pp. 99ff. The section on civil divorce is by far the lengthiest single section in both volumes and constitutes a history of the issue and a discussion of all the complexities inherent in the Reform acceptance of civil divorce. The source of this complexity is the fact that the modern state regulates marriage and divorce, considering them to be matters of civil law; but for Jewish law they are both in the realm of *issur*, although there are matters on *mamon* subsumed within tem. In drawing the dividing line between "civil" and "religious" matters for Jews in the modern state, Reform eliminated the legal aspect from marriage and the religious aspect from divorce. The latter has more serious consequences for individual Jews.,

49. Freehof, p. 118f.

50. Freehof, p. 133ff.

. Freehof, p. 10. Of course, he was far from unique in failing to discern the adaptability of Orthodoxy to modern life and its resurgence both in modern and *haredi* forms.
52. Freehof, p. 11.
53. See "Introduction," *Reform Responsa*, Cincinnati, 1960, pp. 8ff.; "Reform Judaism and the Legal Tradition," Annual Tintner Memorial Lecture, Association of Reform Rabbis of New York City and Vicinity, New York, 1961; "The Reform Revaluation of Jewish Law," The Louis Caplan Lectureship on Jewish Law, Cincinnati, 1972, pp. 13ff.
54. See numerous citations in Elon, vol. I, pp. 13ff.
55. Elon, vol. I, p. 14.
56. The *Landjudenschaften* of this era generally were granted less internal autonomy and were subject to more government supervision than their *medieval counterparts. See e.g., Josef Meisl, ed., Protokolbuch der juedischen Gemeinde Berlins*, 1723-1854, Jerusalem, 1962, pp. 11ff.
57. Those very few *Hofjuden* and other wealthy Jews of the eighteenth century who neglected ritual observances are exceptional. The vast majority of Jews continued to observe the ritual laws, whether or not their courts were allowed jurisdiction in matters of *mamon*.
58. "In the wake of the passage of the Declaration of the Rights of Man, Ashkenazi policy ... changed reluctantly. ... [T]he leaders of the Ashkenazim tried desperately to retain the right to Jewish communal organization. They argued that it could not be the intention of the government to give them the benefit of equality while at the same time demeaning them by taking away their autonomy. Their inherited practices had been their consolation in adversity and they wanted to preserve them in happier times ..." Arthur Hertzberg, The *French Enlightenment and the Jews*, New York, 1968, p. 344. The French Ashkenazim of Alsace-Lorraine were far more similar to the Jews of Germany than they were to the French Sefardic community centered in Bordeaux, and the reaction of its leadership therefore sheds light on attitudes with German Jewry.
59. Freehof, p. 15.
60. See n. 43.
61. This is not the only instance in which Freehof's ideas carry echoes of Mordecai Kaplan's. With regard to his responsa, he was fond of saying that "the past offers guidance, not governance; " a phrase strangely reminiscent of Kaplan's dictum that "the past has a vote but not a veto." Kaplan, however, was a system-builder and Freehof was not. Freehof frequently stated in his correspondence that because the Reform movement had not yet decided how to deal with questions related to Shabbat observance, he could not give official answers to many questions submitted to him as Chairman of the Responsa Committee. AJAA MS-435)
62. Freehof, pp. 13-14.
63. Letter to Rabbi Philip S. Bernstein, October 16, 1963, Temple Brith Kodesh, Rochester, NY. (AJA MS-435)
64. Letter to Rabbi Harold Silver, Temple Emanuel, Pittsburgh, April 16, 1962. (AJA MS-435)

Chapter 5

❖ ❖ ❖

Jewish Law Responds to American Law

Alan Sokobin

Introduction

I begin with three vignettes: The first was a view of a Brooklyn
Hasidic community. The streets were busy with the normal activities of commerce and socializing. The men were uniformly
dressed in their uncorrupted black suits with flapping *tsitsit* and
very broad-brimmed black fedoras. The less-uniformly clothed
women exhibited their individuality in different-colored long
dresses and sleeves that covered their arms. The *sheitles* tended to
be dowdy brown or muted auburn. It was, after all, not Shabbat.
Suddenly there was an inharmonious and charming oddity. A
young boy, *peot* flapping down from his shaved head, ran through
the streets wearing a jacket upon which was boldly emblazoned
the name of a favored team, The Mets. The traditions of the eighteenth century, the traditions of the Pale, had met and succumbed
to one intrusive element of the twentieth century.

Notes for this section begin on page 168.

The second anecdote is from my own personal experience when I was a student at HUC. It was the early 1950's and a major concern of a part of the student body was in the burgeoning civil rights movement. On one occasion two of us joined two or three black members of CORE and went to Fountain Square to a segregated luncheon restaurant diner and we sat at the counter. By previous agreement we rabbinic students wore *kippot* as we wished to be identified as Jews. My companion sat at the counter and ordered a BLT. It is interesting to note, after the passage of over four decades, that I still recall that it was one of the black companions at that "sit-in" that commented on the incongruity of a *kippah* accompanied by an appetite for *hazer*.

My third remembrance is a more recent one. We have friends in Toledo who belong to the Conservative movement and who are, in their own manner of practice, rather traditional. They do, however, ride to Synagogue. We invited them to have Shabbat lunch with us and they refused. They would not interrupt the return journey to their home for any reason.

Whatever our personal attitude toward Jewish practice and religious observances, these disparate examples make the point, I hope, that individuals of all movements and groups in Jewish life are groping to balance, in some measure, the two dynamic poles of our existence. Much like the electrodynamic tow of the North and South Poles of our globe, our Judaism and our modernity often tug at us from the opposite extremes of our existence.[1] The questions that tumble one upon the other are disturbing. The more difficult answers, to those questions, most likely more difficult because we are in a period of intense social flux, will help us define ourselves as Jews in the modern world.[2]

The questions I raise clearly will reflect my own position and predilections as a Reform Jew. Most certainly, they will be greatly influenced by my inclinations which are deeply concerned that essential Jewish matters should be guided, if not by, *halakhah*, by a halakhic process. There are more traditional definitions of *halakhah*.[3] I freely admit, with a small amount of discomfort, although I use the word *halakhah*, I do not use it in a sense, that establishes absolute authority.[4] Rather, I see *halakhah* as representing a Jewishly particular legal process, which has a dynamic, which does, or perhaps more properly, can respond to changes in society. *Halakhah* is a process which affords to both individuals and society the freedom and the mechanisms to develop new norms, standards and criteria[5] by which specific practices, customs and activities can react to changes in culture, technology and attitudes of the general society in which we live and interact.[6]

There are those who see a significant decline in the effect of *halakhah* in modern Jewish life. Over four decades ago the doyen of reform Jewish halakhists, Solomon Freehof, wrote about the development of *halakhah*.[7] Although the word *halakhah* does not appear in the book [8] there is a succinct but sufficient description of the development and influence of *halakhah* through the centuries. The conclusion of the volume with regard to the continuance of this vibrant and constructive legal literature expressed pessimism and lack of expectation with regard to the vitality and effect of responsa, on modern Jewish life.[9]

Of particular pertinence to the theme of this chapter, he noted that the "vigor of the responsa literature depends primarily upon the vitality of Jewish religious life. As long as observant Jewish life continues substantially as it has for centuries, and the people adhere to the inherited laws and customs, then the various circumstances of a widespread religious society are bound to produce a constant stream of questions. But as soon as religious life retreats from a certain field of experience, that field immediately disappears from practical religious Law."[10] He correctly noted that "[f]or centuries the responsa of all the lands were dominated by questions of civil law—problems concerning partnerships, contracts, etc. But during the last century such questions have virtually disappeared from the literature. This is simply a reflection of the fact that the Jewish communities are no longer self-contained and self-sufficient, that Jews no longer bring their business disputes to their own Jewish courts, but to secular courts. There are no civil law responsa nowadays, because there are virtually no questions of civil law brought to the rabbis. A vast field of Jewish observance has thus died out, and the responsa literature reflects the change."[11]

Dr. Freehof's melancholy builds to a dolorous conclusion. "If there is further modern shrinkage in observance, there will be further narrowing of the field of responsa."[12] He perseveres in his distressing analysis: "[a]t present, with widespread nonobservance, and the shrinkage of rabbinic study, the prospects for substantial continuation of the responsa literature are not promising. For the time being 'there is no voice (to ask) and no one answering'."[13]

Time and Dr. Freehof's prodigious productivity and his own matchless knowledge of responsa have contraverted his judgment concerning the development of *Halakhah* in this era.[14] In the next thirty years his books on responsa tumbled one after another from the printing press. He has made a lasting contribution in a period of history, which has seen an exponential growth in a new area of halakhic literature, reform responsa. In largest measure, Dr. Freehof responded to the need for new answers to old questions in the area of personal and communal religious observance. [15] While the broad domain of religious observance involves more than ritual, for our purposes I would use that term to catalog the vast majority of issues he addressed.[16]

During the four decades since Dr. Freehof essentially pronounced *Halakhah* to be moribund, there has been a new creative dynamism in the halakhic process in all the movements of Jewish religious life. The Orthodox and Conservative movements have created, as has the Reform movement, a growing body of literature which is focused on questions of Jewish law responding to new realities in our world. In largest measure, the Conservative movement has used the mechanism of the Committee on Jewish Law and Standards of the Rabbinical Assembly as its means to address the new ritual and ethical dilemmas.[17] Orthodoxy has, in largest measure, continued the century-old pattern of turning to individual rabbis who have acquired authority based upon their knowledge of Jewish law and their moral leadership.[18]

Not quite tangentially, it must be noted that there has been a constant dynamic tension between *halakhah* and the law of the alien jurisdiction under which the Jewish people lived at different times and in different lands. The Jewish legal scholars have grappled with the bipolar tautness created when attempting to define Jewish law that was constricted by the requirements and exigencies of the prevailing law. Initially, it was determined that "any condition contrary to what is written in the Torah is void."[19] In the second century, reacting to the authority of Roman law, Rabbi Judah limited the rule. "This is the rule, any condition contrary to what is in the Torah is invalid if relating to the a matter of *mamon*; if relating to a matter other than *mamon*, it is void."[20] There has been a further development of this concept of the subordination of Jewish law to the prevailing legal system. In the third century CE, Samuel, one of the two preeminent legal scholars of the Babylonian-Jewish community, acknowledged the necessity and legitimacy of Jews to obey the laws of the various lands in which they lived. This still authoritative principle is *dina de-malkhuta dina*;[21] "the law of the government is the law."[22] This doctrine is applicable only if there is no violation of the principles of justice and equity that are the essentials of Jewish law.[23]

The purpose of this paper is to look at both some of the areas where Jewish law is compelled to accommodate to the law of the state[24] as well as at the few examples of the converse, when American law responds to Jewish law. The issues that will be dealt with are marriage and divorce, arbitration, open or closed adoption, post mortem examinations, and the determination of death. The order of the subject matter has been chosen arbitrarily on the basis of the chronology in which these questions touched the American Jewish community.

I

All religious groups within the United States are required to acquiesce to the supremacy of the civil government with regard to marriage and divorce. All movements within American Jewish life accept the authority of the state to license marriages. Originally, the American law of marriage has its origin in English matrimonial law.[25] Until a little over a hundred years ago there was no system of licensing in most of the states or federal[26] jurisdictions.[27] The various legislative or administrative bodies that instituted the licensing procedures[28] did so during the period that the vast number of eastern European Jews was entering this land. Consequently, it appears there was a general acceptance of the licensing[29] requirement.[30] Nonetheless, there is a tension between Jewish law and the law of the land with regard to the appropriate and acceptable minimal age to enter into marriage.

Legal capacity is a major consideration in all systems of law. For the purposes of this chapter the question of capacity will concern itself only with the age that the law requires for legal capacity to be considered sufficient. At what age can a person enter into a contract? Must a person have reached a specific age in order to act as a witness in a legal dispute or to act as a witness to a legal document? The first question, then, is when does a person move from the legal status of a minor to that of an adult?

An early attempt at definition is found in the Mishnah with regard to the legal capacity of a minor to acquire lost or abandoned property found by that minor.[31] In the discussion concerning the definition of a minor, Samuel gives a circumscribed definition stating that no minor is capable (has the capacity) to acquire such property. R. Johanan contends that the definition of a minor is not one of specific age but rather of financial independence from the household: "a minor who is not maintained by his father is regarded as a major."[32]

Both Jewish law and Anglo-American law distinguish between witnesses to an event or crime and witnesses to an agreement or contract. In spite of the distinction drawn above, in the matter of the capacity of a minor to act as a witness to an action, event or crime, the law follows a more clearly defined pattern.

> A person is incompetent as a witness until he reaches the age of 13. Between the ages of 13 and 20, he is competent as a witness with regard to moveable property, but in respect of immovable property he is competent only if he is found to have the necessary understanding and experience (BB 155b; Yad. Edut. 9:8; Sh.Ar. HM 35:3). From the age of 20, all disqualification by reason of age is removed.[33]

The law concerning the legal capacity to be a competent witness to a transaction is the same as that relating to being competent to enter into marriage. As marriage is a legally binding contract, only parties who have legal competence may enter into it. After the groom has reached the age of thirteen years and one day, he is no longer a minor (*katan*) and may contract a valid marriage.[34] As there is legal capacity to enter into a contract, there is legal capacity to be a witness to such a contract. It is immediately apparent that Jewish law subordinates itself to the statutory law in accord with the principle of *dina de-malkhuta dina*, "the law of the government is the law."[35] This principle of Jewish law, *dina de-malkhuta dina*, is a standard by which *halakhah* measures its own ability to maintain its authority in a non-Jewish environment. Thus, Jewish law accedes to the statutes of the various states with regard to the age required for legal capacity to enter into marriage, to enter into other contracts and to act as a valid witness to a legal transaction.

II

Divorce, in the American legal system, is a creature of state or jurisdictional statute.[36] The power of the legislature to legislate divorce is unlimited except as restricted by the Constitution.[37] Civil divorce procedure raises issues in the Jewish community that are not important for governmental courts that issue orders for a civil divorce but may have an immense consequence for divorcing Jews who may wish to remarry in the future.[38] The Reform movement dealt with the issue by negating the need for a Jewish court.[39] The Orthodox and Conservative movements have struggled with several questions.[40] It is obvious that if a divorcing couple chooses to go to a *Bet Din* to receive a *Get*, there is no essential problem in order to find an equitable method to issue that *Get*. The difficulty for Jewish law rises when the couple does not voluntarily present themselves before a *Bet Din*.[41] The Rabbinical Assembly met the issue head on by issuing a rewritten form of the *Ketubah*, the religious marriage document, to include a requirement that the couple will appear before a *Bet Din* to receive a *Get* in the event that the marriage fails.[42] Recently, there have been efforts on the part of some Orthodox Rabbis to achieve the same end by use of a prenuptial agreement.[43] There is a legally binding arbitration agreement, which expands the potent conditions of the marriage.[44] An exceptional example of a secular jurisdiction attempting to respond to the particular needs of the Jewish community is to be found in a modification of the New York domestic relations law to aid Jewish women in the process of receiving a civil divorce.[45]

III

Arbitration has been the legal process of choice in the Jewish community for some two millennia. It has been noted that there is a judicial process within the Jewish community that is "as old as the Bible itself."[46] The first reference to the appointment of judges was prior to reception of law at Sinai.[47] The first post-biblical regulation dealing with the processes of dispute management provided that all disputes over property required a court of three ordained judges.[48] This requirement for a tri-party court was expanded to all matters in private disputes.[49] Ordination was required to function fully as a judge and ordination was limited to Israel.[50] Therefore the communities of the Diaspora utilized non-ordained judges,[51] constituting a court of arbiters.[52] This was clearly the pattern for the hundred generations of the European Jewish experience.[53]

A cursory examination of the literature and legal activities of the early Jewish immigrants to the United States reflects an interesting contradiction. The earliest settlers of New England deliberately chose to have their laws reflect Biblical law.[54] Jewish residents of the colonies, and then of the new republic, took their legal difficulties to the founded courts. [55] Was it in the nature of the Jews who crossed the ocean during those early colonial and American centuries?[56] It may have well been that "[a]ccommodation, after all was an integral part of Jewish history and a pervasive theme of Jewish experience."[57] With the arrival of the first wave of the immense Jewish migration which flooded the United States between 1880 and 1914 there was a subtle but significant change. "Among the various immigrant groups for whom internal dispute-settlement procedures were vital for community cohesion, none migrated with as strong a historical commitment to law, and as deep a distrust of alien legal systems,[58] as the Jews of Eastern Europe."[59] While the principle that the law of the state was supreme[60] had been articulated as a basic legal doctrine for centuries, there had been a strong tradition of avoiding to appear before the European national courts. [61] A guiding principle of the European Jewish community was Maimonides' warning that a Jew who turned to Gentile judges, "caused the walls of the Law to fall."[62] His advice to his community, with its echo through the centuries, was clear. He emphasized his concern that justice be sought through arbitration.

> Jewish law considers it to be commendable at the outset of a trial to inquire of the litigants whether they desire adjudication according to law or settlement by arbitration. If they prefer arbitration, their wish is granted. A court that always resorts to arbitration is praiseworthy. Concerning such a court, it is said: "Execute the justice of peace in your gates."[63] What kind of justice carries peace with it? Undoubtedly, it is arbitration. So, too, with reference to David it is said: "And David executed justice and charity unto all his people."[64] What kind of justice carries charity with it? Undoubtedly, it is arbitration, i.e. compromise.[65]

One of the first efforts to create social order and communal coherence among the thousands of eastern European Jews daily streaming into New York was the establishment of a *Kehillah* presided over by Rabbi Judah L. Magnes.[66] Of evolving importance to the Jews of New York was a need to respond to the labor disputes in the developing areas of trade and manufacture into which the Jews were now entering. The clothing trades were growing and flourishing during these years and a significant number of both employers and employees were Jewish.[67] Derived from the distress in the community because of the level of wages, as well as dramatic and tragic incidents such as the Triangle Shirtwaist Company fire,[68] there was a series of strikes in the clothing industry. Magnes and the *Kehillah* developed a plan for arbitration within the Jewish community.[69] Simultaneously, Magnes successfully lobbied for reform of the New York ordinance, which encouraged easy revocation of arbitration agreements.[70] In 1919 the Jewish Arbitration Court was established.[71] A year later the New York legislature enacted legislation, which upheld the legality of an agreement between two litigants to abide by the decision of a third, non-judicial, party. [72] The Jewish Arbitration Court[73] dealt with no fewer than fifteen thousand cases between 1919 and 1980.[74]

Arbitration is strongly endorsed by public policy.[75] It is essentially a matter of contractual agreement.[76] It has been clearly determined in U.S. law, that arbitration panels or courts may determine the extent or limitations of the questions of the conflict.[77] Questions of law as well as fact may be submitted to arbitration.[78] The extent of the authority of the arbitrators is determined by the wording of the agreement.[79] Moreover, an arbitration agreement may validly provide for arbitration in accordance with the laws of another jurisdiction.[80] Therefore, where arbitration is conducted under the authority and methods of Jewish law, it will normally be enforced by the law of a state or the United States.[81] A statute of New York law, where a significant portion of the Jewish community adheres to rabbinic authority and law, specifically authorizes rabbinical courts utilizing Jewish law to issue decisive legal rulings.[82]

In spite of this clear directive, some New York State courts have refused to accept the decisions of rabbinic courts.[83] In a case involving custody of a child the court was curt, "The basic principles governing the custody of infants are beyond debate. The state…acts as *parens patriae*."[84] Another New York court affirmed the legal authority of a *Bet Din*, "the rabbinical board is compe-

tent to pass on these questions, to hear witnesses, including peti-
tioner and respondent, and to appraise the value given to the testimony of any witness and to render a speedy determination
respecting the rights of the parties. The board can apply the legal,
moral and religious law to the dispute between the parties."[85] A
more recent dispute in Pennsylvania involving millions of dol-
lars was settled in a rabbinical arbitration court.[86] Clearly, there
are cases in which Jewish law can be the law of choice in a dispute in arbitration and that the decision of the arbitrators will be
enforced by the secular jurisdiction.

IV

At first thought, legal adoption[87] of children might well be considered as an area where there is no tension between Jewish law
and the law of the state. In the most popular sense of the word,
adoption is a double *mitzvah*. A childless couple find realization
and contentment as they take a child into their home and hearts,
thus filling their lives and the child's life with richly fulfilling
love.[88] Unfortunately, the reality and the optimistic hope are not
fully congruent.[89] Moreover, relating to the theme of this chapter, modern practices of adoption in many American jurisdictions have created important questions for Jewish law.[90] The
significant issue is concerned with the question of open[91] or
closed [92] adoption. The majority of states have adhered to the
closed adoption position.

There is no national law governing the adoption of children
in the United States, it is one of the functions of law clearly
reserved to the various states.[93] Until this century most adoptions
in the U.S. were arranged without the assistance of the state.[94]
Massachusetts passed the first comprehensive adoption statute in
1851.[95] The early part of this century saw an acceptance by the
various states[96] to actively participate in the adoption process.[97]
State involvement effectively gave full and complete power to
each of the several jurisdictions. It has been characterized as a
legislatively created device.[98]

With the involvement of the states and considering the
mobility of the American people, it became necessary to create
some uniformity between the statutes of the various jurisdictions. In 1953 the National Conference of Commissioners on Uni-

form State Laws prepared a Uniform Adoption Act.[99] It has been twice amended. The 1971 amendment contains language, which offers the potential for "open" adoption.[100] Nonetheless, only the five states of Alaska, Arkansas, Montana, North Dakota and Ohio have adopted the act. [101] In largest measure, therefore, the adoptive process utilized for the vast majority of Americans who are involved in adopting or being adopted is "closed adoption." The adoption statutes in force today are, in largest measure, variants of the 1851 Massachusetts law. The first requirement is the consent of the parents or there must be a pressing need for the courts to effectuate the adoption procedure without that consent.[102] Adoption, in a traditional "closed adoption" transfers the parental rights of the biological parents to the adoptive parents.[103] Traditional adoptions are not revocable.[104] Most importantly, for the purposes of this paper, traditional adoptions in most states involve statutorily imposed anonymity of the parties, secrecy, and sealed records.[105] It truly is a "tangle of state law."[106]

Adoption as a legal concept and process does not exist in earliest Jewish law.[107] Moreover, it "is not known as a legal institution in Jewish law."[108] The reality with regard to an individual or a couple accepting responsibility for the care, growth and future of a child, however, is not the same as the bald statement of Jewish law. While *halakhah* effectively limits the personal status of a child to that of the natural parents, there is an effective pragmatic mechanism to achieve the same results as in adoption. *Halakhah* permits the appointment of a guardian, an *apotropos*[109] (a guardian in all matters).[110]

A vital concern of traditional Jewish law is the personal biological status of each individual.[111] Of particular and direct concern is the status of the *kohen*, the descendant of the ancient priestly caste for whom certain privileges, prerogatives and restrictions apply.[112] The *kohen* is given primacy in the order of those called to read from the Torah on all occasions that the reading takes place.[113] He also invokes the Priestly Blessing in the Synagogue[114] as well as accepts the redemptive money at the ceremony which celebrates the birth of a first-born male.[115] Of greater importance for the theme of this chapter are the limitations and proscriptions placed upon a *kohen*. The rules prohibiting contact with the dead with the exception of his closest of kin are still in effect.[116] Because of this prohibition there are some that would limit the study of medicine for a *kohen*.[117] Most importantly for the purposes of this study, there are important limitations on whom a Kohen may or may not marry. A *Kohen* is prohibited from marrying an unchaste woman, a proselyte or a divorcee.[118]

There is also a clearly defined list of prohibited marriages for all Jews.[119] The first condition for marriage is that a Jew should marry only a Jew.[120] Families considering adoption face the future difficulty of determining whether their adopted child is a Jew. [121] It follows, then, that if a child is adopted and the child's personal status is not known, he may inadvertently enter into a prohibited marriage upon reaching adulthood, he might even enter unknowingly into an incestuous marriage.[122] Such a marriage would have disastrous legal effect upon any offspring of the marriage.[123]

Recognizing that even the most traditional and conservative halakhists have found methods to modify some areas of Jewish law to respond to new technologies and to adjust to the statutory requirements of the state, is there not a possibility that some of the questions which arise with regard to the status of a "closed" adoptee could be disposed of by utilizing new medical techniques? There is a clear and unequivocal opinion by Maimonides that we can accept the new knowledge given by medical technology to determine halakhic questions.[124] He asserts that later generations are not required to accept the level of scientific knowledge of earlier rabbinic authorities.[125] Moreover, *halakhah* will accept the reliability of blood tests.[126]

As a major stumbling block with regard to closed adoptions is the potential for young people who do not know that they are related by blood to wed, could not newly developed sophisticated blood testing deal with that difficulty? Could not the possible blood relationship between a couple planning to be married be determined and authoritatively deal with that question through DNA testing?[127]

V

The oldest and equally, the most modern areas to be addressed are also the most distressing. They fall under the general rubric of bioethical. Both secular American society and Jewish thinkers have struggled with the excruciating moral challenge in what is now termed bioethics.[128] The questions to be addressed are, how does Jewish law respond to the dictates of state law dealing with the definitions of death, hastening or delaying death, and post mortem examinations?[129]

New medical technology, undreamed of in the science fiction literature of my youth, has created a new and sometimes uncomfortable tension between the law of the land and *Halakhah*. The search for patterns of societal assent with regard to some of these technologies and the need of society to give order to the processes by which these technologies are utilized has created an uncomfortable dynamic tension. There is a new word to be found in the lexicon of bioethical concerns, *legisogenic*. [130] This word defines the very present process of legally induced, medically inappropriate treatment. An astute observer of the legal burden which accompanies some of the life and death decisions in modern medicine has defined the difficulty.

> Death is a natural process and a uniquely personal experience. If pressed to categorize it, most would probably term the major controversies surrounding it ethical, rather than medical or legal. Nevertheless, there is an increasing trend to ask the courts whether life-sustaining treatment should be withheld from patients who are unable to make this decision themselves. Judges are asked to decide this question, not because they have any special expertise, but because only they can provide the physicians with civil and criminal immunity for their actions. In seeking this immunity, legal considerations quickly transcend ethical and medical judgments.[131]

Halakhah has had to face the same diverse bioethical issues created in these past decades as had secular law. At times there has been harmony and assent between the two systems of law. In some other tormenting issues there has been disagreement.

The first issue became a legal one in this nation with the confluence of several essential legal factors. In a technologically more naive time the legal definition of death had simply been the absence of life. "Death is the opposite of life; it is the termination of life."[132] Now there was a new medical definition of death by the authoritative Harvard Medical School report.[133] This report was the result of innovations in medical technology which have resulted in machines that artificially maintain cardiorespiratory functions. The use of the new sophisticated respirators makes it possible, in spite of total and irreversible loss of the function of the brain, to maintain the operation of the heart and lungs for a limited period of time.[134] It became clear to practicing physicians that the traditional "vital signs" are not independent indicia of life but are part of an integration of functions in which the brain is dominant. Use of this new medical equipment has led the medical community to consider the cessation of brain activity as the measure of death and compelled a reexamination of the traditional legal and medical criteria for determination of when death occurs.[135] Under the leadership of Harvard Medical School, the medical profession established a multistep test to identify the existence of physical indicia of brain stem activity.[136]

In recent years the general consensus of the legal systems in the United States has been to accept the definition of the Uniform Determination of Death Act. [137] The first statutory recognition of cessation of brain function as a criterion for death was in Kansas in 1970.[138] All fifty states, the District of Columbia, the Virgin Islands, and Puerto Rico now accept some variation on "the complete and irreversible cessation of all functions of the entire brain" as a definition of death.[139]

Dealing, as we are, with the questions that are most basic to our existence, it is not surprising that even within the legal community there has not been immediate or complete acceptance of the Harvard standards for death.[140] Even the acceptance of the standards by state legislatures does not assure uncritical agreement by courts and the populace. Justice Frankfurter is often quoted when he epigrammatically noted that statutory construction is not "a ritual to be observed by unimaginative adherence to well-worn professional phrases."[141] Nonetheless, statutory standards throughout this nation mandate that physicians shall adhere to the criteria of brain death. The new legal standards for determining death placed the traditional definition of death in *halakhah* in an uncomfortable confrontation with the law.

Jewish tradition has come to a definition of death through inductive reasoning. The writers of the Bible did not attempt to define death. The subject is raised in the Gemara as an element of a discussion concerning the value of life in relationship to the fulfillment of biblical mandates. In affirming the sanctity of life, the rabbis agree that the saving of a life has greater religious value than observing the divinely inspired biblical commandment to observe the Sabbath.

Every danger to human life suspends the [laws of] the Sabbath. If debris [of a collapsing building] falls on someone, and it is doubtful whether or not he is there, or whether he is alive or dead, or whether he is an Israelite or a heathen, one should open [even on the Sabbath] the heap of the debris for his sake. If one finds him alive, one should remove the debris, and if he be dead one should leave him there [until the Sabbath day is over].[142]

The discussion continues: Our Rabbis taught: How far does one search [to ascertain whether he is dead or live]? Until [he reaches] his nose. Some say: Up to his heart: If one searches and finds those above to be dead, one must not assume those below are surely dead … life manifests itself principally through the nose as it is written: 'In whose nostrils was the breath of the spirit [breath] of life.' [143]

Moses Maimonides, the twelfth-century legal scholar and philosopher, was also a physician. His codification of Talmudic law defined death. "If upon examination, no sign of breathing can be detected at the nose, the victim must be left where he is [until after the Sabbath] because he is already dead."[144] The still authoritative sixteenth-century Jewish code of law, the *Shulchan Aruch*, states: "Even if the victim was found so severely injured he cannot live for more than a short while, one must probe [the debris] until one reaches his nose. If one cannot detect signs of respiration at the nose, then he is certainly dead."[145]

An eminent modern Orthodox analyst of the law, Rabbi J. David Bleich, has confirmed this definition as being authoritative for traditional Judaism.[146] Rabbi Bleich writes extensively on the subject of bioethics. He insists that Jewish law rejects brain death and irreversible coma as definitions of the end of life.[147] He asserts that only when there is total cessation of both cardiac and respiratory activity can we say that one is dead.[148] Bleich totally rejects the position of the Ad Hoc Committee of the Harvard Medical School.

Responding to the new secular definition of death,[149] some rabbinical authorities sought definitions, which could harmonize the ancient and authoritative Jewish definition of death with the new medical understandings. The Rabbinical Council of Israel stated that "the *halakhah* holds that death occurs with cessation of respiration. Therefore one must confirm that respiration has ceased completely and irreversibly.[150] This can be established by confirmation of destruction of the entire brain, including the brain stem, which is the pivotal activator of independent respiration in humans."[151]

This has not muted the basic conflict of ideologies. Among Jewish scholars and ethicists there is a continuing controversy with regard to what should be the acceptable modern definition of death. Reacting to Anglo-American law which describes irreversible cessation of total brain function as a criterion for death,[152] some Orthodox Jewish scholars following the conclusions of M. D. Tendler, a rabbi and bacteriologist, accept only destruction of the entire brain as a Biblical definition of death.[153] Tendler describes physiological decapitation as "complete destruction of the brain with loss of integrative, regulatory and other functions."[154] Thus, he concludes, "total and irreversible cessation of brain stem function equals destruction of the brain."[155] Another noted Orthodox authority, Rabbi Joseph Soloveichik, Director of the Department of Law at the Hebrew Theological College, categorically denies that only loss of brain function equals death.

Jewish law recognizes the presence of any vital function, including heart action, as indicative of at least residual life. Termination of such life by means of "pulling the plug" or otherwise constitutes an act of homicide. Moreover, a sharp distinction must be drawn between partial and total destruction of the brain. The authors[156] state that the Harvard criteria signify that "when the criteria have been fulfilled, there is widespread destruction of the brain" and that "time must often elapse before morphologic evidence of cellular destruction can be detected." This cannot be equated at all with the state of capitation. Jewish law cannot be cited in support of brain death legislation presently before the legislatures of various states. Jewish law cannot condone the removal of life support systems from any patient in whom any vital sign is present.[157]

To date the conflict between the standards and procedures for the declarations of death based upon the commonly accepted Harvard criteria and those of differing religious traditions, including that of Jewish law, has been addressed by only one state. New Jersey recognizes death as the modern neurological evidence of irreversible cessation of all functions of the entire brain, including the brain stem.1[158] Equally, New Jersey permits an exemption to individuals who reject the definition of death derived from the brain death standard and maintain that death shall be defined on the basis of cardiorespiratory criteria if done so on the basis of a conscientious objection predicated on religious belief.[159] To date there have been no cases before either New Jersey or federal courts testing this statute.

VI

Religion and government not only attempt to define the moment of death, but when death is artificially prolonged, they must attempt to regulate how and when death is permitted. One of the most disturbing and distressing questions of our era is, when can one remove a patient, artificially maintained on life support systems, from that technologically supported existence and permit total death?[160] Even the phraseology of the question utilizing the term "total death" implies that there are or may be circumstances where a person is in an intermediate stage between life and death. Peter Singer's ethically stimulating book[161] challenges the commonly accepted definitions of death. The examples offered are spiritually and morally painful. They bring together the triad of ethical concerns, the legal processes and the humane conscience of people pondering the ultimate verities of life and death as they face an agonizing triangle of moral uncertainty. Singer cites the case of twenty-one year old Joey Fiori who had an accident in 1971. He has been in a medically maintained persistent vegetative state for over twenty years. His mother has petitioned the Commonwealth of Pennsylvania to remove him from his feeding tube but the State Superior Court refused to respond to her request. Singer poses the question, is a non-cognizant, non-responsive, non-thinking but functioning body, alive?[162]

Lord Jakobovits offers a vividly dramatic example of the new ability to maintain some life functions, which expands on Singer's troubling question.

> In an effort to prove that the heart can continue to beat long after the brain has completely ceased to function, an operation was performed where a pregnant sheep was decapitated, maintained by artificial ventilation for several hours and then successfully delivered of a healthy lamb. There can be no argument that the sheep was dead, since it had been decapitated. Medically and halakhically, a dead sheep cannot contain a viable fetus, but this is what happened.[163]

Singer gives examples involving human beings that point to the ethical and legal difficulties that develop from our new technological abilities. In April 1993 a twenty-eight-year-old woman was shot and declared brain dead. She was seventeen-weeks pregnant and placed on life support equipment. Three-and-a half-months later a baby boy was taken from her "dead body" by Cesarean birth. Restating Lord Jakobovits' amazement that medically and halakhically a dead woman cannot contain a viable fetus, but that is what happened; a dead woman was delivered of a live baby.[164]

Responding to the new technologies and the painful moral exigencies that derived from the now extant medical abilities, the Hemlock Society was formed in 1980 to campaign for the right of a terminally ill person to choose voluntary euthanasia its justification is in the book *Final Exit*.[165] The motto of the Hemlock Society is: "Good Life, Good Death."[166] Men and women facing an agonizing terminal illness, coupled with the often accompanying erosion of family welfare, began to contemplate what was termed a suicide that was "rational and reasonable."[167]

Secular American society has struggled excruciatingly with the moral challenge in what is now termed bioethics[168] for over four decades. Since the early 1970s there have been an accelerating number of cases involving the law in the attempt to give legal potency to individuals and families facing the life and death conundrums created by accident or illness.[169] The best-known examples are probably the well-publicized cases of Karen Quinlan[170] and Nancy Cruzan.[171] The twenty years on the legal road from the 1976 *Quinlan* to the 1997 Supreme Court decisions on doctor-assisted suicide[172] have been torturous and painful.

The "seminal decision"[173] in this field is *In re Quinlan*.[174] Karen Ann Quinlan suffered brain damage and lapsed into a coma when she spontaneously and inexplicably stopped breathing.[175] As tests showed some brain activity, she could not be declared to be legally dead and was maintained on a respirator.[176] After an extended period in which she was maintained in this vegetative state, her father requested that the court authorize her physicians to cease life support.[177] The court responded affirmatively and held that a patient's right to refuse treatment is an element of the right of privacy.[178] Where a patient is legally incompetent, a guardian may exercise that right.[179]

A year later Joseph Saikewicz, a sixty-seven- year old severely retarded patient, developed incurable leukemia.[180] His physicians were prepared to attempt to prolong his life with chemotherapy but his guardian requested that he not be treated.[181] The court ruled that the pain of the treatments to Saikewicz would outweigh the benefits.[182] The ruling was based on the presumption that if Saikewicz were competent he would have requested cessation of treatment.[183]

Subsequently, the New York Court of Appeals joined two cases[184] with similar questions. Both involved guardians of incompetent patients who objected to the continued use of medical treatments or measures to prolong the lives of the patients whose diagnosis offered no reasonable possibility of recovery. Brother Fox was an eighty-three-year-old member of a Catholic religious order who was being maintained on a respirator while in a chronic vegetative state.[185] The facts dealing with the request to remove Brother Fox were attested to by his religious superior who testified that Fox had taught ethics, had been aware of the *Quinlan* case, and stated that he would not want his own life extended by extraordinary measures.[186] The court relied on that testimony to find that Brother Fox had made his determination with regard to the refusal of treatment while he was conscious and rational, and found that to be a legitimate request.[187] The court quoted the trial court's decision. "His stated opposition to the use of a respirator to maintain him in a vegetative state was 'unchallenged at every turn and unimpeachable in its sincerity.'"[188]

The companion case dealt with John Storer who was a profoundly retarded fifty-two-year-old with terminal cancer.[189] His mother, who was also his legal guardian, refused consent to administer blood transfusions as they would only prolong his discomfort and would be against his wishes if he were competent.[190] The court noted that physicians could not be held to have violated either legal or professional responsibilities when responding to the right of a competent patient to decline medical treatment.[191] Brother Fox had been competent when he articulated his wish to refuse treatment; Storer was not; mentally he was an infant.[192] The court emphasized the right of an incompetent to medical treatment as well as the limitations placed upon parents and guardians. "A parent or guardian has a right to consent to medical treatment on behalf of an infant. The parent, however, may not deprive a child of lifesaving treatment, however well intentioned."[193]

Two years later a California case[194] expanded the moral dimensions by focusing not on the request of the patient or a guardian but on the action of a physician. Clarence Herbert was a fifty-five-year-old who lapsed into a permanent coma following surgery.[195] At the request of the family the physicians removed the patient from a respirator and discontinued intravenous feeding.[196] Following Herbert's death the physicians were charged with murder and indicted by a trial court.[197] The Court of Appeals interposed a writ dismissing the action on the grounds that withholding life support was a passive omission and there was no duty to treat the patient as there was a lack of consent.[198] In *Cruzan* the court agreed that the due process clause would give a competent adult the right to reject medical treatment but it avoided ruling on the other issues.[199] Some courts have taken the position that lifesaving procedures cannot be ordered for a competent adult who refuses treatment on a religious basis.[200]

Eminent bioethicists who engage in spirited debate have taken and still maintain polar positions in response to the matched, agonizing moral questions of the right of human beings to permit life to cease and to shorten life by hastening death and actively terminating life. Leon Kass argues strenuously against the concept that there is a right to hasten death through assisted suicide or euthanasia.[201] Ronald Green responds directly by affirming the right of competent individuals to make decisions with regard to their own existence.[202] Ronald Dworkin, also an eminent jurisprudential thinker, has defined the issue for those who would grant individuals the right to determine the time to end pain.

> The life of a single human organism commands respect and protection, no matter in what form or shape...[203] Someone who thinks his own life would go worse if he lingered near death on a dozen machines for weeks or stayed biologically alive for years as a vegetable believes that he is showing more respect for the human contribution to the sanctity of his life if he makes arrangements in advance to avoid that, and that others show more respect for his life if they avoid it for him.[204]
>
> Death has dominion because it is not only the start of nothingbut the end of everything, and how we think and talk about dying ... shows how important it is that life end appropriately, that death keeps faith with the way we want to have lived.[205]

Dworkin's analysis implies that society has the moral as well as the legal right to permit removal of life support mechanisms. To this extent it is in agreement with the legally acceptable norms articulated by the report of the President's Commission for the Study of Ethical Problems in Medicine.[206]

A New Jersey court attempted to face up to the ethical conundrums imposed upon society when life is merely existence.[207] Claire C. Conroy was an eighty-four year old who suffered from organic brain syndrome.[208] Miss Conroy died prior to the hearing of the superior court.[209] The court noted that "Conroy's death has rendered the issues that underlie this appeal moot.[210] "Nevertheless, [the court] conclude [d] that the importance of the issues presented by this appeal requires their resolution notwithstanding their mootness."[211] Following the court's statement of its holding it turned to the ethical questions that beset it.[212]

> The ethical question implicit in the decision whether to discontinue life-sustaining measures has traditionally been expressed by the distinction between "ordinary" and "extraordinary" treatment. The standard definition of these terms is given as follows: Ordinary means all medicines, treatments, and operations which offer a reasonable hope of benefit and which can be obtained and used without excessive expense, pain, or other inconvenience. Extraordinary means are all medicines, treatments and operations which cannot be obtained or used without excessive expense, pain or other inconvenience, or if used, would not offer a reasonable hope of benefit.[213]

In response to the fact pattern of this case the court refused to determine the issue of removing a patient from life support system equipment. "The present appeal is not the proper vehicle by which to resolve this issue, and we expressly decline to do so."[214] Nonetheless, it approvingly quoted from the report of the President's Commission that strongly suggests that there could well be situations in which the court would permit such action.[215]

The moral and legal issues presented by increasing requests for removal of terminal patients from life support equipment accelerated. In a 1986 Massachusetts case,[216] Paul Brophy, age 45, suffered extensive brain damage and lapsed into a permanent coma as the result of a burst blood vessel near his brain.[217] His family requested that he be removed from a feeding tube but the hospital and the physicians refused their request.[218] In a Solomonic decision the court ruled that the feeding tube could be removed but that the physicians and the hospital could not be compelled to assist.[219] While Massachusetts had not then adopted the Uniform Rights of the Terminally Ill Act[220] the court's decision paralleled its provision[221] which was designed to "address situations in which a physician or health-care provider is unwilling to make and record a determination of terminal condition, or to respect the medically reasonable decision of the patient regarding withholding or withdrawal of life-sustaining procedures, due to personal convictions."[222] Brophy was moved to another medical facility that acceded to the request of the family.[223] He died shortly thereafter.[224]

That same year a California court extended the parameters of the ethical questions.[225] Elizabeth Bouvia was a twenty-eight-year-old quadriplegic suffering from cerebral palsy.[226] She was bedridden in a hospital and suffered constant pain.[227] She petitioned the court to remove her feeding tube but the trial court refused.[228] The Court of Appeals reversed that court and authorized her to do so,[229] on the basis of the right of a patient to control her own body.[230]

This painful and distressing debate has become a part of the popular ethical challenges that are constantly thrust before us. A former correspondent for the *New York Times* wrote most poignantly about the emotional tautness that results from watching a loved one complete life in constant pain. "My cousin Florence Hosch finally died the Wednesday before Christmas, about a thousand days after she had wished to."[231]

The best-known American exponent of hastening death through euthanasia and assisted suicide is Dr. Jack Kevorkian.[232] He has been an active participant in assisted suicides and has been indicted several times in Michigan for violating that state's law banning assisted suicides.[233] Reacting to the third acquittal of Dr. Kevorkian on assisted-suicide charges in Michigan, the delegates at the American Medical Association voted to continue the group's policy opposing such action on the part of a physician.[234] During the same period of time that Dr. Kevorkian has been active both in advocating changes to the legal status of physicians who assist patients in committing suicide, and in assisting some individuals to commit suicide,[235] ballot initiatives to legalize physician-assisted suicides were before voters in several jurisdictions. Defeated in California[236] and Washington,[237] one such initiative was passed in Oregon[238] but a federal judge struck it down because it failed to ensure equal protection under the law.[239] The law was subsequently rewritten and again was approved by the voters of that state.[240] This action followed the dual Supreme Court decisions on assisted suicide.[241] In the *Washington* case, the Court said that states were free to pursue "the earnest and profound debate about the legality and practicality"[242] of the issue. The significant portion of the electorate that supported such initiatives offers promise that the issue will continue to be ardently debated.

The parliament of Australia's Northern Territory was the first western legislature to enact legislation giving terminally ill adults the right to actively end their lives.[243] The legal right was short-lived. Australia's federal parliament reacted with speed and struck down the territory's voluntary euthanasia law.[244]

In this country there was a recent, important and notable decision. The United States Court of Appeals, Ninth Circuit, sitting *en banc* upheld the decision[245] of a U.S. district court judge who held that "a competent, terminally ill adult has a constitutionally guaranteed right under the Fourteenth Amendment to commit physician-assisted suicide."[246] Responding to the question of whether individuals have the liberty to "determine the time and manner of one's death" the court quoted Justice O'Connor's concurring opinion in *Cruzan*[247] where she questioned whether there exists a rationale for government to enter into the realm of a person's "liberty, dignity, and freedom."[248] In a pointed reference to *Casey*[249] the Ninth Circuit reiterated a fundamental message, "[t]hese matters, involving the most intimate and personal choices a person may make in a lifetime, choices central to personal dignity and autonomy, are central to the liberty protected by the Fourteenth Amendment."[250] The court extended the liberty interest and protection beyond those who are competent to make an informed decision in this critical matter. "Our conclusion is strongly influenced by, but not limited to, the plight of mentally competent, terminally ill adults. We are influenced as well by the plight of others, such as those whose existence is reduced to a vegetative state or a permanent and irreversible state of unconsciousness."[251] While infants and minors were not specifically included in the court's statement, it is reasonable to infer that they are a part of the class intended to be covered in the opinion. Scraping the heels of the Ninth Circuit decision was the even more recent judgment of the U.S. Second Circuit in *Quill*, subsequently reviewed by the Supreme Court.[252] Physicians brought an action to declare unconstitutional two New York statutes penalizing assistance in suicide. The basic argument of the physicians was:

[I]t is legally and ethically permitted for physicians to actively assist patients to die who are dependent on life sustaining treatments .... Unfortunately, some dying patients who are in agony that can no longer be relieved, yet are not dependent on life-sustaining treatment, have no such options under current legal restrictions.[253]

The court rejected the due process-fundamental rights argument of the plaintiffs and reaffirmed that there is no state in the Union that grants a right to assist in suicide.[254] Because the court could not discern a valid distinction between the passive assistance allowed in removing life support systems and the active assistance in prescribing lethal medication, it determined that the New York statutes were in violation of the Constitution's equal protection clause.[255]

In a provocative and innovative concurrence Judge Calabresi accepted the judgment of the court but not its reasoning.[256] He contends that:

[W]hen a law is neither plainly unconstitutional ... nor plainly constitutional, the courts ought not to decide the ultimate validity of that law without current and clearly expressed statements, by the people or by their elected officials, of the state interests involved. It is my further contention, that, absent such statements, the courts have frequently struck down such laws, while leaving open the possibility of reconsideration if appropriate statements were subsequently made.[257]

His analysis pointed out that the rationale for the assisted suicide prohibition had been undermined when suicide and attempted suicide were no longer considered to be crimes.[258] It may be inferred that Judge Calabresi's analysis was an attempt to influence the U.S. Supreme Court in the appeal which was certain to follow the New York decision. Immediately following the two United States Court of Appeals decisions in *Compassion in Dying v. Washington*[259] and *Quill v. Vacco*,[260] the *New York Times* presented a major examination of the issues now confronting the American juridical system in right-to-die cases.[261] "Last week's decision by a Federal appeals court striking down a 19th century New York criminal law against aiding or abetting suicide has thrust a new question to the top of the nation's legal agenda: Do terminally ill patients have a constitutionally protected right to choose physician-accelerated death?"[262] The article was directed to alternate legal theories that might be presented to and considered by the

Supreme Court, but then concluded, "[i]f the Supreme Court wants to address the right-to-die issue without invoking its abortion precedents, Judge Calabresi's analysis shows the way. Even if the Justices decide not to take these two cases, the issue is certain to come back to them—again and again."[263]

The Supreme Court responded to the challenge offered by the Second and Ninth Circuit Courts of Appeals by stepping into the breach. The Court, however, did not close the breach. In *Washington v. Glucksberg*,[264] Chief Justice Rehnquist's unanimous opinion for the Court was forthright and unequivocal. "The question presented in this case is whether Washington's prohibition against 'caus(ing)' or 'aid(ing)' a suicide offends the 14th Amendment to the United States Constitution. We hold that it does not."[265] Concurring opinions, however, would appear to leave a legal door ajar for states to craft changes in the statutes as well as future claims that there is a right to such an action. Justice Souter echoed the opinion of Judge Calabresi's concurrence in the Second Circuit Court of Appeals opinion, *Quill v. Vacco*,[266] "[w]hile I do not decide for all time that respondents' claim should not be recognized, I acknowledge the legislative institutional competence as the better one to deal with that claim at this time."[267]

In responding to the similar issues presented in *Vacco v. Quill*,[268] Chief Justice Rehnquist, again writing for a unanimous Court, reiterated the position that "the question presented by this case is whether New York's prohibition on assisting suicide therefore violates the equal protection clause of the 14th Amendment. We hold that it does not."[269]

Justice O'Connor hesitated to close the door on the issue. "But respondents urge us to address the narrower question whether a mentally competent person who is experiencing great suffering has a constitutionally cognizable interest in controlling the circumstances of his or her imminent death. I see no need to reach that question in the context of the facial challenges to the New York and Washington laws at issue here."[270]

Justice Breyer practically invited new legislation in his concurring opinion.

> The Court describes it [physician assisted euthanasia] as a 'right to commit suicide with another's assistance.' But I would not reject the respondents' claim without considering a different formulation, for which our legal tradition may provide greater support. That formulation would use words roughly like a 'right to die with dig-

nity.' But irrespective of the exact words used, at its core would lie personal control over the manner of death, professional medical assistance, and the avoidance of unnecessary and severe physical suffering—combined.[271]

The Supreme Court in *Cruzan*[272] determined that the critical element in the legal arguments concerning the constitutional right to be allowed to die was dependent upon the competent expression of a wish by the subject not to be maintained in a vegetative state.[273] Jewish law follows a different path.

There is a reference to assisted suicide in Biblical literature but not to euthanasia. It is related as tragic response to a specific incident, not as a resolution to a lingering, painful illness.[274] Biblical reasoning clearly emphasizes the continuing obligation to heal and prolong life. The obligation to save the life of an endangered person is predicated upon the Levitical verse, "nor shall you stand idly by the blood of your fellow."[275] The most eloquent statement of this principle was made with reference to the belief that all humankind was derived from the same primal ancestor.

> For this reason was man created alone, to teach thee that whosoever destroys a single soul of Israel, scripture imputes [guilt] to him as though he had destroyed a complete world; and whosoever preserves a single soul of Israel,[276] scripture ascribes [merit] to him as though he had preserved a complete world.[277]

This principle, however, does not obligate humans to assist others in the process of healing. From the point of view of biblical Judaism, there is hubris in the activity of man in seeking and utilizing medical knowledge. Human interference in the God-ordained process of birth, growth, decline and death may be seen as betraying faithful fulfillment of the commandments. A literal reading of a text in Exodus places all authority and capacity to heal in the hands of God. "I will not bring upon you any of the diseases that I brought upon the Egyptians, for I am the LORD your healer."[278] The Talmudic basis giving physicians the extended responsibility to interpose themselves in situations requiring medical assistance and introduce medical technology is derived from a passage dealing with compensation for personal injury. "When men quarrel and one strikes the other with stone or fist, and he does not die but has to take to his bed—if he then gets up and walks outdoors upon his staff, the assailant shall go unpunished, except he must pay for his idleness and his cure."[279] Whatever the initial intent of the verses, the Talmud expands the rationale and comments, "The School of R[abbi] Ishmael taught: [The words] 'And to heal he shall heal'[280] [is the source] whence it is derived that authorization was granted [by God] to the medical man to heal."[281]

Basic to Jewish law is the principle that there must be a clear distinction between suicide[282] and passive termination of life as well as active and voluntary euthanasia. All three terms share in one basic principle. Human beings have the ability to hasten death. In this context, euthanasia is a word derived from the Greek linguistic elements *eu* plus *thana(os)* to mean to induce a gentle and easy death.[283] The parallel Hebrew term is *mitah yafah*, a pleasant death.[284] This term is first used in a discussion of a judicial execution. As an extension to the Levitical exhortation that one should "love your neighbor as yourself,"[285] it was determined that a condemned criminal should be executed mercifully.[286] The authoritative Talmudic commentator Rashi redefines "nice death" to mean "that he should die quickly."[287] An astute liberal rabbinic scholar links these concepts to assist us in understanding euthanasia.

> The connection between time and suffering brings us to the issue of euthanasia. Were the dying person not suffering, were that person perfectly comfortable, in possession of his/her faculties, the issue would never arise! Suffering causes it to arise. Every human being, after all, every day and every moment, moves toward the grave; if life be free from suffering and full of delight, who would think of speeding there? Euthanasia presents itself as an option only when a person is dying and suffering and there seems no possibility of reversing the first condition or palliating the second. The two elements of euthanasia, then, are death, death which is imminent, and suffering, suffering which cannot be controlled.[288]

The Conservative rabbinate has taken a firm position opposing assisted suicide. Rabbi Elliot Dorff, rector at the University of Judaism, wrote a responsum on behalf of the Committee on Jewish Law and Standards of the Rabbinic Assembly, which resolutely affirms the traditional stance. After an exhaustive discussion of the moral, legal and psychological rationales involved in this painful question, the conclusion is lucid and absolute. A Jew may not commit suicide, ask others to help in committing suicide, or assist in the suicide of someone else.

Withholding or withdrawing machines or medications from a terminally ill patient, however, does not constitute suicide and is permitted. In my view, but not in [the view of a minority member of the committee] one may also withhold or withdraw artificial nutrition and hydration from such a patient, for that too falls outside the prohibitions of suicide and assisted suicide.[289]

There is a tendency in many modern Orthodox Jewish ethics and legal studies to assert as a truism that Judaism is unalterably opposed to euthanasia. "One may not hasten death .... To shorten the life of a person, even a life of agony and suffering, is forbidden ... [I]t is equivalent to murder."[290] This is a direct response to the stricture in the biblically mandated specification of medical ethics. "And provide that he be healed, yes, healed."[291] This leads to the peremptory denial of any form of euthanasia. A prominent scholar of our time has stated this position with vigor. "The practice of euthanasia - whether active or passive - is contrary to the teachings of Judaism. Any positive act designed to hasten the death of the patient is equated with murder in Jewish law ... No matter how laudable the intentions of the person performing the act of mercy-killing may be, his deed constitutes an act of homicide."[292]

An early and oft-quoted example of refusal to accelerate death by euthanasia is that of Rabbi Hananiah ben Teradyon, the second- century martyr who was executed by the Romans in 135 C.E. by burning him at the stake for violating the edict prohibiting the teaching of Jewish law. As the flames were enveloping him his students called out, "Open thy mouth [they said] so that the fire enter into thee [and put an end to his agony]. He replied, 'Let Him who gave me [my soul] take it away, but no one should injure himself [i.e. hasten his own death.]."[293] A modern commentator reminds us that this was a refusal on his part to commit suicide but that Rabbi Hananiah[294] permitted the executioner to remove impediments that were delaying his death.[295]

In another tractate of the Talmud the principle is enunciated with clarity, "a dying person (*goses*) is considered as a living being in all respects."[296] The text elaborates, "one may not bind his jaws, nor plug up his openings, nor place a vessel of metal or an object that cools on his navel until he dies, as it is written (in Ecclesiastes)[297] 'Before the silver cord (i.e. spinal column) is snapped asunder.'"[298] Moreover, one may "not close the eyes of a dying person. One who touches it or moves it is shedding blood. Rabbi Meir used to cite an example of a flickering light. As soon as a person touches it, it goes out. So too, whoever closes the eyes of the dying it is as if he has taken his soul."[299]

The prohibition against hastening one's death is reiterated and emphasized in another Talmudic tractate. The Mishnah states, "one may not close the eyes of a corpse on the Sabbath, nor on weekdays when he is about to die, and he who closes the eyes [of a dying person] at the point of departure of the soul is a shedder of blood (i.e. a murderer because he hastens death.)"[300] The Gemara continues the inquiry, "Our Rabbis taught: He who closes [the eyes of a dying man] at the point of death is a murderer. This may be compared to a lamp that is going out. If a man places his finger upon it, it is immediately extinguished."[301] There is a minority dissenting opinion from Rabbi Simeon Ben Gamliel, which is analogous to termination of treatment. "If one desires that a dead man's eyes should close, let him blow wine into his nostrils and apply oil between his two eyelids ... then they close of their own accord."[302]

Maimonides insisted that a dying person must be regarded as a living being in every respect. "It is not permitted to bind his jaws, to stop the organs of the lower extremities, or to place metallic or cooling vessels upon his navel in order to prevent swelling .... One should wait awhile, perhaps he is only in a swoon."[303] The respected legal codification of the fourteenth century, the *Arba'ah Turim*,[304] prohibits any hastening of death. "Any act performed in relation to death should not be carried out until the soul has departed."[305] As there is disagreement concerning whether one can sanction or facilitate the hastening of death, there is also no agreement that there is no religious obligation to hinder the end of life. The Talmud clearly states that if a person is in the throes of death, and is thus in the legal state of a *goses*, one should stop praying for recovery that the sufferer might know the serenity of death.[306] An often-cited example is that of Rabbi Judah Ha-Nasi, Judah the Prince. He was in agony on his deathbed. The Talmud, reflecting a belief in the possible immediate efficacy of prayer, approvingly tells the tale of his final moments. His soul was prevented from leaving his body because of the ardent and fervent prayers of his students.[307] Rabbi Judah's maidservant, not obsessed with theological considerations nor restrained by legal credentials, abruptly threw an earthen vessel to the ground. The crashing sound distracted the praying rabbis and the soul was then given the opportunity to flee the body and find rest.[308] Other rabbinic authorities assert that no effort can be withheld from attempting to prolong life. To emphasize the importance of this principle, it is stated that even the sanctity of the Sabbath may be desecrated in order to preserve a life.[309] With the exception of the three immoral and heinous infractions of murder, idolatry and sexual offenses, preservation of life takes precedence over all other Jewish principles.[310] Until very recently the attitude of both orthodox and liberal rabbis was that termination of treatment was not permitted.[311] The exigencies of modern life and the pressures created by new medical technologies have caused some modification in the thinking of some rabbis. A reform rabbi asks the fundamental questions when he speculates about those who would choose the hour of their own death. "Increasingly, the time and circumstances of death are no longer entrusted either to chance or to God; unlike every age before, people are planning, preparing, and controlling the circumstances of their death.[312] Equally, there are those who doubt the certainty of those who would affirm ancient principles without doubt and those who would assert modern standards without hesitancy. "The decision is individual but the context is more than personal. The autonomy [to end ones life] is genuine but it is exercised in terms of realities as real as one's self."[313] A creative and authoritative thinker in the orthodox movement, Daniel Sinclair, principal of Jew's College of London, has indicated that *halakhah* permits patients to predetermine their limitations of medical care when faced with a terminal illness.[314] He cites an Israeli case[315] where a dying man's gift was cited in support of a decision to honor the advance directives of a woman not to have her life maintained by artificial means.[316] He noted that "the court cited the Talmudic dictum[317] that 'it is a religious obligation to carry out the instructions of a dying man.'"[318]

Is it possible to affirm that there is a clear difference between the passive acceptance of death and an act, which hastens death which can only be morally judged to be assisted suicide. How does one differentiate when a medication, which is intended as a palliative, accelerates the process toward death? A Jewish physician has written:

> Let me acknowledge that I would prescribe morphine to ease the pain, even though that would probably hasten death ... My primary intent is to give comfort ... but the agent of death is not the

disconnected respirator; it is the disease .... But I have not assisted in a suicide. How different the situation is when persons suffering with fatal illnesses ask and receive help in taking their own lives.[319]

At the same time a radical theological activist with great influence, Rabbi Alvin Reines, has written:

A Reform Jew has a moral right to commit suicide. ... If a person assists, that is, aids and abets a Reform Jew to commit suicide at the request (which, of course, necessarily implies consent) of the latter, the former has behaved morally. (An example of assisting a person to commit suicide is the case where a physician, at the request of the person hands her/him a needle filled with a fatal substance with instructions on how to use it, and she/he then injects her/him-self.)....If a person takes a Reform Jew's life at the request of the latter, then the former has performed a moral act. Another name for such an action is "voluntary euthanasia."[320]

A direct and immediate response to the lenient and permissive theology of Reines is that of Zlotowitz and Selzter, both influential thinkers in the liberal Reform Jewish movement. "It must be therefore stated at the outset that, in keeping with historic Jewish tradition which affirms life, Reform Judaism does not condone the deliberate taking of one's life by someone who is of sound mind."[321]

The distinction between the passive acceptance of death and the active termination of life is a critical one in Jewish law.[322] When the parents of the child whose existence was being artificially maintained sat with the physician and the Jewish chaplain, their inchoate response to the facts and options being offered to them through their miasma of pain had to deal with this essential issue:[323] was the child really dead? Would the removal of the medical support apparatus kill their child? Would their agonizing decision kill their child? If they allowed the hospital to remove their child's organs for transplant, would that action kill their child?

These ethical issues are tangential to the moral problem presented in the case of the infant whose existence was continued by artificial means. Nonetheless, there is a correlation with the essential moral dilemma that faced the parents of the child when they sat with the physician and the hospital chaplain. The distinction between passive acceptance of death and the active termination of life is a critical issue in Jewish law. One must concede that there is not total unanimity with regard to the moral stance of Jewish thinking with regard to this technologically induced critical ethical issue. Nonetheless, in the prevailing and more widely accepted Jewish view, the voluntary removal of medical life sustaining equipment would constitute the hastening of death. But what if the hastening of one person's inevitable death could save the life of other people?

VII

It would appear that there is no or little legal opposition in secular law to the authority of a coroner to order an autopsy.[324] Where there is opposition to an action of a coroner, it is not to the performance of the autopsy. The conflict is based, as in *Brotherton v. Cleveland*,[325] on the action of the coroner in removing a body part from the deceased in violation of the wishes of the deceased and/or the wishes of the family members.[326] Following the autopsy, "the coroner permitted Steven Brotherton's corneas to be removed and used as anatomical gifts."[327] While one of the issues with which the court dealt was the constitutionality of the Ohio statute which allows a coroner to remove the corneas of an autopsy subject without consent,[328] there was no consideration of the right of the coroner to perform an autopsy. *Per contra*, where the circumstances are such as to warrant a coroner's inquiry, as in the case of a child who dies under suspicious circumstances, there is an undisputed statutory duty to perform an autopsy to determine the cause of death.[329]

The function of the medical examiner in deaths in which abuse may have played a part: [C]onsists of (1) determining the cause and manner of death to a reasonable degree of certainty; (2) providing expert evaluation of the presence, absence, nature, and significance of injuries and disease; (3) collecting and preserving evidence; (4) correlating clinical and pathologic findings; and (5) presenting expert opinions in the proper forums.[330]

The autopsy is a critical component in determining the cause of death. A major function of the autopsy performed by the medical examiner is to differentiate between the mechanism of death and the manner of death. The mechanism is a lethal physiologic derangement through which the cause of death acts.[331] The manner of death is the fashion in which the cause of death arises. "The manner of death is an opinion separate from the cause of death."[332] All child abuse deaths are homicidal, the killing of one human being by another. Defining it as homicide, however, does not determine the actuality of criminality. Criminal culpability is determined by the criminal justice system. Jewish law is uncomfortable with post mortem examinations. "Judaism requires that a corpse be accorded every sign of respect ... Physical assault upon the body is, *a fortiori*, forbidden in death as well as in life."[333] The prohibition against violating a body is based upon a biblical verse that refers to the treatment of a body of an executed criminal, " you must not let his corpse remain on the stake overnight, but must bury him the same day. For an impaled body is an affront to God."[334] The logic of Rabbi Ishmael's hermeneutic rule[335] applies. If the rule is applicable for a criminal who is executed for a capital crime, it can be deduced *a fortiori* that it should be applied to others who have not been convicted of heinous offenses.

The Talmud has two instructive references to autopsies. One incident involved the question of whether a corpse could be exhumed and examined to determine whether the deceased was an adult or a minor at the time of death. This examination was requested to determine the disposition of an estate. The petition was denied as the knowledge to be gained would only relate to the disposition of an estate and would not aid in the principle of *pikku'ah nefesh*,[336] the saving of a life.[337]

In the Talmud it is clearly stated that an autopsy may be performed on the victim of a murder in order to establish whether the victim was alive at the time of the assault. If he was not alive at the time of the assault, no charge of murder could be brought against the assailant.[338] This is somewhat different from the statutory regulations governing the coroner, which give authority to examine a body only where there is an unexplained or suspicious death.[339] It is worth noting, moreover, that if there is a disagreement between the provisions of Jewish law and the requirements of the governmental legal system, Jewish law would respond positively to the requirements of the state.[340]

The critical element in the response of Jewish law to the authority of the coroner to perform an autopsy is not in the Jewish attitude toward post mortem examinations. Rather, it is in the operative relationship, which exists between Jewish and governmental law in which Jewish law is subordinate to the law of the land. In the third century C.E., Samuel, one of the two preeminent legal scholars of the Babylonian-Jewish community, acknowledged the necessity and legitimacy of Jews to obey the laws of the various lands in which they lived. This still authoritative principle is *dina de-malkhuta dina*, "the law of the government is the law."[341] Parenthetically, it must be admitted that this principle is not as clear when relating to the intensely difficult moral questions that arise in the matters of brain death or organ donation. The differentiation between the response to post mortem examinations and the definitions of death and the process of giving organ donations relates to the simple reality that the post mortem examination is upon the body of one who is already dead. The other issues impact upon the living.

Dorff and Rosett see the doctrine of *dina de-malkhuta dina* as essentially annulling Jewish law in a situation where it must yield, because of the governing power of the law, to the secular authority. "Samuel's principle effectively abrogates Jewish law in the areas to which it is applied."[342] Elon views it as an accommodation to secular authority not because Jewish law may not be applicable but because it must accede to the regulations of the governing authority.[343] "Abraham b.(en) David (Rabad), a halackhic authority of the twelfth century C.E., laid down as a general proposition that whenever there is a lacuna in the law, it may be filled by resort to non-Jewish law."[344] Thus, the question of resisting the authority of the coroner's determination to perform an autopsy where the law mandates such a procedure would not be raised under the rubric of Jewish law.[345]

The question, which motivated this study, has non-conflicting contradictory answers. Has there been an influence of Anglo-American law upon Jewish law? Has American law been influenced, in any measure, by Jewish law? The response is a clear yes and no! It is obvious that there has been a congruent attempt by both systems of law to deal with the same new ethical and moral dilemma derived from advances in medical technology which confront us. Equally, in those areas of Jewish law which parallel secular law such as marriage and divorce, Jewish law has had to find ways to accommodate to the authoritative secular law. At the same time mechanisms, primarily arbitration, have been accepted by secular law to permit Jewish law to operate in areas of legal conflict.

Of greater import, in response to the question of the interrelationship of Jewish law and American law, has been the revivification of Jewish law in every aspect of American Jewish life. It is not an accident of modern history that the subject of *halakhah* has been given greater academic importance within all the streams of Jewish religious observance. One could well expect this emphasis in the orthodox community; one might anticipate greater stress on *halakhah* in adherents of the conservative movement. Of greater importance to me is the newly strengthened thrust of traditional *halakhic* norms upon the antinomian tendencies of the reform philosophy. *Ken Yirbu!*

Notes

1. "[W]e have had the experience of feeling our souls split—between our commitment to Judaism and our commitment to American life, between the pull of tradition and the insistence of the modern world, between our ties to our family and our need to play out our emerging selves." Harold Kushner, "Forward" to Milton Steinberg, *As a Driven Leaf*, New York, 1987.
2. "Elisha [ben Abuya] said reflectively ... That is the fantastic intolerable paradox of my life, that I have one question for what I possessed initially—a belief to invest my days with dignity and meaning, a pattern of behavior through which man might most articulately express his devotion to his fellows." *Id.* at 474.
3. See 7 *Encyclopaedia Judaica*, 1972, vol. 7, p. 1156. "The word '*Halakhah*,' ..the legal side of Judaism...embraces personal, social, national and international relationships, and all the other practices and observances of Judaism." See also *Random House Dictionary of the English Language*, New York, 1967, p. 637. It defines *halakhah* as "1. The entire body of Jewish law and traditions comprising the laws of the Bible, the oral law as transcribed in the legal portion of the Talmud, and subsequent legal codes amending or modifying traditional precepts to conform to contemporary conditions. 2. A law or tradition established by the *halakah*."
4. "Like other legal systems, the *halakhah* is composed of different elements, not all of equal value, since some are regarded as of Sinaitic origin others of rabbinical." *Encyclopaedia Judaica* 1157, " Sources of Authority."
5. But see 1 J. David Bleich, *Contemporary Halakhic Problems*, KTAV, New York, 1977, p. xiv. He states that "[t]he divine nature of Torah renders it immutable and hence not subject to amendment or modification." He further states that "[a]lthough the Torah itself is immutable, Sages teach that the interpretation of its many laws and regulations is entirely within the province of human intellect. Torah is divine but, '*lo ba-shamayim hi* – it is not in the heavens (Deut. 30:12) is to be interpreted and applied by man."
6. "These sentiments [of the Rabbinical Assembly] bespeak a lack of recognition of the fact that *halakhah* possesses an enduring validity which, while

applicable to changing circumstances, is not subject to change by lobbying or by the exertion of pressure in any guise or form. Nor may independently held convictions, however sincere, be allowed to influence our interpretation of *halakhah*. Normative Judaism teaches that *halakhah* is not derived from any temporal 'worldview' or 'social situation' but expresses the transcendental worldview of the Divine Lawgiver." Ibid., 83.

7. Solomon B. Freehof, *The Responsa Literature*, Jewish Publication Society, Philadelphia, 1955.

8. There is no reference to *halakhah* in the index. The equivalent term utilized is "rabbinic literature." Ibid., 13.

9. Ibid., 268 ff.

10. Ibid., 269.

11. Ibid.

12. Ibid., 270.

13. Ibid., 271.

14. A preeminent orthodox halakhist also comments upon this change in attitude toward halakhah in The United States. Bleich, op. cit., vol. 2, p. xi. It has been said that the page of a Gemara represents in capsule form the long history of Jewish exile. " The *Mishnah* was composed in *Erez Yisra'el*; the text of the Gemara which follows was written in Babylonia; Rashi's commentary hails from France; the *Tosafot* are the product of French and German schools; the marginal glosses represent Polish and Lithuanian scholarship; and finally, the blank space of the margins represent the American contribution to talmudic scholarship. Fortunately, this categorization of the American contribution is no longer correct. *Akhshar dara*; this generation has attained a level of Torah scholarship which far surpasses the fondest anticipations of a previous age."

15. His seminal works dealing with reform Jewish practice are the two volumes of *Reform Jewish Practice*, Union of American Hebrew Congregations, New York, 1955. They thus predate *The Responsa Literature* by two years. It is instructive to note his themes for those volumes. They include marriage and burial customs, synagogue architecture and ornamentation, women and children's participation in the religious services as well as relationships with Christians. Dr. Freehof notes: "[Reform Judaism] has not been creative in such great fields of Jewish law and practice as the dietary laws and the laws of Sabbath observance. This difference can hardly be accidental. The dietary laws and the laws of Sabbath observance, once so vital to Jewish life, have already dropped away from the lives of almost all Jews in the western world. There is still a small percentage of Jews which fully observes them, and a somewhat larger percentage which partially observes them, but at best, they play only a minor role in the actual living of modern Jews." Solomon B. Freehof, *Reform Jewish Practice*, Vol. 2, p. 4.

16. In largest measure the responsa dealt with those areas which parallel the issues found in three of the four sections of the *Shulhan Arukh*: *Orah Hayyim* which deals with the observance of the Sabbath and the Festivals, *Yorea Deah* which concerns mourning customs, and *Even ha-Ezer*, which deals with marriage and divorce.

17. For lists of approved responsa decisions of the Law Committee as well as official correspondence containing Law Committee rulings, see "The Sum-

mary Index of the Committee on Jewish Law and Standards" in *The Rabbinical Assembly*, New York, 1994. There are halakhically developed responsa dealing with such diverse subjects as biomedical issues, conversion, intermarriage, marriage and divorce, mourning and funerals, *kashrut*, women, as well as those dealing with holiday and festival observance.

18. J. David Bleich, *Contemporary Halakhic Problems*, 1977-1999 (a work of 6 volumes); *Responsa of Rav Moshe Feinstein: Translation and Commentary*, David Tendler (tr.), New York, 1998; *Crossroads: Halacha and the Modern World*, Zomet, Gush Etzion, 1987.

19. M. Baba Metzia 7:11.

20. Ketubot 56a.

21. It is explicitly mentioned four times. Nedarim 28a; Gittin 10b; Baba Kama 113a; Baba Basra 54b-55a.

22. Menachem Elon, *Jewish Law: History, Sources, Principles,* Jewish Publication Society, 1994, vol. 1, p. 59 1994. The legal rationale given by various later authorities for the source of the binding force of the king's law was that this binding force flows from an agreement between the people and the king, under which the people yield up to the king their prerogatives in all matters falling within the king's law, while the king obligates himself to preserve and protect the people. This rationale applies to every form of government, and certainly to one chosen by the people."

23. Ibid., 72.

24. "In theory the Jewish legal system [during the middle ages] was regarded as self-sufficient, but in practice the Jewish courts and jurists (i.e., the halakhists) did not entirely disregard legal rulings and enactments emanating from non Jewish sources." Jacob Katz, *Exclusiveness and Tolerance*, 1961, p. 53.

25. See State *ex rel.* Fowler v. Moore, 46 Nev. 65, 207 (1922).

26. "An act of Congress providing that the power of every territory shall extend to all rightful subjects of legislation not inconsistent with the Constitution and laws of the United States has been construed as operating as a delegation of authority to control marriages." Simms v. Simms, 175 U.S. 162 (1899).

27. Examples abound of court cases, which assert the power of a legislature to issue a license to officiate at a marriage to an officer designated by statute. *See* Brewer v. Kingsberry, 69 Ga. 754 (1882). There were, as well, cases asserting that the officiant must be in full compliance with the authorizing statute. *See* People v. Schoonmaker, 119 Mich. 242 (1917).

28. "The state has the sovereign power to regulate marriages." Henderson v. Henderson, 199 Md. 449 (1952).

29. "Marriage is a civil contract entered into by a male and a female not under such disability as to render the ceremony void…the marriage must be duly solemnized. Besides the agreement of the parties there must be a license and a ceremony performed by an authorized person before witness…without a license and a ceremony there is no marriage." People v. MacDonald, 24 Cal. App. 2d 702 (1938).

30. "Rabbis should not officiate without a state license, for when they perform *kiddushin* they are considered to act as officers of the state who give the union standing in civil law." *Rabbi's Manual*, Central Conference of American Rabbis, New York, 1988, p. 246.

31. M. Baba Metziah 1:5.

32. Baba Metziah, 12a-12b.
33. *Encyclopaedia Judaica*, vol. 16, p. 586.
34. Kid. 50b.
35. See Elon, op. cit., note 22.
36. "There is no common-law right of divorce. Divorce is purely a matter of statute." Jelm v. Jelm, 155 Ohio St. 226 (1951). See also Larsen v. Ericson, 222 Minn 363 (1946)(stating that " [i]n the United States, all divorce jurisdiction is statutory"). People *ex rel*. Doty v. Connell, 9 Ill.2d 390 (1956); Bernatavicius v. Bernatavicius, 259 Mass. 486 (1927).
37. Coleman v. Coleman, 32 Ohio St.2d 155, 161 (1970).
38. The *Get* is considered to be a bill of divorcement but it is, more properly, an authorization to remarry. "Thus do I see free, release thee, and put thee aside, in order that thou may have permission and the authority over thyself to go and marry man though may desire. No person may hinder thee from this day onward, and thou art permitted to every man." *Encyclopaedia Judaica*, vol. 6, p. 131.
39. "Reform congregations recognize civil divorce as completely dissolving the marriage, and permit remarriage of the divorced persons." Freehof, *Reform Jewish Practice*, vol. 1, p. 99.
40. A major difficulty is the *Agunah*, a "married woman who for whatsoever reason is separated from her husband and cannot remarry, either because she cannot obtain a divorce from him or because it is unknown whether he is still alive." *Encyclopaedia Judaica*, vol. 2, p. 429 . Rabbi Emanuel Rackman, an eminent leader in the orthodox community, has attempted to ameliorate this difficulty by establishing a unique Bet Din which convenes only for the purpose of granting women whose husbands refuse to grant them a religious divorce an annulment in lieu of a *Get*. This action has him "embroiled in a bitter dispute that has pitted him against virtually the entire spectrum of the Orthodox rabbinate." Nadine Brozan, "Annulling a Tradition: Rabbis Stir Furor by Helping 'Chained Women' to Leave Husbands," *N.Y.Times*, Aug. 13, 1998.
41. A most unusual example of a traditional halakhic method for dealing with a recalcitrant woman who refuses to accept a *get* was recently reported in the news. "Mrs. [Chayie Singer…filed suit last month in Supreme Court in Manhattan against the Union of Orthodox Rabbis of the United States and Canada; the Bed Din Zedek of America, a rabbinical court, and five individual rabbis … She is seeking $13 million in damages…[Mrs. Sieger said,] I got a letter from Chaim's attorney, Abe Konstam, stating, 'As you are aware, a rabbinical divorce has already been granted.' Without informing her, the rabbis had used the Heter Meah Rabonim, which was introduced centuries ago to give men whose wives are mentally incapacitated, unconscious or unwilling to accept a *get* the right to take a second wife. It is not technically a Jewish divorce but is a way of releasing a man in an untenable situation from the bonds of marriage. It requires the signatures of 100 rabbis in three countries attesting to the woman's inability to accept the *get*." Nadine Brozan, " Women Sue Rabbis, Alleging Betrayal in Divorce Cases," *N.Y. Times*, December 14, 1998.
42. "*Hatan* and *kallah* agreed that should there be any contemplation of the dissolution of this marriage, or in the event of its dissolution in the civil courts, they will respond to the summons each may make to the other to appear

before the *Beit Din* of the Rabbinical Assembly and the Jewish Theological Seminary of America or its representative. They are committed to abide by its rulings and instructions, so that they both may live according to the laws and teachings of our sacred Torah." *Ketubah*, in Rabbinical Assembly, 1990.

43. The text that follows has no statement of authorship. "Prenuptial Agreement, Husband's Assumption of Obligation. I, the undersigned husband to be, hereby obligate myself to support my wife to be in the manner of Jewish husbands who feed and support their wives loyally, If, God forbid, we not continue domestic residence together for whatever reason, then I obligate myself, as of now, to pay to her $....per day (indexed to the consumer price index as of December 31st following the date of our marriage) for food and support (*parnasa*) for the duration of our Jewish marriage, which is payable each week during the time due, under any circumstances, even if she has another source of income or earnings. Furthermore, I waive my *halakhic* rights to my wife's earnings for the period that she is entitled to the above-stipulated sum. However, this obligation shall terminate if my wife refuses to appear upon due notice before a *Bet Din* for purpose of a hearing concerning any outstanding disputes between us, or in the event that she fails to abide by the decision or recommendation of such *Bet Din*. I execute this document as an inducement to the marriage between myself and my wife to be. The obligations and conditions contained herein are executed according to all legal and halachic (*sic*) requirements. I acknowledge that I have effected the above obligation by means of a *kinyan* (formal Jewish transaction) in an esteemed (*chashuv*) *Bet Din*.

    I have been given the opportunity, prior to executing this document, of consulting with a rabbinic advisor and a legal advisor.

44. The text that follows has no statement of authorship. Only the pertinent sections are quoted. Should a dispute arise between the parties after they are married, Heaven forbid, so that they do not live together as husband and wife, they agree to refer their marital dispute to an arbitration panel, namely, the *Bet Din* of....for a binding decision. Each of the parties agrees to appear in person before the Bet Din at the demand of the other party. The decision of the panel, or a majority of them, shall be fully enforceable in any court of competent jurisdiction. (c) The parties agree that the Bet Din shall apply the equitable distribution law of the State/Province of...., as interpreted as of the date of this agreement, to any property disputes which may arise between them, the division of their property and to questions of support. This agreement constitutes a fully enforceable arbitration agreement. The parties acknowledge that each of them have been given the opportunity prior to signing this agreement to consult with their own rabbinic advisor and legal advisor.

45. "In any decision made pursuant to this subdivision the courts shall, where appropriate, consider the effect of a barrier to remarriage, as defined in subsection six of section two hundred and fifty three of this article, on the factors enumerated in paragraph (d) of this sub-division." N.Y. Dom. Rel. Law § 236B:5 (McKinney 1992). §253 (6) limits "barriers to remarriage" to situations where a *get* is withheld. *See* Michael Broyde, The Pursuit of Justice and Jewish Law 139 (1996).

46. *Rabbinical Courts: Modern Day Solomons*, 6 Colum. J.L. & Soc. Probs. 49, 50 (1970).

47. Ex. 18:13-27.

48. M San. 1:1.

49. Ibid., 1:1, 3:1.

50. San. 14a " R. Joshua b. Levi said: 'There is no ordination outside Palestine.' What is to be understood by, 'There is no ordination?' Shall we assert that they have no authority at all to adjudicate cases of *kenas* outside Palestine? But have we not learned, 'The *Sanhedrin* has competence both within and without Palestine?' This must therefore mean that ordination cannot be conferred outside Palestine."

51. The need to establish this quasi-judicial authority in the Diaspora was resolved by the Talmudic rabbis in Babylon. Our rabbis taught:" Monetary cases are decided by three, but one who is a recognized *Mumheh* may judge alone. R. Nahman said: One like myself may adjudicate monetary cases alone. And so said R. Hiyya." The following problem was consequently propounded: Does the statement "one like myself" mean that as I have learned traditions and am able to reason them out, and have also obtained authorization, so must he who wishes to render a legal decision alone , but that if he has not obtained authorization, his judgment is invalid? Come and hear! Mar Zutra, the son of R. Nahman, judged a case alone and gave an erroneous decision. On appearing before R. Joseph he was told: If both parties accepted you as their judge, you are not liable to make restitution. Otherwise, go and indemnify the injured party. Hence it can be inferred that the judgment of one, though not authorized, is valid. Rav said: Whosoever wishes to decide monetary cases by himself and be free from liability in cases of erroneous decision, should obtain authorization from the Resh Galuta. And Samuel said the same thing San 4b ff. See also R. Judah Lowe (1520- 1609): "In some countries and in some communities they turn justice into wormwood. They have set up ignorant men as authorities, men who know not the meaning of justice and law. It has reached a point where those who are qualified, the real scholars, see with their own eyes the perversion of justice ... and they are helpless even in redressing the cause of an orphan or a widow ... The true sages have no opportunity to correct the vile conditions of this generation, for those in power tell them 'you are not our *Ab Bet Din* that we need be obliged to listen to you.' It is indeed more difficult to bear their yoke than the yoke of the gentiles. For when they sense that there be one who does not respect them and does not want to recognize their authority, they seek to subdue and oppress and persecute him with every kind of persecution ... It is indeed a virtuous deed to show contempt for such men. The hands of Esau ordained them." Ben Zion Bokser, *From the World of the Cabbalah*, New York, p. 39.

52. Arbitration is encouraged in various Talmudic sources and utilization of the court system is discouraged. M. Baba Metzia 20, Moed Katan 18 as well as Sanhedrin,t , 2b–3a, 3b, 6a–6b.

53. David M. Shochet, Jewish Court in the Middle Ages , New York, 1931. Israel Goldstein, *Jewish Justice and Conciliation*, New York, 1981.

54. The settlers in colonial New England "deliberately chose as their governing legal systems the laws of the ancient Hebrew." BERNARD MEISLIN, JEWISH LAW IN AMERICAN TRIBUNALS 1 (1976).

55. Morris Schappes, *A Documentary History of the Jews of the United States*, Jewish Publication Society, Philadelphia, 1971, p. 20.

56. "The American Jew was not ghettoized. He was not separated by an act of state from his fellow man. He desired to be an American in spirit. Concerned for integration, he sought it and attained it." Jacob Rader Marcus, *Memoirs of American Jews*, 1955, vol. 1, p. 15.

57. Jerald S. Auerbach, *Justice Without Law*, 1983, p. 73.

58. "Perhaps the most important reason for their inhibition from going to the courts for the vindication of their grievances was their lack of confidence that non-Jewish judges were possessed of the ability to understand in a mean-ingful way – to pierce through the 'veil' of – the particularly Jewish charac-ter or background of the subject matter which was the core of their differences with the other party to the controversy." Simon Agranat, "Pref-ace" to Goldstein, note 53, xvi.

59. Auerbach, op. cit., note 57, p. 76.

60. *Dina de-malkhuta dina*, "the law of the government is the law." Elon, op. cit., vol. 1, note 22.

61. Auerbach, Op. Cit., note 57p. 77; Shochet, Op. Cit., note 53, p. 96.

62. Yad Hil. San. 26:7.

63. Zechariah 8:16.

64. II Sam. 8:15.

65. Yad, Hil. San. 22.4.

66. "Magnes developed a plan for neighborhood rabbinical judges to answer questions of ritual and mediate minor disputes. Their participation in dis-pute settlement was intended to restore a traditional rabbinical function, but it could not restore the rabbinate to its traditional place in the Jewish com-munity. The rabbis resolved a restricted sphere of ritual issues for a dwin-dling constituency." Auerbach, Op. Cit., note 57, p. 79.

67. "Jews have shown a special preference for the clothing trades. According to official reports, three-fourths of the workmen in these trades in New York are Jews…The instability of the Jewish unions has been ascribed to the Jew, who has in inborn desire to be 'his own boss.' …The clothing trade in its begin-nings requiring little capital, the development of the clothing industry in New York within recent years has been marked, in contrast with the general trend of the time, by a tendency toward small-scale production." "Trade-Unionism," *Encyclopaedia Judaica*, vol. 12, p. 217 .

68. Robert St. John, *Jews, Justice and Judaism* , New York, 1959, p. 269.

69. Auerbach, op. cit., p. 80.

70. B.H. Hartogenesis, *A Successful Community Court*, 12 J. Amer. Jud. Soc. (1929).

71. Goldstein, op. cit., p. 88

72. New York State Arbitration Law and Civil Practice Act 1920

73. The title of the court was changed to Jewish Conciliation Court in 1930 and was later amended to Jewish Conciliation Board of America. Goldstein, Op. Cit., p. xvii.

74. Ibid., xvii.

75. Riess v. Murchison, 384 F.2d 727, 734 (9th Cir. 1967); Sewer v. Paragon Homes, 351 F. Supp. 596, 598 (D. V.I. 1972).; *In re* Columbia Broad. Sys., Inc., 205 N.Y.S.2d 85, 89 (Sup. Ct. 1960).

76. United Steelworkers of America v. Warrior & Gulf Nav. Co., 363 U.S. 574, 582 (1960).

77. Erving v. Virginia Squires Basketball Club, 468 F.2d 1064, 1068 (2d Cir. 1972) (stating "[w]here federal law is applicable, it should be implemented in such way as to make arbitration effective and not to erect technical and insubstantial barriers," and "[w]here parties have elected to submit their differences to arbitration, courts should not by hair-splitting decisions hamstring its operation"). *But See* Franks v. Franks, 1 N.E.2d 14, 15 (Mass. 1936) (stating "[c]ompliance with statute regarding arbitration is jurisdictional requirement to validity of final award"). Hous. Auth. of New Orleans v. Henry Ericsson Co., 2 So.2d 195, 200 (La. 1941) (stating "[g]enerally a submission to arbitration under a statute must conform to statute in every essential particular").

78. Lundgren v. Freeman, 307 F.2d 104, 109 (9th Cir. 1962); Acme Cut Stone Co. v. New Center Dev. Corp., 281 Mich. 32 (1937).

79. Funk v. Funk 6 Ariz. App 527, 531 (1967). ; Maxwell Shapiro Woolen Co. v. Amerotron Corp., 158 N.E.2d 875, 880 (Mass. 1959).

80. Wachusett Spinning Mills, Inc. 183 N.Y.S.2d 601, 603 (App. Div. 1959).

81. New York case law recognizes the authority of Jewish law by analogy as it is a foreign system of law. "A foreign arbitration is valid and will be enforced where the parties voluntarily appear, where opportunity for a hearing is given, where the arbitrators are shown to have been appointed and to have acted in a manner valid under the laws of the place of arbitration, and where no prejudice or fraud is shown." Coudenhove-Kalergi v. Dieterle, 36 N.Y.S.2d 313 (Sup. Ct. 1942).

82. " A Board of rabbinical arbitrators selected by husband and wife to settle their marital and financial disputes may apply legal, moral and religious law to the dispute between the parties as to recovery of an alleged sum lent by the wife to her husband." Berk v. Berk, 171 N.Y.S.2d 592, 593 (Sup. Ct. 1957).

83. "Whatever position the Jewish law may take today regarding the probating of wills and settling of estates, the civil law of the State of New York must be applied and is the only law this court can consider." *In re* Will of Jacobovitz, 295 N.Y.S.2d 527, 531 (Sur. Ct. 1968).

84. Agur v. Agur, 298 N.Y.S.2d 772, 776 (App. Div. 1969).

85. *Berk*, 171 N.Y.S.2d at 592-93.

86. Steve Levin, *Disputes Resolved in Jewish Courts, Pittsburgh Post-Gazette,* Aug. 10, 1997.

87. "Legal process ... in which a child's legal rights and duties toward his natural parents are terminated and similar rights and duties toward his adoptive parents are substituted." *Black's Law Dictionary,* 1979, (ed. 5th), p. 45.

88. "[Adoption] ... whereby a person takes another person into the relation of a child and thereby acquires the rights and incurs the responsibilities of parent." *In re* Adoption of Robert Paul P., 63 N.Y.S.2d 233, 236 (1984).

89. "The most reliable and recent data comes from 1992...The number of adoptions reported was 127,441 [of which] two thirds were adopted by stepparents or relatives...the other third, or about 43,000 [are adaptable]...and less than 2 percent of unmarried pregnant women are placing their babies for adoption." Laura Mansnerus, *Market Puts Price Tags on the Priceless: In Search of a Child,* N.Y. TIMES, Oct. 26, 1998, at A14.

90. Ibid. "A tangle of state law has made adoption all but impossible to navigate without professional help. Disparate provisions govern, among other things, lawyers roles, residency requirements and birth mothers' consent."

91. "'Open adoption' is one in which final judgment incorporates parties' pre-adoption written agreement that the child will have continuing contact with one or more members of his or her biological family after adoption is competed." New Jersey Div. of Youth and Family Servs. v. B.G.S., 677 A.2d 1170, 1177 (1996).

92. Tammy M. Somogye, *Opening Minds to Open Adoption*, 45 Kan. L. Rev. 619 (1997).

93. U.S. Const. amend. X.

94. John M. Stoxen, *The Best of Both "Open" And "Closed" Adoption Worlds: A Call for the Reform of State Statutes*, 13 Notre Dame J. Legis. 292 (1986).

95. Burton Z. Sokoloff, *Antecedents of American Adoption, in* 3 The Future Of Children 17 (Richard E. Behrman ed., 1993).

96. "Adoption has been characterized a status created by the state acting as *parens patriae*." 2 Am. Jur. 2d *Adoption* § 1 (1986).

97. All States had enacted adoption statutes by 1931. Stoxen, *supra* note 95, at 298.

98. Lisa Diane G., 537 A.2d 131, 132 (R.I. 1988).

99. Unif. Adoption Act, 9 U.L.A. 15 (1969).

100. "(2) all papers and records pertaining to the adoption whether part of the permanent record of the Court or of a file in the [Department of Welfare] or in an agency are subject to inspection only upon consent of the Court and all interested persons; or in exceptional cases, only upon an order of the Court for good cause shown; and (3) except as authorized in writing by the adoptive parent, the adopted child if [14] or more years of age, or upon order of the court for good cause shown in exceptional cases, no person is required to disclose the name or identify of either an adoptive parent or an adopted child." *Id.* at § 16.

101. Alaska Stat. §§ 25.23.005 to .240 (Michie 1974); Ark. Code Ann. §§ 9-9-201 to -224 (Michie 1977); Mont. Code Ann. §§ 40-8-101 to -202 (1957); N.D. Cent. Code §§ 14-15-01 to -23 (1971); Ohio Rev. Code Ann. §§ 3107.01-.19 (Banks-Baldwin 1995).

102. Joan Heifetz Hollinger, *Adoption Law, in* 3 The Future of Children, *supra* note 96, p. 43.

103. *See* 3 Ibid. p. 49.

104. *See* 3 Ibid. p. 50.

105. *See* Sokoloff, *supra* note 96, p. 21.

106. Mansnerus, *supra* note 89.

107. "The evidence for adoption in the Bible is so equivocal that some have denied that it was practiced in the biblical period." *Encyclopaedia Judaica*, vol. 2, p. 298.

108. 2 Ibid., p. 301.

109. *Encyclopaedia Judaica*, vol. 3, p. 217.

110. M. Git. 5:4.

111. "And they assembled all the congregation together on the first day of the second month, and they declared their pedigrees after their families." Num. 1:18 and Gunther Plaut, *The Torah: A Modern Commentary*, Union of American Hebrew Congregations, New York, 1981, Num. 1:18: "And on the first day of the second month they convoked the whole community, who were registered by the class of their ancestral houses."

112. "All the rights and privileges of the *Kohen*, as well as the prohibitions apply among Orthodox Jews today." *Encyclopaedia Judaica*, vol. 13, p. 1089.
113. *Shulkhan Arukh, Orah Hayyim* 23: 9.
114. *Kitzur Schulhan Arukh Even ha-Ezer* 100:1.
115. *Shulkhan Arukh, Hoshen Mishpat* 164:1.
116. Ibid., 202:1.
117. "Even nowadays, a priest is prohibited from becoming ritually defiled. The highest grade of such defilement occurs if a *kohen* touches a dead body or is present under the same roof with a dead body. Therefore, a *kohen* should not study to become a male-nurse [or physician]." Abraham Steinberg, *Medical-Halachic Decisions of Rabbi Shlomo Zalman Auerbach (1910-1995)*, Assia, Jan. 1997, at 37.
118. *Kitzur Schulchan Aruch.*
119. *Rabbi's Manual*, p. 235.
120. "There are t hree [persons] who drive the *Shekhinah* from the world…[the second is]he who cohabits with the daughter of a gentile." Bleich, Op. Cit., 2, p. 268 (quoting *Zohar, Shemot* 3b).
121. "The Halakhah with regard to the children of a union between a Jew and a non-Jew is well established. The child acquires the religious status of the mother." Ibid., 103. *See also Kiddushin* 68b. "Your son by an Israelite woman is called your son, but your son by a heathen is not called your son [but her son.]"
122. "The general prohibition against incest with one's 'near of kin' (Lev. 18:6) has been held to be limited to the following degrees on consanguinity: parents (18:7); mother-in-law (20:14); stepmother (18:8); sister and half sister (18:9)…" *Encyclopaedia Judaica*, vol. 8, p. 1316 .
123. "According to *Halakhah*, a bastard is defined as a child born of an adulterous or incestuous relationship and may marry only a person of similar birth or a convert. A *mamzer* [bastard] is forbidden to marry a Jew of legitimate birth." Bleich, Op. Cit., vol. 1, p. 159.
124. "[Sages] did not make pronouncements based upon traditions derived from the prophets, which they had in those matters, but rather because they had knowledge on these subjects in terms of the general level of knowledge of those generations, or they became aware of those opinions from those who were knowledgeable in those generations." Dov I. Frimer, "Establishing Paternity By Means of Blood Type Testing," *Assia*, May 1989, p. 22.
125. Moses Maimonides, *Guide to the Perplexed*, (Chaim Rabin tr.), 1947.
126. "We would not need a 100% reliability of blood test results. Inasmuch as a 'majority' is sufficient (e.g. 'a majority of a woman's sexual unions are [held to be]with her husband'), the *halachah* would accept reliable blood test results together with other evidence, whether positive or negative, which have a greater than 50% degree of reliability." Frimer, Op. Cit., p. 27.
127. This would not make determinations with regard to such questions as personal status as a *kohen*. It would, however, eliminate the potential for incest.
128 Van Rensselaer Potter, *Bioethics*, New York, 1971.
129. Alan M. Sokobin, "A Child Was Killed: Shaken Baby Syndrome; A Comparative Study: Anglo-American Law and Jewish Law; Legal, Moral and Ethical Issues," University of Toledo Review, 1998, vol. 29.

130. Marshall Kapp, "Treating Medical Charts near the End of life," Ibid., p.. 524. (1997).

131. George J. Annas, "The Incompetent's Right to Die: The Case of Joseph Saikewicz," Hastings Center Report, 1978, vol. 8, Feb, p. 21.

132. Evans v. People, 49 N.Y. 86, 90 (1872).

133. "Report of Ad Hoc Committee of Harvard Medical School to Examine the Definition of Brain Death," JAMA, 1968, vol. 205, p. 337.

134. Immanuel Jakobovits, "Halakhic Debate on Brain Death," 41 *Le'ela*, 1996, p. 29 .

135. *Report of President's Commission for Study of Ethical Problems in Medicine and Biomedical and Behavioral Research on Defining Death,* 1981; Compton, "Telling the Time of Human Death by Statute," Wash. & Lee Law Rev, 1974, vol. 31, p. 521; Alexander M. Capron & Leon R. Kass, "A Statutory Definition of the Standards for Determining Human Death: An Appraisal and a Proposal," U. Pa. Law. Rev., 1972, vol 121, pp. 87, 87-92.

136. "Report of Ad Hoc Committee of Harvard Medical School to Examine the Definition of Brain Death," p. 134.

137. Unif. Determination of Death Act § 1, 12A U.L.A. 593 (1996).

138. 1970 Kan. Sess. Laws ch. 378, § 1 (codified as amended at KAN. STAT. ANN. § 77-204 (1995).

139. Thirty-two states, the District of Columbia, and the Virgin Islands have statutorily adopted the Uniform Determination of Death Act. UNIF. DETER-MINATION OF DEATH ACT, 12A U.L.A. 589 (1996). *See* ARK. CODE ANN. § 20-17-1010 (Michie 1995); CAL. HEALTH & SAFETY CODE § 7180 (West 1997); COLO. REV. STAT. ANN. § 12-36-136 (West 1997); DEL. CODE ANN. tit. 24, § 1760 (1996); D.C. CODE ANN. 1981 § 6-2401 (1997); GA. CODE ANN. § 31-10-16 (1997); IDAHO CODE § 54-1819 (1997); IND CODE § 1-1-4-3 (1997); KAN. STAT. ANN. § 77-204 to 77-206 (1996); ME. REV. STAT. ANN. tit. 22 §§ 2811 to 2813 (West 1997); MD. CODE ANN., HEALTH-GEN. § 5-202 (1997); MICH. COMP. LAWS ANN. §§ 33.1031 to 33.1034 (1997); MINN. STAT. ANN § 145.135 (West 1997); MISS. CODE ANN. §§ 41-36-1, 41-36-3 (1997); MO. ANN. STAT. § 194.005 (West 1996); MONT. CODE ANN. § 50-22-101 (1996); NEB. REV. STAT. §§ 71-7201 to 71-7203 (1996); NEV. REV. STAT. § 451.007 (1995); N.H. REV. STAT. ANN. §§ 141-D1, 141-D2 (1996); N.M. STAT. ANN. § 12-2-4 (1997); N.D. CENT. CODE § 23-06.3-01 (1997); OHIO REV. CODE ANN. § 2108.30 (Banks-Baldwin 1997); OKLA. STAT. ANN. tit. 63, §§ 3121 to 3123 (1997); OR. REV. STAT. § 432.300 (1995); PA. STAT. ANN. tit. 35, §§ 10202 to 10203 (1996); R.I. GEN LAWS § 23-4-16 (1996); S.C. CODE ANN. §§ 44-3-450, 44-43-460 (1997); S.D. CODIFIED LAWS § 34-35-18.1 (Michie 1997); TENN. CODE ANN. § 68-3-501 (1997); UTAH CODE ANN. §§ 26-34-1, 26-34-2 (1997); VT. STAT. ANN. tit. 18, § 5218 (1997); V.I. CODE ANN. tit. 19, § 869 (1996); W. VA. CODE §§ 16-10-1 to 16-10-4 (1997); WIS. STAT. ANN. § 146.71 (1997); WYO. STAT. ANN. §§ 35-19-101 to 35-19-103 (1997). Alabama has adopted the Uniform Brain Death Act. UNIF. BRAIN DEATH ACT, 12 U.L.A. 63 (1996). *See* ALA. CODE § 22-31-1 (1996). Twelve states and Puerto Rico have adopted statutes which include a variation on the "cessation of all functioning of the brain" among other indices of death, especially when a patient's cardiac or respiratory functions are supported by artificial means. *See* ALASKA ADMIN. CODE tit. 9 § 68.120 (1997); CONN. GEN. STAT. ANN. 19a-279h (West 1997); FLA. STAT. ANN. § 382.009 (West 1997); HAW. REV. STAT. § 327C-1 (1997); IOWA CODE ANN. § 702.8

(1996); Ky. Rev. Stat. Ann. §446.400 (Banks-Baldwin 1997); La. Rev. Stat. Ann. § 9:111 (1997); N.J. Stat. Ann. § 26:6A-3 (1997); N.C. Gen. Stat. § 90-323 (1996); P.R. Laws Ann. tit 18, § 731a (1994); Tex. Health & Safety Code Ann. § 671.001 (West 1997); Va. Code Ann. § 54.1-2972 (Michie 1997). In five states, despite inaction by the state legislature, the courts have determined death to occur in a manner consistent with the Uniform Determination of Death Act. *See* State v. Fierro, 603 P.2d 74 (Ariz. 1974); *In re* Longeway, 549 N.E.2d 292 (Ill. 1990); Commonwealth v. Golston, 366 N.E.2d 744 (Mass. 1977); People v. Eulo, 472 N.E.2d 286 (N.Y. 1984); *In re* Bowman, 617 P.2d 731 (Wash. 1980).
140. In decisions where a court could not find nor apply a definition of brain death, the courts have generally been willing to uphold the conviction of an accused that caused the brain death of a victim. *See* Commonwealth v. Golston, 366 N.E.2d 744 (Mass. 1977), *cert. denied,* Golston v. Massachusetts, 434 U.S. 1039 (1978).
141. Felix Frankfurter, "Some Reflections on the Reading of Statutes,"Colum. L Rev. 1947, vol. 47, pp. 527, 529.
142. Yoma 83a.
143. Yoma 85a.
144. Yad, Hil. Shabbat 2.19.
145. Shulhan Arukh, Orah Hayyim, 330.5.
146. J. David Bleich, *Time of Death in Jewish Law*, New York, 1991.
147. Fred Rosner, "On Death and Dying," *Assia*, Jan. 1991, p. 42.
148. Ibid.
149. *President's Report.*
150. "Completely and irreversibly" conforms with the "Report of the Ad Hoc Committee of Harvard Medical School."
151. 151. Tanhumim , 1986, vol. 7, p. 187; Yoel Jakobovitz, "Brain Death and Heart Transplants," *Tradition*, Summer 1989, p. 24.
152. P. Byrne et al., *Brain Death—An Opposing Viewpoint*, 242 JAMA 1985 (1979).
153. M.D. Tendler, *Reply to Letter on Jewish Law and the Time of Death*, 240 JAMA 109 (1978).
154. Ibid.
155. Ibid.
156. Aaron Soleveichik, *Jewish Law and Time of Death*, 240, JAMA 109 (1978).
157. Ibid.
158. N.J. STAT. ANN. §26:6A-3 (1997)
159 N.J. STAT. ANN. §26:6A-5 (1997)(religious exemption clause).
160. Sokobin, Op. Cit.
161. Peter Singer, *Rethinking Life and Death: The Collapse of Our Traditional Ethics*, New York, 1994.
162. Ibid., 63.
163. Jakobovits, Op. Cit.
164. Singer, Op. Cit., p. 11.
165. Derek Humphry, *Final Exit: The Practicalities of Self-Deliverance and Assisted Suicide for the Dying*, Boston, 1991.
166. Ibid., 180.
167. Ibid., 13.
168. Potter, Op. Cit.
169. Cruzan v. Dir., Mo. Dep't of Health, 497 U.S. 261, 270 (1990).

170. Quinlan, 355 A.2d 647 (N.J. 1976).
171. Cruzan v. Dir., Mo. Dep't of Health, 497 U.S. 261 (1990). Nancy Cruzan was seriously injured in an automobile accident. *Id.* at 265. Her injuries placed her in a vegetative state. *Id.* Her parents sought to have her removed from life support, allowing her to die. *Id.* at 267. The court asserted that the Constitution does permit someone "to refuse lifesaving hydration and nutrition." *Id* at 279. In Nancy Cruzan's case, however, the court did not permit her removal from life support, because her parents failed to meet a "clear and convincing evidence standard," that removal was what Nancy wished. *Id.* at 284.
172. The Supreme Court ruled in two separate opinions that state prohibitions on doctor-assisted suicide do not violate the equal protection clause of the Fourteenth Amendment if rationally related to legitimate government interests. *See* Washington v. Glucksberg, 117 S. Ct. 2258 (1997); Vacco v. Quill, 117 S.Ct. 2293 (1997).
173. *Cruzan,* 497 U.S. at 270 (discussing *In re Quinlan,* 355 A.2d 647 [N.J. 1976]).
174. 355 A.2d 647 (N.J. 1976).
175. Ibid., 654.
176. Ibid., 654-655.
177. Ibid., 656.
178. Ibid., 662-664.
179. Ibid., 671.
180. Superintendent of Belchertown St. Sch. v. Saikewicz, 370 N.E.2d 417, 420 (Mass. 1977).
181. Ibid., 419.
182. Ibid., 430.
183. Ibid., 432.
184. Eichner v. Dillon, 426 N.Y.S.2d 517 (App. Div. 1980); *In re* Storar, 420 N.E.2d 64 (N.Y. 1981).
185. *Storar,* 420 N.E.2d at 67.
186. Ibid., 68.
187. Ibid., 70.
188. Ibid., 68.
189. Ibid.
190. Ibid.
191. Ibid.
192. Ibid., It was estimated that he had a "mental age of about 18 months."
193. Ibid., 73 (citations omitted).
194. Barber v. Superior Ct., 147 Cal. App.3d 1006 (1983).
195. Ibid., 1010.
196. Ibid., 1011.
197. Ibid., 1011-1012.
198. Ibid., 1022.
199. Cruzan v. Dir., Mo. Dep't of Health, 497 U.S. 260, 261 (1990).
200. Brooks, 205 N.E.2d 435 (Ill. 1965). *See also In re* President & Directors of Georgetown College, 331 F.2d 1010, 1015 (D.C. Cir. 1964) (Burger, J. dissenting).
201. Leon R. Kass, "Death With Dignity and the Sanctity of Life," *The Ethics of Choice; A Time to Be Born and a Time to Die,* (Barry S. Kogan, ed.), 1991, p. 128.

202. Ronald Green, "Good Rules Have Good Reason: A Response to Leon Kass," *The Ethics of Choice; A Time to Be Born and a Time to Die*, p. 147.

203. Ronald Dworkin, *Life's Dominions: An Argument About Abortion, Euthanasia and Individual Freedom*, New York, 1993, p. 84.

204. Ibid., 215.

205. Ibid., 199.

206. *President's Report.*

207. *In re* Conroy, 464 A.2d 303 (N.J. 1983).

208. Ibid., 304. Organic brain syndrome is a "syndrome resulting from diffuse or local impairment of brain tissue function." *Melloni's Illustrated Medical Dictionary*, 1979, p. 347.

209. *Conroy*, 464 A.2d at 304.

210. Ibid., 305.

211. Ibid.

212. Ibid., 312.

213. Ibid., quoting G. Kelly, *Medico-Moral Problems*, 1958, p. 129.

214. *Conroy*, 464 A.2d at 313.

215. *President's Report.*

216. Brophy v. New Eng. Sinai Hosp., Inc., 497 N.E.2d 626 (Mass. 1986).

217. Ibid., 628.

218. Ibid., 628-629.

219. Ibid., 638. There is an irony in this decision and an interesting difficulty with the moral and legal conundrum created by it. New England Sinai Hospital, a Jewish Hospital, and its ethics committee found itself bound by their interpretation of the restrictions in Jewish law which resisted removing the life support equipment. By acceding to the wishes of the family to move Paul Brophy to another facility they sanctioned the violation of the Noachide laws which are legally binding on non-Jews by Jewish law. The Rabbis held that while Jews are subject to the full panoply of Biblical legislation, all non-Jews are obligated to observe six basic humane regulations. "Man may not worship idols; he may not blaspheme God; he must establish courts of justice; he may not kill; he may not commit adultery; and he may not rob" Plaut, a note 112, at 71. By passively permitting the staff of another medical center to violate the proscription not to kill, the hospital may be thought to have facilitated a violation of that basic Noachide law by a gentile. *See* Michael Broyde, *Assisting In A Violation of a Noachide Law*, 8 JEWISH L. ASS'N STUD. 11 (1996).

220. UNIF. RIGHTS OF THE TERMINALLY ILL ACT, 9B U.L.A. 609 (1987).

221. Ibid., § 7.

222. Ibid.

223. "Appeals Exhausted, Firefighter to be Moved to Die," *Associated Press*, Oct. 14, 1986.

224. "Comatose Man Dies," *Newsday*, Oct. 14, 1986 at 14.

225. Bouvia v. Superior Court, 225 Cal. Rptr. 297 (1986).

226. Ibid., 299.

227. Ibid., 300.

228. Ibid., 298.

229. Ibid., 298-299.

230. Ibid., 300. "A person of adult years and in sound mind has the right in the exercise of control over his own body to determine whether or not to submit to lawful medical treatment." *Id.* (quoting Cobb v. Grant, 502 P.2d. 1 [Cal. 1972]).

231. Dudley Clendinen, "When Death Is a Blessing and Life Is Not," *New York Times,* Feb. 5, 1996, A11.

232. "See *Jury Acquits Kevorkian in Common-Law Case,*" Ibid., May 15, 1996, A14.

233. People v. Kevorkian, 534 N.W.2d 172 (Mich. Ct. App. 1995), *appeal denied,* 549 N.W.2d 566 (Mich. 1996), *cert. denied,* Kevorkian v. Michigan, 117 S. Ct. 296 (1996).

234. "A.M.A. Keeps Its Policy against Aiding Suicide, " *N.Y. Times,* June 26, 1996, B10.

235. Justin Hyde, "Doctors Group Opposes Assisted Suicide: The State Medical Society Doesn't Want a Ban on It, But Jack Kevorkian Helped Prompt the Policy Change," *Grand Rapids Press,* May 5, 1997, B3.

236. Sandi Dolbee, "Right-to-Die Measure Rejected by State Voters," *San Diego Union-Tribune,* Nov. 4, 1992, A3.

237. Jane Gross, "The 1991 Election: Euthanasia," *N.Y. Times,* Nov. 7, 1991, B16.

238. Oregon Death with Dignity Act, OR. REV. STAT. §§ 127.800-.897 (1997). The Oregon Supreme Court in a decision relating to the wording of the title to be used on the ballot for the "Oregon Death with Dignity Act" abridged and synopsized the proposed law. "The proposed measure creates a statutory regime that permits an adult resident of Oregon, who has been diagnosed as suffering from an incurable and irreversible disease that will, in the reasonable medical judgment of two physicians, cause that person's death within six months, to obtain and take lethal medication. The choice of the incurably ill person must be voluntary and informed, not the product of psychiatric or psychological disorder or of depression that is impairing the person's judgment." Kane v. Kulongoski, 871 P.2d 993, 995 (Or. 1994).

239. Lee v. Oregon, 891 F. Supp 1429 (D. Or. 1995).

240. David Garrow, "The Oregon Trail," *N.Y. Times,* Nov. 6, 1997, A27.

241. Washington v. Glucksberg, 117 S.Ct. 2258 (1997); Vacco v. Quill, 117 S.Ct. 2293 (1997).

242. Glucksberg, 117 S. Ct. at 2275.

243. "Around the World," *Detroit News,* Feb. 22, 1996, A1.

244. "Euthanasia Law Struck Down in Australia, " *N.Y. Times,* Mar. 27, 1997 A15.

245. Compassion in Dying v. Washington, 79 F.3d 790 (9th Cir. 1996), *rev'd sub nom.,* Washington v. Glucksberg, 117 S.Ct. 2258 (1997)

246. Ibid., 797.

247. Cruzan v. Dir., Mo. Dep't of Health, 497 U.S. 261 (1990).

248. *Compassion in Dying,* 79 F. 3d at 799 (quoting *Cruzan,* 487 U.S. at 278 [O'Connor, J., dissenting]).

249. Casey v. Planned Parenthood, 505 U.S. 833 (1992) (upholding the right of privacy in a woman's choice to have an abortion).

250. *Compassion in Dying,* 79 F. 3d at 799 (quoting *Casey,* 505 U.S. at 851).

251. Ibid., 816.

252. Quill v. Vacco, 80 F.3d 716 (2d Cir. 1996), *rev'd,* Vacco v. Quill, 117 S. Ct. 2293 (1997).

253. Quill, 80 F.3d at 721.

254. Ibid., 724 (referencing Yale Kamisar, *Are Laws against Assisted Suicide Unconstitutional?*, 23 HASTINGS CTR. REP. 32 [1993]).

255. Ibid., 726.

256. Ibid., 731 (Calabresi, J., concurring).

257. Ibid., 738 (Calabresi, J., concurring).

258. Ibid., 739 (Calabresi, J., concurring).

259. 79 F.3d 790 (9th Cir. 1996).

260. 80 F.3d 716 (2d Cir. 1996).

261. David J. Garrow, "The Justices' Life-or Death Choices," *N.Y. Times*, April 7, 1996, E6.

262. Ibid.

263. Ibid.

264. 117 S. Ct. 2258 (1997)

265. Ibid., 261 (alteration in original).

266. 80 F.3d at 731 (Calabresi, J., concurring).

267. Glucksberg, 117 S. Ct. 2258, 2293 (Souter, J., concurring).

268. 117 S. Ct. 2293 (1997).

269. Ibid., 2296.

270. Washington v. Glucksberg, 117 S. Ct. 2302, 2303 (1997) (O'Connor, J., concurring).

271. Ibid., 2311 (Breyer, J., concurring).

272. Cruzan v. Dir., Mo. Dep't of Health, 497 U.S. 261 (1990).

273. Ibid.

274. I Samuel 31:4. Saul begged his armor-bearer to kill him but was rebuffed and fell upon his own sword. *Id.* The most famous act of suicide and assisted suicide in Jewish history was the mass self-immolation of the garrison of Masada in 73 C.E. as reported by Josephus. The husband/father in each family group first killed his family and was then assisted in suicide by a companion. Flavious Josephus, "The Works of Josephus,"(William Whiston trans.), 1987, . 8. 769.

275. Leviticus 19:16.

276. The phrase "'of Israel' is absent in some texts." Sant 37a.

277. San 37a.

278. Exodus 15:26.

279. Exodus 21:18.

280. Exodus 21: 19 (a literal translation.)

281. Baba Kamma 85a.

282. There is a distinction in Jewish law between willful suicide and one induced by mental illness. Only when there is clear and unequivicable evidence of intent is the suicide considered to have been of sound mind. The Talmud states the principle with clarity. "Who is a suicide of sound mind? It is not so regarded if a man climbed a tree or a roof and fell to his death, but only where he states, 'I am climbing the roof or the tree and I am going to throw myself to my death,' and one sees him acting accordingly ... a man found strangled or hanging from a tree or cast upon a sword is regarded as a suicide of unsound mind." *Tractate Semachot, in* TALMUD, *supra* note 20, at 2:2-3. *Semachot* (joys) is named with ironic humor. It is the classic rabbinic text on death and mourning. It is appended to the Babylonian Talmud. The fourteen-chapter text begins with the legal status of a dying person and asserts

that the dying must be considered as living in every respect. A suicide is termed *shekhiv me-ra,* which denotes a person who is so severely ill as to be facing imminent death. *See* 1 ELON, *supra* note 22, at 1877.

283. *Oxford English Dictionary,* Oxford, 1089, p. 444 .

284. "R[abbi] Nahman said in Rabbah b[en] Abbahu's name: Scripture says, 'Love thy neighbor as thyself': Choose an easy death for him." San 45a.

285. Leviticus 19:18.

286. San 45a.

287. Commentary to San 45a.

288. Leonard Kravitz, "Euthanasia," *Death and Euthanasia in Jewish Law: Essays and Responsa,* (Walter Jacob & Moshe Zemer eds), Pittsburgh, 1995, p. 11 ff.

289. Elliot N. Dorff, "Teshuvah on Assisted Suicide," *Conservative Judaism,* Summer 1998, pp. 3ff.

290. Abraham S. Abrahams, *The Comprehensive Guide to Medical Halachah,* Jersualem, 1990, p. 177.

291. Exodus 21:19.

292. Fred Rosner, *Modern Medicine and Jewish Ethics,* New York, 1991, p. 211.

293. A.Z. 18a.

294. Hananiah was a second-century C.E. rabbinic scholar. He was executed by the Romans during the Hadrianic repression of Jewish life in Judea. Hanania, when arrested, admitted that he was teaching Torah in violation of the emperor's edicts. "He was sentenced to be burnt at the stake ... he was burnt at the stake wrapped in the *Sefer Torah* [a scroll on which was written the Five Books of Moses] which he had been holding when he was arrested. In order to prolong his agony tufts of wool soaked in water were placed over his heart so that he should not die quickly...It is stated that the executioner (*quaestionarius*), moved by his sufferings, removed and increased the heat of the fire." *Encyclopaedia Judaica,* vol. 7, p. 1254.

295. David Feldman, "The End of Life," *Hippocrates,* May/June 1988, p. 24.

296. Semahot 1.1.

297. Ecclesiastes 12:6.

298. Semahot 1.2.

299. Ibid., 1:4.

300. Shab. 37a.

301. Ibid.

302. Ibid.

303. Fred Rosner and J. David Bleich, *Jewish Bioethics,* New York, 1979, p. 262.

304. Jacob ben Asher (1270?-1340) *Turim.*

305. *Turim Yoreh Deah,* 339.

306. Ned. 40a.

307. Ket. 104a.

308. Ibid.

309. Yoma 85a.

310. San 74a.

311. Israel Bettan in W. Jacob, *American Reform Responsa,* New York, 1983, p. 263.

312. Yoel H. Kahn, "On Choosing the Hour of Our Death," *Reform Jewish Quarterly,* Summer 1994, p. 65.

313. Eugene Borowitz, *Choices in Modern Jewish Thought,* New York, 1983, p. 271.

314. Daniel B. Sinclair, "Patient Self-Determination and Advance Directives," 8 *Jewish Law Association Studies,* vol. 8, 1994, p. 173.
315. C.A. 759/92 (T.A.), Zadok v. Beth Haelah, P.M. (unpublished).
316. Sinclair, Op. Cit., p. 180.
317. Ket. 70a.
318. Sinclair , Op. Cit., 181.
319. Harvey L. Gordon, *Assisted Suicide, Bio-Ethics: Program/Case Study,* Union of Am. Hebrew Congregations, Summer 1994.
320. Alvin J. Reines, "The Morality of Suicide: A Surresponse," *Journal of Reform Judaism,* Winter 1991, p. 74.
321. Bernard Zlotowitz and Sanford Seltzer, "Suicide as a Moral Decision," *Journal of Reform Judaism,* Winter 1991, p. 66.
322. Ibid.
323. See supra text accompanying notes 4-13.
324. Board of Comm'rs v Bond, 88 Ind. 102 (1882).
325. 923 F.2d 477 (6th Cir. 1991). For a situation with an almost identical fact pattern, see Whaley v. County of Tuscola, 58 F.3d 111 (6th Cir. 1995).
326. Ibid.
327. Ibid.
328. OHIO REV. CODE ANN. §§ 2108.01-.09 (Banks-Baldwin 1995).
329. OHIO REV. CODE ANN § 313.121 (Banks-Baldwin 1997).
330. Michael Graham, "The Role of the Medical Examiner in Fatal Child Abuse," *Child Maltreatment,* (James A. Monteleone & Armand E. Brodeur eds.), NEW YORK, 1994, P. 431.
331. Ibid. 433.
332. Ibid.
333. Bleich, Op. Cit., p. 162.
334. Deuteronomy 21:23.
335. "Inference from minor to major, or from major to minor." *The Authorized Daily Prayer Book,* (Joseph H. Hertz trans. rev. ed.), London, 1959, p. 43.
336. See *Pikku'ah Nefesh* supra note 283.
337. Baba Basra 154a f.
338. Hullin 11b.
339. OHIO REV. CODE ANN. § 313.12 (Banks-Baldwin 1997).
340. The state also accommodates religious beliefs in performing an autopsy. If an autopsy is contrary to the deceased's religious beliefs, but is a "compelling public necessity," the coroner must wait forty-eight hours before performing the procedure. This waiting period is designed to allow the relatives of the deceased to petition for an injunction against the autopsy. OHIO REV. CODE ANN. § 313.131 (Banks-Baldwin 1997).
341. ELON, Op. Cit., vol. 1, supra note 22.
342. Elliot N. Dorff and Arthur Rosett, A Living Tree: *The Roots and Growth of Jewish Law,* New York, 1988, p. 516.
343. Elon, Op. Cit., vol. 1, p. 71.
344. Ibid.
345. The principle of *dina de-malkhuta dina* would not be operative in matters of defining death or in questions of organ donation. There is no conflict with regard to organ donation as it is not a statutory requirement. In the future there may be a dispute between secular law and Jewish law if the two sys-

tems of law focus in on the agonizing moral conundrum. As has been noted, the decisive definition of death is still in the process of determination in both the Anglo-American legal system as well as in Jewish law.

Contributors

Joan S. Friedman served as Jewish Chaplain and Instructor in religion at Colgate University in Hamilton, New York. She has served on the Responsa Committee of the Central Conference of American Rabbis since 1994. She is currently preparing a doctoral dissertation on Solomon B. Freehof.

Walter Jacob is Senior Scholar of Rodef Shalom Congregation, Pittsburgh, Pennsylvania. President of the Abraham Geiger College in Berlin/Potsdam, Past President of the Central Conference of American Rabbis, President of the Solomon B. Freehof Institute of Progressive *Halakhah*, and the Associated American Jewish Museums. Author and editor of twenty-seven books including *Contemporary American Reform Responsa* (1987), *Liberal Judaism and Halakhah* (1988), *The Healing Past*: *Pharmaceuticals in the Biblical and Rabbinic World* (1993), *Not by Birth Alone, Conversion to Judaism* (1997), *Gender Issues in Jewish Law* (2000).

Richard S. Rheins is Rabbi of Temple David in Monroeville, Pennsylvania, a member of the Responsa Committee of the Central Conference of American Rabbis. He has written in the field of *halakhah*.

Alan Sokobin is Rabbi Emeritus of Temple Israel in Toledo, Ohio, and Professor at the University of Toledo School of Law. He has written extensively in both Jewish and general law, most recently "Child Abuse: a Study in Comparative American and Jewish Law" in *The University of Toledo Law Review*.

MARK WASHOFSKY is Professor of Rabbinics, Hebrew Union College-Jewish Institute of Religion in Cincinnati, Ohio. He is Chair of the Responsa Committee of the Central Conference of American Rabbis. He has published a number of studies in the field of Jewish law and legal theory. His books include *Teshuvot for the Nineties* (1997), and *Jewish Living, A Guide to Contemporary Reform Practice* (2000).